The Political Themes of Inter-American Relations

The Political Themes of Inter-American Relations

Edward J. Williams
University of Arizona

Duxbury Press
A Division of Wadsworth Publishing Company, Inc.
Belmont, California

Duxbury Press
A Division of Wadsworth Publishing Company, Inc.

L. C. Cat. Card No.: 74-150361

ISBN 0-87872-006-5

Printed in the United States of America

1 2 3 4 5 6 7 8 9 10 - 75 74 73 72 71

Preface

This book catalogs, explicates, and analyzes the political themes of inter-American relations. The political issues set out in the study have caused Hemispheric controversy for 150 years, and they will continue to play a major role in the seventies. The possibilities of a Haitian intervention, the continuing debate concerning United States assistance to the dictatorial Brazilian regime, the arguments over military assistance, and the fear of another Soviet intrusion into the Hemisphere are cases in point.

Although many problems of contemporary relations are cast in economic terms, politics is still the master science. Inter-American disagreements over trade agreements, investment policies, and styles of economic development are crucially affected by the political environment and obviously have important implications for political decision makers. The book discusses economic problems only when they impinge directly on political themes or when their absence would present a distorted image of the theme.

By showing the evolution of several political themes, it may be possible to anticipate the controversies of the 1970s; by noting the arguments of the North Americans and Latin Americans, it may be possible to further pinpoint the specific forms these controversies will take and the specific apologies they will elicit.

The five basic themes of inter-American political intercourse are complementary. The cry of *imperialism* is long-lived in Hemispheric relations. Its major catalyst in the postwar years has been *the Cold War and Communist issue.* The Cold War and the imputed ambitions of the Communist powers, moreover, have added new dimensions and increased cogency to two older themes — *intervention* and *aid to dictatorships.* The propaganda battle of the Cold War and the reaction of the nonaligned states has also aided in the evolution of the last theme — the rich nations and the poor nations, or *the increasing adherence of Latin America to the poor nations' political power bloc.*

In a sense, then, the themes of imperialism and the Cold War and communism are the context for the other, more specific issues of inter-American relations. These two factors define the environment in which the other problems are acted out. In any given diplomatic situation, more than one theme influences U.S. action and Latin American reaction. A case in point may elucidate the mutually reinforcing connection of the themes. For example, when the United States sponsored and assisted the Cuban exiles' Bay of Pigs invasion in 1961, Yankee policy makers were obviously motivated by the theme of the Cold War and communism. Latin American reaction to the invasion was influenced by a different interpretation of the threat of communism. The intensity of Latin American criticism, however, was also motivated by the long history of U.S. intervention. Both Latin American and Afro-Asian condemnation of the intervention, furthermore, evolved from the fact that they saw Cuba as a small, poor nation that had suffered at the hands of the rich and powerful. The whole messy business, finally, was depicted as yet another example of Yankee imperialism that had been the context of inter-American relations for 150 years.

However interconnected the themes may appear in the nexus of any specific event, they are also separate and distinct political factors and currents of thought. Sorting them out may increase understanding of the nuances of inter-American relations. This book attempts to do exactly that.

This book is first a personal exercise in attempting to understand the political issues of inter-American relations. It has provided me with a framework for filing the seemingly endless masses of data from diplomatic historians and the impassioned rhetoric from political polemicists.

It was also written as a teaching tool for the course on inter-American politics offered at many universities and colleges. I don't think that a book has ever been written specifically for that course. The instructor is compelled to piece together a number of works to help the students understand what inter-American relations is all about. The works used may be good in their own right, but they are too specialized, too historical, too polemical, too expensive, or too dated for the course. In that sense, the book is intended for students; it is written specifically for them and because of them.

Lastly, the book was written for all those interested in hemispheric relations. Though never so tightly organized nor so influential as the "China Lobby," a group interested in helping Latin America and improving inter-American relations has always existed in the United States. It is hoped that this book may prove useful to them.

However personal the original intention of this book, it is far from a private effort. The ideas of many and the assistance of many more have contributed to it. Their help demands acknowledgment. Anne O'Connor, then a graduate student, assisted in the conceptualization of the idea several years ago. We originally intended to do the book together, but personal tragedy forced her to put her academic work aside. My friend and colleague, Freeman Wright, read most of the manuscript with a combination of good grace and critical intelligence. My inter-American politics classes (especially the fall 1969 group) contributed much through their questions, arguments, ideas, and snotty remarks. To these people, I am especially grateful.

Many others read parts of the manuscript as it progressed. They saved me from errors of fact and interpretation and infelicities of organization and style. For that assistance, I thank Rudolph de la Garza, Fred Hellberg, Milton Jamail, Darrell Krueger, Robert Lawrence, Michael Sullivan, and Charles White. My thanks also to Donald Bray of California State College at Los Angeles, Howard Wiarda of University of Massachusetts, and John G. Freels, Jr., of University of Florida, who reviewed the final manuscript.

Terry Nash edited and typed the first four chapters. Barbara Harrison and Eleanor Abney did the same for the last two chapters. All were efficient; to all my grateful appreciation.

Finally, my thanks to the Institute of Government Research at the University of Arizona for financial support, which provided time for research and writing during the summers of 1969 and 1970.

Whatever good their gracious assistance contributed to this endeavor, none of them can bear responsibility for what may be wrong with it. The final decisions on form and content were mine. It is I who must answer for them.

Edward J. Williams
Tucson, Arizona

To my father and mother:

Edward Cleveland Williams
Cecilia Pankowski Williams

Contents

One

Imperialism

Introduction

The history of relations between the two Americas has centered on the accusation of imperialism by the Latin Americans and the responses of the North Americans. Both charge and defense have ranged from rather accurate to fairly ludicrous, but the important fact is that imperialism has been a central theme of inter-American politics.

Much of the confusion surrounding the whole question of imperialism emanates from the absence of agreement on a working definition. Many equate "imperialism" with "economic imperialism." It is more than that. Some limit the definition of imperialism to overt intervention, but intervention is only one manifestation of a much more comprehensive policy or practice. (Intervention as imperialism is discussed later in this book.) Most commit the opposite sin and posit imperialism as applying to all relations among nations. Still others identify several types of imperialism.

The rhetoric too frequently befogs rather than enlightens the issue. It is difficult, for example, to decipher the differences among "economic imperialism," "Wilsonian imperialism," "defensive imperialism," "patronizing imperialism," and "Imperialism." Comprehension is not increased by adding terms like "interposition," sometimes qualified by "temporary" and other times not. The mind is equally boggled by the imperialistic implications of No-Transfer, the Monroe Doctrine, the Polk Corollary, the Roosevelt Corollary, and the Johnson Doctrine.

Imperialism, in short, is employed to define and damn practically every aspect of hemispheric intercourse. It is applied with bewildering promiscuity to political, economic, military, and cultural relations. Imperialism, for Latin

Americans, and some North Americans, defines both the territorial acquisitions of the Mexican War and the scholarly acquisitions of North American researchers in Latin America. It encompasses the shoddy grab of the Panamanian isthmus and the youthful idealism of Peace Corps volunteers. Its variations are limitless, implications boundless, and nuances countless.[1]

Recognizing that only a minimal step toward clarity is involved, this effort will employ Webster's definition. Imperialism is "the policy, practice, or advocacy of seeking to extend the control, dominion, or empire of a nation."[2] The only addition to that definition is the warning that imperialism need not be characterized by "conscious" calculation. The British, it is said, amassed an empire in a fit of absentmindedness. Other "fits" better explain American imperialism, but the almost accidental nature of some aspects of U.S. imperialism is similar to the British experience.

The term "imperialism" is laden with pejorative connotations. Few would deny that some men are evil or that some nations are consciously and selfishly imperialistic. The point of this chapter, however, is not necessarily to damn the United States, but merely to relate what seems, in fact, to have been the situation and to describe the Latin American and U.S. responses to it. "Imperialism" is used in a neutral sense except where Latin Americans themselves imply a pejorative connotation.

With that point made, two facts about American imperialism demand postulation. First, U.S. imperialism is a profound reality for Latin Americans. Gonzalo Barrios, a moderate Venezuelan social democrat, charges that it has caused many evils. That point could be debated. What cannot, however, is Barrios' further charge that "attitudes toward imperialism are, among Latin Americans, the touchstone of political and moral positions and an unavoidable aspect of any discussion of political and social matters."[3] Second, the fear of Yankee imperialism among Latin Americans is well founded. Historically, the United States has pursued imperialistic policies and has officially advocated and practiced the extension of its control and dominion over Latin America.

---

1. It should be noted that confusion on the meaning of imperialism is not limited to its applications in the Western Hemisphere. In his well-known text, Hans J. Morgenthau charges that the term "has lost all concrete meaning." He devotes the first four pages of the discussion to setting out "what imperialism is not." See *Politics among Nations,* 3rd ed. (New York: Alfred A. Knopf, 1960), pp. 44–47.

2. *Webster's New Collegiate Dictionary* (Springfield, Mass.: G. & C. Merriam Co., 1956), p. 416.

3. Quoted in Luigi Einaudi, *Changing Contexts of Revolution in Latin America* (Santa Monica, Calif.: The Rand Corporation, 1966), p. 8.

A Historical Sketch of American Imperialism[4]

Though the historical evolution of inter-American relations contains many examples of U.S. imperialism, the record is uneven. At times, the United States was simply uninterested in Latin America; at other times relations were rather intimate, but not poisoned by the imperialistic issue; at still other times the full force of Yankee imperialism endangered diplomatic amity; and finally, some periods were marked by ambiguity. Using U.S. imperialistic ventures in Latin America as the determining factor, the history of the hemisphere counts seven periods.

The period beginning with colonization of the two continents and ending with the promulgation of the Monroe Doctrine was marked by good, if rather peripheral, relations between the Americas. Commercial contacts began very early and increased slowly over almost two centuries. Enlightened groups in Latin America were sympathetic to the American war of independence and were in no small part inspired by it. Though officially neutral, U.S. contributions to the Latin American wars of independence included harboring of rebel ships, provision of munitions, and diplomatic defense against European intervention.[5]

Two pronouncements with imperialistic implications were issued during this period. The No-Transfer Resolution in 1811 prohibited the transfer of hemispheric territory from one European nation to another. Though of little immediate significance, the principle had imperialistic connotations that were acted out later in inter-American history. In this resolution, the United States made a first tentative pronouncement that its decisions were binding beyond its territory.

The Monroe Doctrine of 1823 was, of course, even more important. The doctrine, literally the root of U.S. hemispheric policy, was originally directed at European intervention, but soon sprouted a series of branches. The Polk and Roosevelt corollaries to the doctrine were supplemented by countless congressional resolutions and presidential decrees that anticipated, justified, and implemented U.S. imperialistic control in the Western Hemisphere.

In the second period of inter-American history, 1823 – 1845, the United States refused to enforce the Monroe Doctrine. Brazil and Colombia were denied treaty arrangements to implement Monroe's pledges; several European

---

4. For more complete descriptions and analyses of the historical evolution of inter-American politics, see Samuel Flagg Bemis, *The Latin American Policy of the United States* (New York: W.W. Norton & Co., 1943); Edwin Lieuwen, *U.S. Policy in Latin America: A Short History* (New York: Frederick A. Praeger, 1965); J. Lloyd Mecham, *A Survey of United States – Latin American Relations* (Boston: Houghton Mifflin Co., 1965); Dexter Perkins, *A History of the Monroe Doctrine* (Boston: Little, Brown and Co., 1963); or Graham H. Stuart, *Latin America and the United States,* 5th ed. (New York: Appleton-Century-Crofts, 1955).

5. See Benjamin Keen, *Americans All* (New York: Dell Publishing Co., 1966), p. 223.

forays into the Western Hemisphere went unchecked. The United States had neither the will nor the power to push a dynamic Latin American policy.

With the promulgation of the Polk Corollary in 1845, however, the United States began a generation of imperialistic muscle-flexing. Manifest Destiny was the official dogma of the period and territorial expansion the official policy. The Polk Corollary broadened the definition of the No-Transfer Resolution to prohibit transfer of territory from an American nation to a European one. The United States forbade Mexico to sell California to Britain.

In 1845, the United States annexed Texas and the following year fought an imperialistic war with Mexico. The war cost Mexico one third of its territory when the United States annexed New Mexico and Upper California. U.S. imperialism had claimed its first tangible fruits.

Several other episodes signalled the emergence of U.S. hemispheric domination and imperialistic ambitions. The United States' strong opposition to French intervention in Mexico and to Spanish re-annexation of the Dominican Republic ended the threat of European intervention in the Western Hemisphere. European power did not again transgress the U.S. sphere of influence until 1961, when the Soviet Union aided Fidel Castro in Cuba. (The presence of Great Britain in Guyana could be considered an exception to this statement.)

The United States' increasing interest in the isthmus of Panama was more directly ominous for the Latin American nations. In late 1846, a treaty with Colombia gave the United States its first rights to use of the isthmus. Protection of the Panama Canal eventually became the foremost rationale for U.S. imperialistic control of the Caribbean and Central American states.

Thus, the period from 1845 to 1870 introduced all major aspects of American imperialistic influence. Manifest Destiny presaged other ideological apologies; European power was repulsed; and the groundwork for the strategic imperialism surrounding the Canal was laid.

The fourth period of inter-American relations (1870 – 1895) was relatively quiet. British sea power protected the area from incursions by other European nations. The United States concentrated on internal development. The growing industrial might of the United States was ultimately to cause serious problems for Latin America, but few important exchanges between the Americas occurred. The only minimal exception was Secretary of State James G. Blaine's half-aborted Washington Conference of American Nations, which convened in 1889. The import of that conference, however, was more potential than actual.

In the fifth period of hemispheric history, encompassing approximately the first third of the present century, North American imperialism achieved unequaled heights. The period began with the United States' reaction to a dispute between Great Britain and Venezuela over the boundary between Venezuela and British Guiana. President Grover Cleveland's Secretary of State, Richard Olney, forced the British to accept arbitration. In a note to the

British Foreign Secretary in 1895, Olney set out an incredible claim of North American competence.

> Today the United States is practically sovereign on this continent, and its fiat is law upon the subjects to which it confines its interpositions. . . . It is because, in addition to all other grounds, its infinite resources combined with its isolated position render it master of the situation and practically invulnerable as against any or all other powers.[6]

Events of the next quarter century supported Olney's claim. Through the Spanish-American War of 1898, the United States annexed Puerto Rico, acquired the Guantanamo Bay naval installation, and imposed the Platt Amendment, formally recognizing the right of the United States to intervene in Cuban domestic affairs.

The inspiration and material assistance that Theodore Roosevelt provided the Panamanian independence movement in late 1903 was little more than a ploy to establish the U.S. protectorate that led to the construction of the Panama Canal.

Only a year later, the Roosevelt Corollary pronounced the United States to be keeper of hemispheric morals.

> Chronic wrongdoing, or an impotence which results in a general loosening of the ties of civilized society, may in America, as elsewhere, ultimately require intervention by some civilized nations, and in the Western Hemisphere, the adherence of the United States to the Monroe Doctrine may force the United States, however reluctantly, in cases of wrongdoing or impotence, to the exercise of the international police power.[7]

A series of interventions were undertaken and protectorates established during the following years. United States military forces imposed varying degrees of control on Cuba, the Dominican Republic, Haiti, Honduras, Nicaragua, and Panama. There were also two forays into Mexico; and the Lodge Corollary, barring foreign companies from buying land in the Western Hemisphere, was issued.

Though differing nuances sometimes animated imperialist policy, the effort was bipartisan, encompassing the terms of four presidents. Theodore Roosevelt's "police power" was exercised in much the same way as Woodrow Wilson's attempts to impose democratic regimes on the Latin American nations.

The Latin Americans responded vehemently to this imperialism. Although some degree of fear and suspicion had characterized the entire history of inter-American relations, this epoch evoked the full force of the anti-Yankeeism that continues to exist in inter-American politics today.

---

6. Quoted in Milton S. Eisenhower, *The Wine Is Bitter: The United States and Latin America* (New York: Doubleday & Co., 1963), p. 173.

7. Quoted in Lieuwen, *U.S. Policy*, p. 42.

If the imperialism connected with Theodore Roosevelt meant the nadir of inter-American relations, the sixth period, popularly identified with Franklin Roosevelt's term of office, signaled the introduction of a new amity that one author sees cresting with the Rio Conference in 1947, "when inter-American relations were at the highest level in history."[8] The change in policy was partially conceived and implemented by the series of Republican administrations between 1921 and 1933. As early as 1923, Secretary of State Charles Evans Hughes began to back away from the "right" of intervention, though still clinging to the prerogative of "temporary interposition." The Republican administrations also began the liquidation of American occupations in the Caribbean and Central America. President Herbert Hoover reverted to the Jeffersonian policy of de facto recognition, ending the previous de jure policy of stipulating requirements that nations had to meet before U.S. recognition was offered. The reintroduction of the de facto policy recognized governments with no qualifications except that those governments were in control of the country. At about the same time, moreover, the extravagant claims of United States citizens for protection were repudiated and a new policy of more limited protection was introduced. The United States government no longer responded indiscriminately to calls for its protection. American citizens living and operating abroad were compelled to follow strict procedures if they wished to call on Washington for its assistance in protecting their lives and property. Most importantly, an entire new appraisal of inter-American politics and of the Monroe Doctrine was outlined in late 1928 by the Clark Memorandum. The memorandum essentially disavowed the interpretations of inter-American relations that had evolved in the previous 30 years and returned to a much less ambitious role for the United States.

The Good Neighbor policy highlighted this period of inter-American politics. The Roosevelt administration continued the initiatives of the previous Republican administrations. All military occupations and protectorates were officially liquidated. American troops and financial officials were withdrawn. The hated Platt Amendment was repudiated. Furthermore, new policies were undertaken that contributed to the increasing cordiality of hemispheric relations. Perhaps most important was U.S. agreement, long sought by the Latin American countries, to non-intervention pledges. The first step was taken in 1933 at the Inter-American Conference at Montevideo, Uruguay. Secretary of State Cordell Hull agreed that no nation had the right to intervene in the internal affairs of another. A reservation to Hull's statement was erased at the subsequent conference in Buenos Aires in 1936. At that meeting, the United States repudiated its long-held and oft-exercised right of intervention.

The good faith of the United States was put to the test almost immediately. Bolivia in 1937 and Mexico in 1938 nationalized oil industries owned

---

8. William Manger, "Reform of the OAS: An Appraisal," *Journal of Inter-American Studies,* 10: 1 (January 1968), 5.

in part by U.S. interests. The Bolivian nationalization involved minor sums and evoked relatively little opposition. The Mexican case was much different, however. The socialistic proclivities of the Mexican Revolution had long been opposed in the United States. Nationalization of the oil industries seemed to be one more indication of alien philosophies and policies encroaching at the borders. Both the oil interests and a significant part of the population pressed for intervention. The Roosevelt administration withstood the political pressure, however, and another important step was taken in the increasing friendship nurtured by the Good Neighbor policy. Until the early 1950's, inter-American relations continued to be characterized by cordiality and mutual trust.

The contemporary period of inter-American relations is ambiguous. Relations are more strained than during the 1930's, but conversely, numerous initiatives have evoked hopeful responses from Latin American and North American alike. Beyond the immediate significance of particular programs and policies, moreover, there are some indications that the entire tone of inter-American politics is more promising than in the past. Whatever the future promise may be, however, the period from the early 50's has been inconsistent and contradictory.

Historically, relations disintegrated rapidly during the late 1940's and 50's. The crumbling of relations was dramatically manifested by the riotous displays of anti-Americanism evoked by Vice-President Nixon's visit to several Latin American countries in 1958. Even more publicized, though certainly no more portentous, was the course of Fidel Castro's revolution during the early 1960's.

Simultaneously, however, Washington responded to the growing disaffection of the Latin American nations by agreeing to the foundation of the Inter-American Bank in 1958 and launching the Alliance for Progress in 1961. These initiatives, coupled with the sympathetic personality of President John F. Kennedy, brought an upswing in relations.

That resurgence of inter-American amity was vitiated by the United States' intervention in the Dominican Republic in 1965. The late 1960's also witnessed the burgeoning of Latin American nationalism, inevitably increasing strains on hemispheric rapport. The upshot of these developments is a heated controversy anent the import and intentions of U.S. policy and the present status of inter-American relations. The post World War II record, it is safe to say, is mixed.[9]

---

9. For some arguments that the mix is basically bad, see John Gerassi, *The Great Fear in Latin America* rev. ed. (New York: Collier Books, 1965); and James Petras, "The United States and the New Equilibrium in Latin America," *Public Policy,* 18: 1 (Fall 1969), 95 – 135. For the opposing view, see Roberto de Oliveira Campos, "Relations between the United States and Latin America," in Mildred Adams, ed., *Latin America: Evolution or Explosion?* (New York: Dodd, Mead & Co., 1963), pp. 23 – 57; and John P. Powelson, *Latin America: Today's Economic and Social Revolution* (New York: McGraw-Hill Book Co., 1964).

The Explanations of North American Imperialism

Hemispheric history has been characterized by varying degrees of United States' control over the Latin American countries. In attempting to explain, defend, and sometimes reject that relationship, numerous theories, arguments, and apologies have been propounded. This section catalogs those theories and arguments to decipher some of the overriding themes of hemispheric politics.

Economic Imperialism

Though the economic problems and theories of inter-American relations are not within the scope of this book, the fundamental importance of the economic interpretations of imperialism compel some discussion. Economic interpretations of imperialism are the best known, the most widely propagated, and probably the most generally accepted explanations of why strong nations attempt to control weak ones. It will be argued below[10] that other interpretations are even more cogent in understanding North American imperialism in Latin America, but there is no question that the economic explanation is convincing.[11]

The basic argument is that powerful nations control weak ones to insure a source of raw materials and a market for manufactured goods. The powerful nations also force the weak to sell cheap and buy dear. The strong nations are controlled (or greatly influenced) by powerful economic trusts that manipulate political policies for their own selfish ends. Thus, the argument goes, Wall Street, or the oil companies, or the sugar trusts, or the agri-businesses dictate Washington's imperialistic policy in Latin America. The purpose of that policy is to insure economic domination.

Specific charges may elucidate the point. A Bolivian student charges that "Imperialism has used, and continues to use, different means depending on circumstances of time and space [but] the objective is always economic domination."[12] A North American damns Yankee intervention:

> Never, unfortunately, did we do so to bring a better life to our neighbors; always did we intervene for purely economic or territorial gain, or as the strong-arm agents for wealthy companies or high-class adventurers.[13]

---

10. See especially the "Strength vs. Weakness" and "National Security" explanations.

11. In Latin America, the best known formulation of the argument is V. I. Lenin, *Imperialism: The Highest Stage of Capitalism.* For some recent examples of the basic position, see Gerassi, *The Great Fear;* Irving Louis Horowitz et al., eds., *Latin American Radicalism* (New York: Random House, 1969); Carlos Fuentes et al., *Whither Latin America?* (New York: Monthly Review Press, 1963); and most editions of the *North American Congress on Latin America (NACLA) Newsletter.*

12. Quoted in Powelson, *Latin America,* p. 2.

13. Gerassi, *The Great Fear*, p. 231.

A Brazilian intellectual interprets the Monroe Doctrine in purely economic terms. It was, he says, devised solely to protect the commercial interests of the United States and Great Britain.[14]

In economic interpretations of imperialism, the entire history of inter-American relations is explained by the desire of the United States to protect and expand its economic interests in Latin America. The long campaign to establish influence in the isthmus was to reduce trading costs and enrich the merchants of the East Coast. Beginning at the turn of the century, North American interventions in Central America and the Caribbean were carried out to assist in the economic exploitation of that area. Even Franklin Roosevelt's developmental loans are seen as being motivated by economic imperialism. An economic interpreter depicts the object of the loans as "forcing those nations to become totally dependent, economically, on the United States." The 1965 Dominican Republic intervention is explained within the context of economic imperialism.

> The forces determining United States priorities and objectives in the Dominican Republic were rooted in powerful American economic interests and domestic political considerations. The United States corporations with a direct and indirect stake in the outcome of Dominican events had ready access to United States administration officials, and when the April 1965 rebellion broke out, they most likely expressed their deep concern. A considerable number of individuals with financial, legal and social connections to the East Coast sugar complex were well stationed throughout the upper echelons of the United States Government.[15]

According to this theory, a web of economic interests explains both inter-American relations and internal politics in Latin America. North American foreign policy is dictated by the trusts. A critic presents some bombastic evidence, quoting "a much-decorated United States patriot: Major General Smedley D. Butler of the United States Marine Corps." General Butler reveals the economic motivations of United States policy in the early part of the present century.

> I helped make Mexico and especially Tampico safe for American oil interests in 1914. I helped make Haiti and Cuba a decent place for the National City Bank boys to collect revenue in . . . I helped purify Nicaragua for the international banking house of Brown Brothers in 1909 – 12. I brought light to the Dominican Republic for American sugar interests

14. Otto María Carpeaux, "Battles and the War in Latin America," in *Latin American Radicalism,* p. 441.

15. For the charges and quotations, see Carpeaux, *ibid.,* p. 444; Gerassi, *The Great Fear*, p. 238; and Fred Goff and Michael Locker, "The Violence of Domination: U.S. Power and the Dominican Republic," in *Latin American Radicalism,* p. 280.

> in 1916. I helped make Honduras "right" for American fruit companies in 1903.[16]

U.S. foreign aid is also informed by selfish economic interest, say the economic interpretations. It is used to dump capitalist surpluses on Latin Americans. It is used to favor the Yankee investor, the Yankee exporter, and the Yankee shipping industry. It is employed to intimidate Latin Americans who might stray from the capitalistic path.[17] Even the Alliance for Progress is explained as a means of furthering United States economic control in Latin America. The Punta del Este Charter contains a clause committing the signers to the promotion of "conditions that will encourage the flow of foreign investments." "Though these brief words are inconspicuous in the charter as a whole," says a critic, "they are, from the point of view of Washington, the main purpose of the Alliance."[18]

The effects of economic imperialism on the Latin American countries are also criticized. The powerful capitalist interests from the United States have contributed greatly to the poverty of Latin America. They have plundered the wealth of the continent with little regard for the consequences. They have taken out disproportionate profits to be distributed in the United States. They have reinvested far too little and cared nothing for the balanced development of the Latin American countries.

Moreover, the economic trusts have corrupted Latin American politics. In earlier times, Yankee interests overtly and blatantly interfered in domestic politics by backing the side that seemed most favorable to them. In more recent times, U.S. businessmen have been more subtle, but no less harmful, say their detractors. A powerful, close-knit group of native entrepreneurs, "landowning elites, foreign investors, and United States influenced international financial institutions" control the Latin American countries.[19]

Merle Kling, a leading North American scholar, has presented other political consequences of United States economic interests in Latin America.[20] Professor Kling postulates that political instability derives from the fact that the government is the only economic resource at the disposal of most Latin Americans, because the land is owned by the firmly-entrenched *hacendado* class and business is owned by foreign trusts. Hence, the government is constantly fought over by ambitious interests who have been boxed out of other possible sources of economic satisfaction. The result is endemic political insta-

16. Gerassi, *The Great Fear*, p. 231.

17. See Powelson, *Latin America*, p. 8; and J. P. Morray, "The United States and Latin America" in James Petras and Maurice Zeitlin, *Latin America: Reform or Revolution?* (Greenwich, Conn.: Fawcett Publications, 1968), pp. 113–114.

18. Morray, *ibid.,* p. 108.

19. Petras, "The United States and the New Equilibrium," 105–106.

20. See Merle Kling, "Toward a Theory of Power and Political Instability in Latin America," *Western Political Quarterly,* 9:1 (March 1956).

bility as one group attempts to replace another in a battle for economic spoils and social standing.

Finally, one other theory of inter-American economic relations demands discussion within the context of economic imperialism. The Prebisch Thesis,[21] published in 1950, is not a theory of economic imperialism, but it has supplied much valuable ammunition to those who charge the United States with economic exploitation. Dr. Raúl Prebisch and his colleagues in the United Nations Economic Commission for Latin America charge that inequities in trade relations have enriched the United States (and other industrialized countries) while impoverishing Latin America. Prebisch argues against the classical theories of trade, which posit that technological advances in industrialized countries are beneficial to poor nations because they result in lower prices for finished products. He proposes, to the contrary, that the poor pay more and more of their primary goods for the finished products of the industrialized countries. It cost more bags of coffee to buy a tractor in 1970 than it did in 1930. Hence, the terms of trade have benefited the rich United States and contributed to the economic exploitation of Latin America.

There are two basic responses to economic theories of imperialism. Some meet the argument head-on and attempt to show that the good done by economic imperialism far outweighs the bad. Others admit that imperialism is frequently motivated by economic considerations but then argue that the importance of economic motivations has been grossly exaggerated. Other explanations of imperialism are equally, if not more, important in understanding the influence of the strong over the weak or the rich over the poor.

The explanations that follow this discussion of economic imperialism focus on that argument. Other explanations of imperialism are offered as crucially important for a balanced understanding of U.S. imperialism in Latin America. Furthermore, it is proposed that national security considerations have been the most important determinant of U.S. imperialism in the Western Hemisphere.

Before proceeding to alternative explications of imperialism, however, it is necessary to set out the response of those who defend U.S. imperialism on the grounds of its contributions to Latin America. In a book entitled, *Foreign Investment in Latin America,* Marvin D. Bernstein[22] lists some contributions of North American business. He proposes that "foreign investments have almost always aided the economic growth of the Latin American nations, creating jobs and stimulating business internally." U.S. interests employ over 2 million Latin Americans. They contribute technological expertise and efficient business methods. "They purchase power, use transport facilities and

---

21. For an explanation of the thesis, see Albert O. Hirschman, "Ideologies of Economic Development in Latin America," in Hirschman, ed., *Latin American Issues* (New York: The Twentieth Century Fund, 1961), pp. 13–23; and Powelson, *Latin America*, pp. 72–75.

22. (New York: Alfred A. Knopf, 1966), 16ff. See also *Time,* July 11, 1969, p. 26, for some of the arguments and figures presented below.

local supplies, and pay taxes." U.S. business pays more than one-fifth of the continent's taxes. It also creates foreign exchange. American business has often exploited and developed areas that were beyond the capacity of the Latin Americans. There would be no (or at least much less) Venezuelan oil, Chilean copper, Bolivian tin, or Ecuadorian bananas if it were not for Yankee ingenuity and Yankee money. Latin America, it is argued, would be worse off economically than it is today had the United States not contributed private investment.

Many Latin Americans recognize the importance of U.S. public and private assistance. A leading statesman has noted that the economic cooperation of the United States is "fundamental" for the "economic development and future prosperity" of Latin America as well as for the "well-being of its peasant, industrial, and mining masses." Those who encourage hatred between the two continents, he warns, are sacrificing the people. Another leader of the Democratic Left recognizes that "a certain resistance" exists, but advises his fellows to import U.S. technicians to further economic growth. President José María Velasco Ibarra of Ecuador has stated that "Ecuador has no native capital. Only foreign investments will bring in such capital, needed to develop the country." The Peruvian Aprista movement argues that "foreign capital . . . is essential for the development of the resources of Latin America."[23]

Finally, many have challenged the validity of the Prebisch Thesis as a description of United States-Latin American trade relations.[24] It has not been proved, say the critics, that Latin Americans' primary products are worth comparatively less than in the past. Some charge that statistical data have been incorrectly manipulated or that incomplete data have been used. Moreover, Prebisch has failed to recognize the qualitative improvement in manufactured products that the poor nations purchase for essentially the same primary goods. Venezuelan oil, for example, is no different now than it was 30 years ago, but the refrigerator it buys is much improved. "The same coffee or tin that was previously exchanged for streetcars or wood-stoves is today used to buy airplanes and electrical appliances."[25] Finally, even if Prebisch's conclusions are correct, say some, he has not specified the right causes. These causes may not be monopoly control of trade or strong labor unions in developed countries, as he suggests. Rather, the unfavorable balance of trade may be caused by more easily rectified factors.

---

23. For the allusions and quotations above, see Edward J. Williams, *Latin American Christian Democratic Parties* (Knoxville: University of Tennessee Press, 1967), p. 148; Rómulo Betancourt, *Posición y Doctrina* (Caracas: Editorial Cordillera, 1958), pp. 149–50; Morray in Petras and Zeitlin, *Latin America*, p. 106; and Harry Kantor, *The Ideology and Program of the Peruvian Aprista Movement* (Washington: Saville Books, 1966), pp. 40–41.

24. For the following discussion, see Charles W. Anderson, *Politics and Economic Change in Latin America* (Princeton, N.J.: D. Van Nostrand Co., 1967), pp. 79–81; and Powelson, *Latin America*, pp. 72–75.

25. Anderson, *ibid.,* p. 80.

Strength vs. Weakness

Explaining the history of U.S. imperialism as the unequal power of the two continents may appear unsophisticated. Nonetheless, it may well be the most profound way to understand that relationship. Lord Acton's classic proposition that "power tends to corrupt" is irrefutable. The corruption of American power is American imperialism. Senator J. William Fulbright's charge of the arrogance of American power is a variation on the basic theme. American imperialism, in other words, inevitably emanates from U.S. strength and Latin American weakness. However trite and however sad, the strong rule the weak; all other considerations are beside that basic point.[26] Arguments looking to strategic or economic explanations, for example, are secondary in nature. The protection of the Panama Canal or the search for raw materials and markets only helps to explain the way that strength was rationalized or activated.

Though certainly not the major focus of hemispheric literature on Yankee imperialism, the "strength vs. weakness" explanation has frequently been discussed, Felipe Herrera, former president of the Inter-American Bank, explained the imperfection of inter-American multilateralism by alluding to the "essential inequality of the countries" and decrying the "power relationship between the mightiest nation in the world and 21 developing and disunited countries." A Colombian former minister echoes the same theme in commenting on negotiations concerning world commodity agreements on coffee. "The results could have been worse," he said, "as always occurs in business talks between unequals. The weak ought to be thankful that the strong do not abuse their power every time that they are able to abuse it."

Stripped of its rhetoric, the same argument was proposed by United States Ambassador Spurille Braden in his confrontation with the Perón regime in Argentina. Non-intervention, said Braden, was a legal fiction because the overwhelming wealth and power of the United States automatically meant intervention. If the United States acted, it intervened; if the United States did not act, it also intervened. The lesson for Braden was that the United States ought to intervene on the side of good, rather than not intervene and give its tacit approval to evil.[27]

This concept of United States power has resulted in a delightful Animal

---

26. The classic formulation is that propounded by the Athenians to the Melians during the Peloponnesian War. "We believe that heaven, and we know that men, by a natural law always rule where they are stronger. We did not make the law nor were we the first to act on it; we found it existing, and it will exist forever, after we are gone." Sir Richard Livingstone, ed. and trans., *Thucydides: The History of the Peloponnesian War* (New York: Oxford University Press, 1960), p. 270.

27. See "Remarks by Felipe Herrera at the closing session of the tenth annual meeting of the bank's board of governors," Guatemala City, April 25, 1969, p. 3, mimeo.; " ¿Fué en realidad un mal menor?" *Visión*, 13 de octubre de 1967, p. 48; George I. Blanksten, *Peron's Argentina*, reissued (New York: Russell & Russell, 1967), p. 411.

Farm of images created by various contemporary writers. The best-known beastly analog is Juan José Arévalo's *The Shark and the Sardines,* which notes that "it is the natural function of the shark to devour the sardine." A Cuban writer introduces another denizen of the deep when anticipating the possible reaction of American recognition of its loss in Vietnam. "I hope," he worries, "it will not be like Moby Dick. A bewildered monster who flicks his tail and wipes us off the island." Alberto Lleras Camargo evokes a third brute in his essay "El Paquidermo" (The Elephant). Lleras rejects the charge that U.S. policy is consciously imperialistic. Like the elephant, however, the United States is a great, clumsy beast that is sometimes imperialistic owing to "the inevitable, terrible, and vexatious consequence of a great disorientation."[28]

Though differing in specifics, the same point is dramatized by the increasing cultural imperialism of the United States in Latin America. Imperialism transcends American military and economic presence; even the cultural values of North American society, including baseball and racial prejudice, are impinging on Latin America. U.S. technology, management techniques, administrative organization, political campaigning methods, academic research techniques, and artistic styles are all increasingly diffused in Latin America. These, of course, are added to the more mundane influence of Yankee clothing, recreation, and speech.[29]The lesson for the student of inter-American relations in these examples of cultural imperialism seems to be the same as the political or military implications of the "strength vs. weakness" argument. A strong, dynamic nation inevitably dominates weaker ones.[30]

---

28. For the quotes, see Lawrence T. King, "On Arévalo's *The Shark and the Sardines*" in Alan F. Westin et al., *Views of America* (New York: Harcourt Brace Jovanovich, 1966), p. 320; Renata Adler, "Cultural Life in Cuba Thriving despite Regime," *New York Times,* February 10, 1969; *Visión, 13 de octobre de 1967, p. 21. With the reader's indulgence, I am compelled to complete the bestiary by noting two other descriptions of the power of the United States. Lin Piao on United States imperialism: "...like a mad bull dashing from place to place." Pierre Elliot Trudeau on living next door to the United States: "...like sleeping with an elephant. No matter how friendly and even-tempered is the beast..., one is affected by every twitch and grunt." See Norman Gall, "The Legacy of Che Guevara," A Commentary Report with Study Guide, 1967, p. 14; and "U.S. – Canada Talks — With a Cuban Accent," Miami Herald,* March 27, 1969.

29. On the diffusion of North American cultural influences as an indication of the profound power of the American society, see John N. Plank, "The Two American Cultures: Coexistence, Competition, or Cooperation?" address to the Inter-American Forum, St. Louis, 1968, mimeo.; and "Latin American Intellectuals Speak Out," in *The First Conference of the Latin American Solidarity Organization,* a staff study prepared for a subcommittee of the Senate Committee on the Judiciary (Washington, D.C.: Government Printing Office, 1967), p. 117.

30. Daniel Cosío Villegas, though not exactly responding to the "strength vs. weakness" theme, has noted that one lesson of Castro's successful flouting of U.S. power "is the fantastic vulnerability of the U.S.: Cuba, its former slave, and furthermore, small, poor, and disunited, has literally immobilized it, speechless, in a corner." Although the point is well taken, it should be noted that it was made before either the Bay of Pigs or the Missile Crisis. *Change in Latin America: The Mexican and Cuban Revolutions* (Lincoln: University of Nebraska Press, 1961), pp. 43 – 44.

Shared Values

If the "strength vs. weakness" proposition is first logically in understanding North American imperialism, then the "shared values" argument is first historically of the many philosophical rationales for the U.S. sphere of influence. The concept of the two spheres, the Old World and the New World, as set out by President James Monroe in the Monroe Doctrine, became the basis for a series of philosophic and propagandistic initiatives that grouped the Americas together. On the political level, the Pan-Americanism of James G. Blaine pushed the image. On the historical-philosophical level, Herbert Eugene Bolton's thesis that understanding North and Latin American history demands that they be treated as parts of a whole teaches the same message. More recently the anti-communism of the Cold War has also assumed some of the same implications, resulting in what one student has called the "harmony of interests" ideology.[31]

The concept, most simply stated, proposes that the United States and Latin America share a common historical and philosophic heritage, common contemporary interests, and a common destiny. The Old World, moreover, is intrinsically different, intrinsically evil, and its intrusion into the New World would have dangerous philosophic and political results. Most recently, the idea was proposed by President John F. Kennedy in his famous Alliance for Progress speech:

> We meet together as firm and ancient friends, united by history and experience and by our determination to advance the values of American civilization. For this new world of ours is not merely an accident of geography. Our continents are bound together by a common history—the endless exploration of new frontiers. Our nations are the product of a common struggle—the revolt from colonial rule. And our people share a common heritage—the quest for the dignity and the freedom of man.
>
> The revolutions which gave us birth ignited, in the words of Thomas Paine, "A spark never to be extinguished." And across vast, turbulent continents, these American ideals still stir man's struggles for national independence and individual freedom.[32]

The concept has also been widely accepted and propagated in Latin America. The Preamble to the 1961 Charter of Punta del Este evoked the image of "the long struggle for freedom [in this hemisphere] which now inspires people in all parts of the world." As recently as 1952, a leading Mexican thinker alluded to the "community of neighbors" of the hemisphere that "share in common an idea about the organization of society." A Christian Democrat ideologue proposes that "both Americas are heirs of Western and Christian civilization. From that trunk was born two branches, so that they

---

31. See Petras, "The United States and the New Equilibrium."

32. *President Kennedy Speaks on the Alliance for Progress* (Washington, D.C.: Agency for International Development, n.d.), pp. 3–4.

have the same profound origin and, in spite of many differences, a substantially common mind and a similar conception of man." Even Luis Carlos Prestes, a leading Latin American Communist, wrote that "the war against Nazism served to strengthen the bonds of Pan-American solidarity.[33]

Opposition to the "shared values" concept has focused on two major critiques. The first charges that, in practice, the concept has been a crass device of U.S. imperialism. Pan-Americanism, notes one North American student of Latin America, "may be said to consist of the Washington government's attempts to organize all of the American republics in support of the foreign policy of the United States." José Vasconcelos feared the diplomacy of Pan-Americanism, which he typified as "more dangerous than the cannon of the old English pirates." Indeed, the connotations of the "Pan" movement in the Western Hemisphere are similar to those of Pan-Slavism and Pan-Germanism, which were clearly guises for the imperialistic ambitions of Russia and Germany.[34]

The second critique is more profound; it questions the entire validity of "shared values" and, therefore, repudiates all political and policy implications that may flow from it. It proposes that "North American and Latin American cultures are so radically different that any expectation of really effective understanding, communication, and cooperation between the two parts of the Hemisphere is probably illusory."[35] A Latin American Communist is more bombastic in his denial of the concept:

> So-called Pan-American brotherhood, it is clear, lacks social and economic foundations of any kind; only effervescent charlatans, unprincipled quislings, and the power-hungry can unabashedly assert that the downtrodden Indian or Creole of Latin America has a communion of interests with the limitless wealth of Wall Street or the millionaire set on Park Avenue.[36]

For whatever reason the idea is rejected, it is evident that neither the United States nor Latin America has ever seen the concept as having opera-

---

33. For the quotations, see O. Carlos Stoetzer, *The Organization of American States* (New York: Frederick A. Praeger, 1965), p. 145; Luis Quintanilla, quoted in Arthur P. Whitaker, *The Western Hemisphere Idea: Its Rise and Decline* (Ithaca, N.Y.: Cornell Paperbacks, 1965), p. 4; Eduardo Frei Montalva, *La Verdad Tiene su Hora* (Santiago de Chile: Editorial del Pacífico, 1955), p. 130; Luis Carlos Prestes, "Brazilian Communists in the Fight for Democracy," in Luis E. Aguilar ed., *Marxism in Latin America* (New York: Alfred A. Knopf, 1968), p. 141. Whitaker's *The Western Hemisphere Idea* is entirely given over to the concept. Many favorable evaluations from Latin Americans also appear in Donald Marquand Dozer, *The Monroe Doctrine: Its Modern Significance* (New York: Alfred A. Knopf, 1965).

34. See Blanksten, *Perón's Argentina,* p. 8; Vasconcelos, quoted in William Rex Crawford, *A Century of Latin-American Thought,* rev. ed. (New York: Frederick A. Praeger, 1966), p. 267; and Manger, "Reform," p. 11.

35. Plank, "The Two Americas," p. 3.

36. Rodney Arismendi, "The End of the War and the New American Imperialism," in Aguilar, *Marxism in Latin America,* p. 150.

tional validity. The Monroe Doctrine may allude to shared values, but that declaration was essentially unilateral, protecting U.S. security. The Polk and Roosevelt corollaries make the same point. The Pan-American Union and the Organization of American States might well be seen as the manifestation of Pan-Americanism, yet until recent years all important political and administrative posts were held by North Americans. In 1966 the United States Senate Foreign Relations Committee rejected commodity stabilization and free trade agreements, because they might be interpreted as a "permanent commitment to Latin America."[37]

Reinforcing this denial of "shared values" between the two Americas, a strong case can be made that the two continents share more with other parts of the world than with each other. The ethnic makeup, cultural traditions, political institutions, and strategic designs of the United States are obviously more intimately tied to Western Europe than to Latin America. The vast majority of North Americans trace their political institutions, language, culture, and ancestry to Western European countries. Moreover, the foreign policies of the United States have most often been determined by events in Western Europe.

For Latin America, a number of other affinities seem at least as strong as those highlighted by the "shared values" concept. Both Pan-Hispanicism and Pan-Latinism are deeply engrained in the Latin American mind. Pan-Hispanicism has been implemented through the concept of *Hispanidad,* launched by Spain around the turn of the present century. *Hispanidad,* which emphasizes the cultural similarities of the Hispanic nations, has been well received in Latin America, tapping a reserve of goodwill for the former colonial master.

Charles De Gaulle's 1964 tour of Latin America revealed the strong undercurrent of Pan-Latinism. Had the material resources of France been adequate, De Gaulle might well have been successful in his attempts to wean Latin America from the United States.

The growing identification of Latin America with the underdeveloped nations of Afro-Asia also belies the "shared values" and Pan-Americanism ties. Finally, a strong element of universalism exists in Latin American political thought and diplomacy that has been manifested by a strong attachment to both the League of Nations and the United Nations.[38]

---

37. "Kennedy's Prescription for Latin America," *New Republic,* May 28, 1966, p. 9.

38. See Clarence H. Haring, *Latin America Looks at the United States* (New York: Macmillan Co., 1928), Chapter 8, "Pan-Hispanicism and Pan-Latinism," pp. 168–92. On the De Gaulle trip, see *Hispanic American Report* (November 1964), p. 17. On the attachment to Europe more broadly, see Edward J. Williams, "Comparative Political Development: Latin America and Afro-Asia," *Comparative Studies in Society and History* 11:3 (June 1969) 342–354. On Latin America and the rest of the Third World, see pp. 131–156 of this study. Though the emphasis in this discussion has been on the socio-cultural and philosophic affinity, Latin American affinity to these movements has also, of course, been politically motivated. It has been propagated quite consciously to offset the influence of the United States.

Manifest Destiny and the White Man's Burden

The rhetoric of "shared values" and Pan-Americanism implies partnership and equality. That implication of equality has been corrupted in the evolution of hemispheric history, but the ideal has never been repudiated within the context of that tradition. Another tradition, Manifest Destiny and the White Man's Burden, however, is in direct contradiction.

It states in clear, unequivocal terms that the United States is superior to the Latin American nations and carries the right and the moral obligation to spread its benign influence among the backward peoples of the southern continent. Although some variations of the Manifest Destiny theme seem to lack benevolent connotations, it is almost always interpreted in terms of the White Man's Burden.

As with the other justifications for North American imperialism discussed in this section, the Manifest Destiny and White Man's Burden apology winds its way through the entire history of inter-American relations.[39] The image of guardian presented in the Monroe Doctrine, for example, clearly assumes a superior-inferior relationship; a strong United States was to protect its weak Latin American cousins from the evil intentions of corrupt Europe. The same theme informs the evolution of American self-consciousness throughout the nineteenth century and is best seen in the sense of mission that surrounded the Mexican War (1846–1848), and the post-Civil War attitude toward Cuba, Mexico, Santo Domingo, and other Caribbean and Central American states. During that period, the United States first began to explain its imperialistic policies as a moral obligation to carry a superior culture to lesser peoples. The concept was clearly set out in the Roosevelt Corollary, which alluded to the United States as a "civilized nation" compelled to exercise "international police power" in the Western Hemisphere in the event of a "general loosening of the ties of civilized society" in Latin America. The task of Woodrow Wilson was scarcely less ambitious. He proposed the mission of "teaching the Latin Americans to elect good men."

The formal tone of more contemporary relations became less patronizing, but the same basic theme continues to play a major role. Although the United States has officially termed the Alliance for Progress a "cooperative effort" in which the United States is the junior partner,"[40] it is more correctly conceived as another attempt by the United States to save the benighted Latin Americans from their own inefficiency and incompetence.

The White Man's Burden has been undertaken in numerous spheres and with varying degrees of commitment. Wilson's policy is the best example of

---

39. For an excellent history of the concept, see Frederick Merk, *Manifest Destiny and Mission in American History: A Reinterpretation* (New York: Vintage Books, 1963).

40. Teodoro Moscoso, "Address before the Wisconsin Union of the University of Wisconsin" (Washington, D.C.: Agency for International Development, March 28, 1963), p. 4.

the Burden being interpreted in political terms. As a good political scientist, Wilson concentrated on teaching the political arts to the Latin Americans. In the Dominican Republic and Haiti, direct guidance by American mentors was employed; in Mexico, the indirect pressure of non-recognition was used to encourage the success of politicians espousing Wilson's philosophy. Wilson used U.S. influence to topple those he defined as dictators and to champion those he defined as liberal democrats.

Economically, the Burden has usually been defined as an obligation to teach Latin Americans the virtues of North American economic theory and practice.[41] The lessons have included the superiority of free trade over protective tariffs, monetary stability over inflation, micro-economics over macro-economics, free market over planned systems, and the innate rightness of the complementary relationship of Latin America's primary products to U.S. manufactured goods over the ambition of Latin Americans to build their own industrial economies.

In the socio-cultural sphere, the interpretation of the White Man's Burden has been the same. The United States lectured the Latin Americans about the superiority of the U.S. educational system, liberal individualism, social voluntarism, egalitarianism, Protestantism, and many other aspects of Americanism that seemed to set off the superior society and culture of the United States.

Latin American response to the implications of the White Man's Burden has generally ranged from sullen criticism to vehement repudiation. Simón Bolívar anticipated the feelings of many at the very beginning of inter-American relations. "The United States," he said, "appears to be destined by Providence to plague America with misery in the name of liberty." The White Man's Burden, say the Latin Americans, has all too often been a guise for the imperialistic designs of the Yankee and an excuse for imposing Yankee social values, economic practices, and political theories.

To provide perspective, however, it should be noted that a strong current in Latin America has favored the cultivation and importation of Yankee virtues, even if it frequently opposed some specific connotations of the White Man's Burden. Domingo Sarmiento, the great teacher-president of Argentina, was profoundly inspired by the American educational system and transferred much of what he saw to his native country. The Uruguayan ethical philosopher José Enrique Rodó, usually critical of the United States, taught his students to nurture the "greatness and dignity of labor," the "glory" of Yankee civilization. The Chilean, Francisco Bilbao, talked of the advantages of Protestant liberty, and José Martí of the superiority of Anglo-Saxon liberalism.[42]

In more recent times, many have praised the advances of U.S. technology

---

41. For an excellent discussion of the differing interpretations of economics, see Powelson, *Latin America.*

42. See Crawford, *A Century,* and José Enrique Rodó in Westin, *Views of America.*

and looked to the United States to export its sophisticated technology. Rómulo Betancourt makes the point:

> We are obligated to give an audacious, sustained impulse to the entire process of Venezuelan education. But while this process is undertaken, we must think about the transitory importation of *técnicos.* Perhaps this plan causes a certain resistance. . . . The United States, in the epoch of its industrial revolution, imported European capital and *técnicos.* Soviet Russia has utilized many knowledgeable Germans for its advances. We, then, shall have to import *técnicos* in a limited and transitory form just as we import meat, potatoes . . .[43]

A balance sheet of the mission of the White Man's Burden would seem to be inconclusive, with the stronger evidence inclining toward failure. On the positive side, the defenders of economic imperialism have argued that the United States has contributed to Latin American economic growth. The United States has also offered diplomatic support, established schools, trained police and labor union leaders, improved sanitation, and eradicated diseases.[44]

In the more difficult arts of building nations and implanting democracy, however, the accomplishments have been less noteworthy. After the liquidation of U.S. occupations in the 1920's, the Caribbean and Central American nations seemed to go from bad to worse. In the Dominican Republic and Nicaragua, Rafael Trujillo and Anastasio Somoza, American-trained military men, soon imposed long-lived dictatorships. Haiti fell into political chaos pockmarked by repressive regimes. Cuba suffered dictatorships and deep-rooted corruption that eventually led to the reaction of the Castro takeover. Panama evolved into an oligarchical state characterized by corruption and increasing political instability.

Among the states that had felt the pressure of American idealism, only Mexico progressed in the political, social, and economic arts. But the cause was the sweeping implications of the Mexican revolution and not the contributions of the White Man's Burden. Indeed, Mexico may have prospered in spite of the United States rather than because of it.

But this attempt at balancing the record is, in a sense, beside the point. Miles of roads built or nations not built are only the surface manifestations of more profound and clearly negative implications of the White Man's Burden. A student of inter-American politics says:

> Let us be altogether honest with ourselves: there has been something psychologically degrading to the Latin Americans in the way we have customarily interacted with them, whether in the cultural sphere or any

43. Betancourt, *Posición y Doctrina,* pp. 149 – 150.

44. For some representative arguments, see Rayford W. Logan, "The United States in Haiti, 1915 – 1952," in Harold A. Bierck, ed., *Latin American Civilization* (Boston: Allyn and Bacon, 1967), pp. 257 – 263; Mecham, *A Survey*; Dana G. Monro, *Intervention and Dollar Diplomacy in the Caribbean, 1900 – 1921* (Princeton, N.J.: Princeton University Press, 1964); and Perkins, *A History.* See also the defense of United States economic imperialism offered above.

> other. Even if all that we had conveyed to them of our wisdom through our preaching, chastising, cajoling had been useful and relevant — and we know, of course, that much of it has not been — the relationship has been intrinsically an unhealthy one.[45]

National Security, Self-Defense, Self-Preservation

The basic political explanation of United States imperialistic ventures is probably what one Latin American statesman has called "defensive imperialism." A leading North American scholar emphasizes the point when he argues that early twentieth-century imperialistic policies "must be explained in terms of fulfilling the security requirements of the United States."[46] The United States exercised imperialistic control because it thought that its national security was threatened. The threat was defined as the possibility of an unfriendly power gaining control of one of the weak nations near the borders. U.S. domination of Cuba, Haiti, or Nicaragua was necessary to prevent possible German, French, or Soviet control. An unfriendly Germany, France, or Soviet Union would be a threat to the lives and well-being of the American people. The scope and necessities of self-defense may have been shoddily defined, but that, obviously enough, is a measurement of political sophistication, not moral intention.

The argument is compelling. A survey of the geographic location, historical periods, and circumstances of U.S. imperialism lends credence to the premise. First, the imperialistic moves that have elicited the most criticism have occurred almost entirely in the Caribbean and Central America. Two facts explain the restricted geographic application of U.S. imperialistic military power. Control by unfriendly governments or big powers of areas close to U.S. borders dramatizes the possibility of a threat to American security. As early as 1845, the Polk Corollary established geographic propinquity as a definition of the applicability of the Monroe Doctrine. That is, an unfriendly Bolivia is less dangerous than an unfriendly Cuba. Bolivia is far away; Cuba is not.

One argument surrounding the Dominican intervention of 1965 exemplifies the point. Some military strategists opposed it on grounds that Soviet missiles in the Dominican Republic were no more a threat than Soviet missiles on submarines patroling the east coast or long-range missiles in Kiev. That is, the sophistication of modern weapons systems abolishes considerations of distance. United States policy makers, nonetheless, obviously rejected the argument. The overriding opinion does indeed envisage distance as an important criterion in a strategy of national security. Now, as in the past, the United States must insure that no unfriendly regimes are established near American

45. Plank, "The Two Americas," p. 12.

46. Campos, in Adams, *Latin America*, p. 24; and Mecham, *A Survey*, p. 263.

borders. American security demands therefore that American power be used to prevent the possibility of unfriendly regimes in Central America and the Caribbean.

The second, and even more important, fact explaining American imperialism in that area is the Panama Canal. American control of the canal has historically been interpreted as an essential ingredient of American security. Forty years before the canal was built, President U. S. Grant was influenced in his attempt to buy Santo Domingo because of "its strategic position commanding 'the entrance to the Caribbean Sea and the Isthmus transit of commerce.' "[47] The strategic necessities (and imperialistic connotations) were "officially" propounded by Charles Evans Hughes in 1923.

> By building the Panama Canal we have not only established a new and convenient highway of commerce but we have also created new exigencies and new conditions of strategy and defense. It is for us to protect that highway. . . . I believe that the sentiment of the American people is practically unanimous that in the interest of our national safety we could not yield to any foreign power the control of the Panama Canal, or the approaches to it, or the obtaining of any position which would interfere with our right of protection or would menace the freedom of our communication.[48]

More contemporary pronouncements of American policy exemplify the same ongoing concern for the security of the canal. In 1954, the United States CIA supported Carlos Castillo Armas in overthrowing Jacobo Arbenz Guzmán in Guatemala because of supposed Communist influence in the Arbenz government. The significance of Communist influence for Secretary of State John Foster Dulles and others was as a possible threat to the safety of the canal. Soviet arms being shipped to Guatemala, the argument was, were to be used to sabotage the canal.[49] Fidel Castro's importation of Soviet offensive missiles, which led to the crisis of 1962, also evoked fear for the security of the canal.

Security, not economic exploitation, primarily motivated Yankee imperialism. In Central America, for example, the two countries that have suffered most are Panama and Nicaragua — Panama because the canal is there, Nicaragua because a canal might have been or might yet be there and because it is very close to Panama. Concern for the security of the canal is also seen in the liquidation of American imperialism in Cuba and Panama in the 1930's. In Cuba, where much more American money was invested, the Platt Amendment was abolished with scarcely a ripple. The Panamanian liquidation of treaty rights, however, was much more difficult; only after three years was the Senate

---

47. Jackson Crowell, "The United States and a Central American Canal, 1869 – 1877," *Hispanic – American Historical Review* 49: 1 (February 1969), 35.

48. Charles Evans Hughes, "The Monroe Doctrine Officially Defined," in Dozer, *The Monroe Doctrine,* p. 93.

49. Philip B. Taylor, Jr., "The Guatemalan Affair: A Critique," in Bierck, *Latin American Civilization,* p. 269.

finally convinced that American security was not threatened by the new arrangements.[50]

The timing of North American imperialism can also be explained by the concern for security. Imperialism was most pronounced during periods when an extra-hemispheric threat seemed possible. When the United States was complete master of the hemisphere, when extra-hemispheric powers were too weak to involve themselves in the Americas, imperialism faded. The United States was least imperialistic during the period from the end of World War I to the mid-1950's. World War I had left the strong nations of Western Europe weak; the Soviet Union was launching its revolution. No nation posed a threat to United States hegemony in the Western Hemisphere. The United States could afford to be a Good Neighbor. Both before and after that time, however, possible challengers were relatively much stronger and the United States, therefore, exercised "defensive imperialism."[51]

Finally, the circumstances of U.S. imperialism lend credence to the security argument. In almost every instance of imperialism, genuine fear that failure to act defensively would result in a threat to American security seemed to motivate U.S. actions. In the traditional circumstances, a Latin American nation mismanaged its funds or was duped into going into debt to a European country. The nation then expressed a belligerent attitude and threatened action to insure payment of the debt. The United States then intervened to forestall an imperialistic foray by another power. More recently, North American imperialism has been evoked by fear of the entry of Soviet power into the Americas. To keep Soviet influence out of the United States' backyard, as it were, the United States has begun another round of defensive imperialism.

Many charge that U.S. fears of extra-hemispheric challenges have been flagrantly exaggerated. Although the charge may be correct, circumstances indicate that Washington genuinely felt it was acting defensively. But if the response has been far in excess of the potential threat, that only proves that American policy makers are none too perceptive; it does not prove they are evil.

Whether evil or stupid, however, "security" as a justification for U.S. defensive imperialism has been rather loosely defined. The American response in the Cuban missile crisis was elicited on the grounds of "self-preservation." The original Monroe Doctrine and many of the measures that have flowed from it have claimed "self-defense" of the United States. Self-defensive measures have responded to "threatened aggressions," which are "dangerous to our peace and safety," or are a "manifestation of unfriendly disposition," or "endanger our peace and happiness." Secretary of State Olney charged that the

---

50. Mecham, *A Survey,* pp. 118, 324.

51. One possible reservation to this argument is that the benign policy of the United States may have been an attempt to cultivate Latin American opposition to some minimal fascist threat in the late 1930's and early 40's. That threat was never so serious as those of the traditional powers in the early part of the century or of the Soviets later on, however.

"safety and welfare" of the United States demanded the independence of all hemispheric states. Secretary of State Robert Lansing later dissuaded Cuban rebels from destroying the sugar harvest by noting that "all disturbances which interfere with this production must be considered as hostile acts." The protection of the American war effort, for Lansing, was implicit in Monroe's "self-defense." "National safety," according to Hughes, "could not yield to any foreign power the control of the Panama Canal, or the approaches to it, or the obtaining of any position which would interfere with our right of protection or would menace the freedom of our communication."[52] President Kennedy's definition of security was equally broad.

> . . . if at any time the Communist buildup in Cuba were to endanger or interfere with our security in any way, including our base at Guantanamo, our passage to the Panama Canal, our missile and space activities at Cape Canaveral, or the lives of American citizens in this country, or if Cuba should ever attempt to export its aggressive purposes by force or the threat of force against any nation in this hemisphere, or become an offensive military base of significant capacity for the Soviet Union, then this country will do whatever must be done to protect its own security and that of its allies.[53]

These concepts, "self-preservation," "self-defense," "safety," "welfare," and "happiness," have never been concretely defined. The 1928 Clark Memorandum on the Monroe Doctrine admits as much.

> . . . there is a broad domain occupied by self-preservation which is incapable of definite boundary as to its extent, or of definition as to the kind of act which lies within it, because new conditions, new advances in the arts and sciences, new instrumentalities of international contact and communication, new political theories and combinations, vary from age to age and cannot be certainly foretold. As the law now stands, whatever falls within the necessities of self-preservation, under existing or future conditions, lies within the boundaries of the domain of the principle.[54]

The activities of the United States in pursuit of security mirror both the comprehensive applicability of the principle and the profound importance of the policy. The United States has used every measure from diplomatic pronouncements to annexation in search of security. The policy pronouncements began as early as the No-Transfer Resolution and have progressed through the Monroe Doctrine, the Polk and Roosevelt corollaries, the Olney Declaration, the Clark Memorandum, Dulles' Caracas Resolution, the Johnson Doctrine,

---

52. For the quotations, see Hughes in Dozer, *The Monroe Doctrine*, p. 93; and Mecham, *A Survey*, pp. 50, 64, 301.

53. Robert N. Burr, *Our Troubled Hemisphere: Perspectives on United States-Latin American Relations* (Washington, D.C.: The Brookings Institution, 1967), p. 29.

54. J. Ruben Clark, "Memorandum on the Monroe Doctrine," in Dozer, *The Monroe Doctrine*, p. 117.

and hundreds of other presidential decrees, congressional resolutions, and administrative fiats covering almost 175 years of diplomatic intercourse.

Diplomatic accords and mutual defense pacts include the establishment of the Pan-American Union, the Gondra Treaty, the Central American Court of Justice, the Bryan-Chamorro Treaty, the Act of Chapultepec, the Rio Treaty, the Pact of Bogotá, the Act of Bogotá, and dozens of other treaties, accords, acts, and pacts designed to increase the security of the Western Hemisphere and the United States.

The list continues with the encouragement or the provision of loans through the National City Bank of New York, the Export-Import Bank, the Inter-American Bank, the International Monetary Fund, and the World Bank. It also includes preventing international or inter-American control of the canal, keeping the United Nations out of the hemisphere, bolstering dictatorships, blockading Cuba, annexing Puerto Rico, attempting to annex the Dominican Republic, and buying President Francois Duvalier's vote in the Organization of American States (OAS).

In short, the explanation of North American influence and imperialism on security grounds is impressive. It is possible to postulate that almost every example of inter-American relations has some security manifestations for the United States. The entire history of hemispheric interaction could be written from the premise that U.S. actions have been motivated by security from the promulgation of the Monroe Doctrine to the establishment of the Alliance for Progress.

The Straw Man Argument

The "straw man" explanation or apology for Yankee imperialism posits essentially that the issue of imperialism has been grossly exaggerated in Latin America. A contemporary North American scholar outlines the argument:

> The charge of imperialism is very useful politically, for although its precise meaning is hazy, it is certainly a "bad thing." Its use is calculated to exploit the conviction that "something is wrong" — which it is — while simultaneously placing the blame at the doorstep of some detested foreigner and avoiding the need for action on the personal or national level. For the many adherents of the conspiratorial view of history, the charge of "imperialist" plays in Latin America a role identical to the cry of "communist" in the United States.[55]

There are several gradations of the charge. One contention is that selfish politicos use the imperialism straw man to further their personal ambitions. A journalist, for example, writes that "Peru's military dictator, General Juan Velasco Alvarado, is following a well-worn Latin American tradition. He is making a political career out of pulling the American eagle's tail feathers." The

---

55. Burr, *Our Troubled Hemisphere,* p. 107.

image proposed is of the selfish demagogue appealing to the baser passions of the people to recruit a political following.

A second nuance of the argument claims that the burgeoning nationalism of the Latin American countries invariably leads to charges of Yankee imperialism. The obvious target of Castro's revolution, for instance, could be nothing other than U.S. power and influence on the island.

A third gradation of the straw man apology centers on Latin American incompetence or inferiority. Here, in the words of a statesman-scholar, "Latin Americans used invective against the Yankees to divert attention from emerging social and economic problems at home." The United States becomes a whipping boy and receives the blame for what is in reality the incompetence of Latin American governments.

A further nuance again switches from conscious manipulation to natural response. The Latin American inferiority complex leads to criticism of the Yankee.[56] The point is that "this Latin American attitude is a reflection, of course, of a lack of self-confidence and of a kind of inferiority complex. Nationalism is one of the manifestations of these phenomena. Another is the tendency to blame somebody else for one's troubles."[57]

Finally, a contemporary Latin American has gathered most of the arguments set out above and added still another — conscious Soviet manipulation of anti-Yankeeism.

> And the anti-Yankeeism of Fidel? What object does it have? To defend the sovereignty and independence of Cuba? Events have demonstrated the contrary. His anti-Yankeeism originated in xenophobia and an inferiority complex. It is not today a part of the Latin American anti-imperialistic struggle. It is an arm of communist imperialism directed at the United States of North America and serves the Iron Curtain countries in order to infiltrate the underdeveloped countries.[58]

The Moods of Interpreting North American Imperialism

The way that people think about the universe obviously has meaning for the way that they approach concrete problems. The way that North Americans

---

56. Everett E. Hagen, in his fascinating and controversial *On the Theory of Social Change* (Homewood, Ill.: Dorsey Press, 1962), suggests that the response of Latin Americans, their feeling that others are manipulating rather than helping them, may be part of their personality. See pp. 429–430.

57. For the quotations and other commentary, see Richard Dudman, "Peru Dictator Follows Anti-United States Tradition," *St. Louis Post Dispatch,* February 19, 1969; Eisenhower, *The Wine Is Bitter,* p. 177; Cosío Villegas, *Change in Latin America,* p. 44; Rollie E. Poppino, *International Communism in Latin America* (New York: Free Press, 1964), p. 46; and Pat M. Holt, *Survey of the Alliance for Progress: The Political Aspects,* a staff study prepared for a subcommittee of the Senate Committee on Foreign Relations (Washington, D.C.: Government Printing Office, 1967), p. 13.

58. Luis Alberto Monge, "Unas lecciones del bloqueo a Cuba," *Combate,* 3:25 (noviembre y diciembre de 1962), 58.

and Latin Americans have conceived the nature of imperialism has just as obviously had real meaning for political policies designed to effect imperialism. Two moods or theories, "determinism" and "voluntarism," are present in interpretations of U.S. imperialism.

Determinism depicts the whole history of U.S. imperialism as being natural or inevitable, part of the scheme of things. U.S. hegemonic policies flow naturally from U.S. power. It does no good to be indignant about it or to try to change it. Changes are only a result of the grand sweep of history that men had no ability to affect.

Voluntarism sees imperialism and any other policy as a willful, planned choice made by men who can be influenced. Therefore, it is both right and useful to harrangue against it and work to change it. Policies can be modified and even reversed through the activity of men who muster intelligent arguments against them, actively encourage trends toward their change, or combine power blocs to oppose them. In inter-American history there have been varying degrees and types of both positions.

Determinism

The deterministic mood appeared at the very outset of hemispheric independence from Europe, clothed in the doctrine of the Two Spheres that identified the Western Hemisphere as the New World or the Promised Land. The concept implied deterministic patterns of political and social evolution.[59] It was preordained that the Western Hemisphere should be separate from the corruption and decadence of Europe; the New World would bring forth new ideas, new organizations, new dignity, and, indeed, a new utopia. Though it did not logically entail North American imperialism, the Two Spheres idea laid a philosophic foundation for the development of a U.S. sphere of influence. The policies of the United States, after all, were in tune with the evolution of history. That evolution was right; therefore, policies in pursuit of the idea were equally right.

Although a deterministic interpretation of inter-American relations was sketched out in the early part of the nineteenth century, the entire picture did not appear until the second half of the century. In both North and South America theories, doctrines, and ideologies emerged that emphasized the immanent nature of North American hegemony. Certainly the best known in the United States was the Manifest Destiny ideology. Mexico, during the 1830's and 40's, was the first Latin American target of that determinism. Expansion into and acquisition of Mexican territory was not judged as right and wrong; it was part of the natural law that impelled higher civilizations to rule backward peoples.[60]

---

59. See Whitaker, *The Western Hemisphere Idea,* Chapter 1, pp. 1 – 20.
60. See Merk, *Manifest Destiny*, Chapters 2 – 5; pp. 24 – 143.

After a period of quiescence, the deterministic implications of Manifest Destiny again contributed to the ideology of American imperialism beginning at the turn of the twentieth century. The ideology had been buttressed by the pseudo-scientific social Darwinism, which popularized the idea of the survival of the fittest. The fit, in the evolution of natural history, were destined to rule the unfit. Imperialistic ventures were only implementing the obvious determinism of the law.

Strangely enough, the same strain of determinism was significant in Latin America at the time. Social Darwinism was well known and widely accepted. Though Darwinism was usually put to other uses, some applied it to the relations between nations. The Argentine José Ingenieros wrote of the strength of the races and concluded that it was inevitable that the weak would suffer the rule of the strong. Eugenio Hostos agreed. Hostos, in the words of a scholar, proposed that "Latin America must develop civilization or die. It is a case of a strong culture absorbing a weak one." The choices were "civilization or death."[61] Though both men admitted the possibility of eventual redemption, they obviously thought that immediate relationships between the two Americas were intrinsically determined. There was a natural inevitability to the rule of the Yankee over the Latin.

A more recent strain of determinism in Latin America derives from the diffusion of Marxism. Marxist thought appeared in Latin America during the last part of the nineteenth century, but did not achieve widespread popularity until after the Soviet revolution of 1917. Since that time, several strains of Marxism have been important in Latin American thought, and the deterministic characteristics of that theory have informed the literature on inter-American relations. Particularly in the period immediately following the Bolshevik triumph in Russia and the more recent triumph of Castro in Cuba, Marxist or Communist determinism was well publicized. José Carlos Mariátegui, one of the most important of the early Communist apologists, posited the argument in 1927.

> North America, by feats of historical strength that are superior to the will of its own people, has set out upon a vast imperialistic venture, from which it cannot turn back. . . .
>
> And on this plane North American capital, still internally vigorous and prosperous, ceases to function as a national, autonomous phenomenon and is subordinated to an inescapable historical destiny.[62]

In the post-Castro contemporary period, the issue of determinism has again been brought to the forefront by the polemic between the old, Soviet-style Communists and the New Left. Soviet-style Communists hold that objective conditions must be ripe before the revolution or the liquidation of Ameri-

---

61. Crawford, *A Century*, pp. 124, 241.

62. José Carlos Mariátegui, "Yankeeland and Marxism," in Aguilar, *Marxism,* pp. 98, 99.

can imperialism. For them, the appearance of revolutionary conditions depends on the deterministically ordained evolution of history. American imperialistic power will remain until the Marxist dialectic unfolds another epoch.[63]

A last example of determinism might be called "contemporary pessimism." There seem to be two varieties. The first type has been brought about by the seeming inability of U.S. aid and good intentions to effect change or gain friends in Latin America or elsewhere. President Nixon's 1969 policy speech on Latin America reflected the pessimistic attitude.

> For years, we in the United States have pursued the illusion that we could remake continents. Conscious of our wealth and technology, seized by the force of our good intentions, driven by our habitual impatience, remembering the dramatic success of the Marshall Plan in postwar Europe, we have sometimes imagined that we knew what was best for everyone else and that we could and should make it happen.
>
> But experience has taught us better.[64]

This strain of contemporary pessimism has, of course, been strengthened by the tragedy of the Vietnam war. A popular feeling of unease, if not disgust, has evoked a political policy of neo-isolationism that looks to increasing attention to the problems at home.

Although not deterministic in the strictest sense, contemporary pessimism is a step backward from the dynamic, activist mentality that has always characterized American foreign policy. The United States has been chastened, as it were, and now is beginning to doubt its ability to work wonders. The international political world is not so malleable as it was thought to be. The unhappy, if not unhealthy, result is to view the international political universe in more deterministic ways. The new currents of history, goes the despairing argument, are communism, nationalism, Soviet or Chinese power, burgeoning population, irresponsibility among the poor, and wrongheadedness among our European allies. These problems are unmanageable and have determined the necessity for retreat.

The implications of this variety of contemporary pessimism spell the decline of North American imperialism in Latin America. As the inability to control the situation becomes more apparent and the frustrations attendant to changing the situation more striking, pressures on policy makers may force the United States to quit the area, just as it is now quitting Vietnam.

The Nixon administration's policy, announced in October 1969, seemed to indicate a reduced role for the United States in Latin America. The policy

---

63. For some examples of the argument and counter-argument, see Aguilar, *Marxism,* "Introduction," pp. 45–46, and "Documents" 21, 23, 27, 28, 29, and 36.

64. "Text of President Nixon's Address to the Inter-American Association," *New York Times,* November 1, 1969.

was in tune with the overall unobtrusive character of the Nixon image, but it may also indicate the more profound modification of U.S. policy emanating from contemporary pessimism.

The second variety of contemporary pessimism has a different focus and connotes different results. It is based on the proposition that U.S. culture, society, economy, and polity have become so complex and dynamic that they are overwhelming Latin America. A leading student of the area proposes that "what emanates from us is so manifold as almost altogether to escape meaningful coordination and control."[65] The image here is of a sort of original sin that emphasizes the limitation of man's ability to predict the consequences of his actions. Its implications are similar to that of the Animal Farm presented earlier in this chapter.[66] In evoking the elephant, for example, Lleras Carmargo is not saying that the beast is evil or rationally determined. Rather, he says that the United States, like the elephant, is a great, clumsy, stupid beast that is bound to do some harm no matter how well intentioned. He is saying that even when United States official political policy is becoming less imperialistic, the dynamic strength of the United States is exporting even more technology, organization, and life style than before. Therefore, in a very poignant sense, U.S. imperialism is determined by the nature of U.S. society. It will, moreover, probably become even more overbearing in the future.

Voluntarism

It is rather more difficult to specify the voluntaristic responses to North American imperialism, but three general schools or foci seem evident. First, Latin American thinkers and politicos have always attempted to reform their own societies. In earlier periods, these reform movements had only infrequent allusion to the threat of U.S. power. Later, however, reform was often consciously defended on the grounds that it was the only way to meet the United States on more equal footing and, thereby, to discourage imperialistic control. Whatever the rationale, however, the result was to be a stronger Latin America, better able to counter U.S. power.

The second position centered more concretely on imperialism. In both North America and Latin America, individuals and groups set out to change the imperialistic policies of the U.S. government. They viewed the hegemonic ventures and ambitions of the United States as being amenable to reasonable argument and political pressure.

The third position is represented by the Castroite New Left. This school looks to revolutionary change within the domestic societies of Latin America and the physical defeat of American power through guerrilla warfare. This

65. Plank, "The Two Americas," p. 4.

66. See p. 14.

"supervoluntaristic" position propounds that small groups of guerrillas can cause the final defeat of Yankee imperialistic might.

The goal of Latin American reformers has always been to change and strengthen their societies. Even before independence in 1825, Simón Bolívar and others had analyzed the Latin American malady and prescribed constitutional remedies. Later the Argentines Domingo Sarmiento and Juan Alberdi called for education and immigration to eradicate the weakness of the Southern continent. The positivists looked to science as the redeeming tool.[67] Recently, Communists have sometimes seen revolution as the answer. Aprista Social Democrats and Christian Democrats have proposed comprehensive reform programs covering social, economic, and political areas.

Whatever the interpretation of the malady, the Latin Americans have been obviously engaged in attempting to strengthen their polities. Even more to the voluntarist point is that they believe in the efficacy of their activity to reform and empower their societies. Furthermore, reforms leading to increased strength would change the power equation in the hemisphere and decrease the possibility of U.S. imperialism. Whereas that result was only implicit in the earlier programs of reform, it has been made an explicit goal by contemporary political forces. Aprista Social Democrats and Christian Democrats are the two most important progressive movements in Latin America today. Both point to their reform programs as increasing their independence from the United States. The economic and social strength gained by internal reform ultimately signifies increased international power and increased ability to withstand the imperialism of the United States.[68]

The second focus of voluntaristic thought has looked to a change in U.S. policy. In refutation of the deterministic arguments, this position holds that imperialistic ventures are political policies wrought by men and therefore changeable. The Aprista Social Democrats have reflected this position. Aprista thought showed a strong deterministic strain during the 1920's, but the advent of the New Deal and the Good Neighbor policy led to a revision of the position "along reformist lines à la Kautsky." Víctor Raúl Haya de la Torre, the father of the movement, "proclaimed that *imperialism was a policy,* and one that could be changed or reversed."[69] The agents for change have frequently been depicted as "advanced" or "progressive" groups in the United States. Those groups, say the Latin Americans, understand the problems of their Latin

---

67. See particularly Bolívar's Jamaica Letter and Angostura Message in Harold A. Bierck, Jr., ed., *Selected Writings of Bolívar* (New York: Colonial Press, Published by Banco de Venezuela, 1951), I, pp. 103 – 22, 173 – 97. On Sarmiento and Alberdi, see Crawford, *A Century,* pp. 18 – 51. On the positivists, see Leopoldo Zea, *The Latin American Mind* (Norman: University of Oklahoma Press, 1963), Part II, "The New Order."

68. For allusions to the point, see Williams, *Latin American Christian Democratic Parties,* p. 148; and Víctor Raúl Haya de la Torre, "Indo-America," in Paul E. Sigmund, Jr., ed., *The Ideologies of the Developing Nations* (New York: Frederick A. Praeger, 1963), p. 288.

69. Einaudi, *Changing Contexts,* p. 21, emphasis in Einaudi.

neighbors; their growth and influence spell a change in policy. The Mexican thinker José Vasconcelos explains:

> Within the Anglo-Saxon and Latin-American communities the better elements can fight the good fight against imperialism and *caudillismo;* it is the worst elements of each race that cause trouble, and there is hope that men of good will can be brought to work together. There are still men in North America, heirs of the spirit of a day before imperialism, when the United States was example and mentor to two continents.[70]

Most recently, this position received a major boost during the short Kennedy administration. Kennedy was popular in Latin America, and many saw his administration as the triumph of those "better elements" outlined by Vasconcelos. The editor of the Aprista-sponsored *Combate* wrote that "groups there (in the United States) who are friendly to our demands have grown in strength." At the same time, a leading Christian Democrat proposed that "in Washington there are influential politicos capable of understanding the times" who were ready to "identify with the forces of progress rather than those of reaction." A Mexican thinker saw the restraint of the United States in the face of Castro's Cuba as "praiseworthy, for strength that does not resort to force in order to resolve its difficulties inspires sympathy and confidence."[71]

A North American scholar has also identified the rise of the "better elements," though his position falls somewhere between the deterministic and voluntaristic poles. He argues that a real change in American policy has resulted from the U.S. domestic revolution beginning with the New Deal.

> Social change takes place at home before it finds its mark abroad. By the mid-fifties the Unites States had not yet adapted its foreign policy to include the trends that had already taken shape in domestic affairs. . . . The shift in policy toward Latin America was precipitated by Castro but it was built on a profound domestic revolution.[72]

Finally, in the last ten years a school of "supervoluntarists" has evolved in Latin America. The movement is informed by Maoist and Guevarist doctrines and inspired by the success of Castro's Cuban revolution and U.S. failure in Vietnam. The New Left denies the possibility of a change in imperialism, but also denies the pessimism of those who see the United States as undefeatable. Their position is confident of the eventual defeat of U.S. imperialism. The process is to be initiated by small guerrilla bands attacking the domestic oligarchy and the United States agents of imperialism. These small groups will change the "subjective" mentality of the Latin American masses, leading to

---

70. Crawford, *A Century,* p. 268.

71. Monge, "Unas lecciones," pp. 57–58; Radomiro Tomic, "Un vistazo al los Estados Unidos de hoy," *Política y Espíritu* 16: 27 (abril de 1962), 23; Cosío Villegas, *Change in Latin America*, pp. 43–44. Remember that Cosío was writing before the Bay of Pigs.

72. Powelson, *Latin America*, p. 31.

a wholesale revolutionary repudiation of Yankee power. The skill, tenacity, and seemingly superhuman efforts of these small groups, goes the theory, are the catalyst for change in Latin America. Their victory signals the end of Yankee imperialism.

Conclusion

Apart from some aspects of Manifest Destiny, deterministic explanations of history and politics have never been well received by North Americans. For the United States, the cause of Latin American weakness or underdevelopment must lie in the unwillingness of the Latins to make the most of their potential. On the popular level, the stereotype of the sombrero-clad, slumbering figure tells the story of Latin American weakness. Even on the more academic level, the literature seems to depict a wrongheadedness or incompetence that Latin Americans stubbornly defend despite the teaching of their U.S. mentors.

North Americans also vehemently deny any preordained pattern to their own imperialism. Whatever imperialism there has been, they have argued, derives from some unfortunate side effects of a U.S. foreign policy rationally designed to protect Latin America as well as the United States. The North American, in sum, naturally repudiates deterministic thought and instinctively accepts voluntarism.

In truth, of course, both arguments have some merit. Philosophers, psychologists, and sociologists have long ago concluded that man's activities are both determined and voluntary. The same point holds concerning the relations between the Americas. American policy has changed in the past and will surely change in the future because men have decided it prudent to change it.

However voluntaristic that policy, two important contextual determinants have been suggested in the preceding discussion. First, imperialism in Latin America has been very directly conditioned by the U.S. interpretation of its security interests. The possibility of extra-hemispheric intrusion has been answered by imperialistic forays. At the beginning of the century, when the Western European powers were strong enough to challenge the United States, a policy of defensive imperialism resulted in a number of interventions and occupations. More recently, when Soviet power began to intrude into the hemisphere, the United States intervened in Cuba, the Dominican Republic, and Guatemala.

Conversely, U.S. imperialism retreated only when there was little possibility of a threat to its control of the hemisphere. From about 1920 to 1954 is the longest period in which the United States has not been involved in imperialistic ventures in Latin America. Then U.S. security was insured because it was the undisputed master of the hemisphere. The Western European powers were prostrate after World War I and soon became primarily concerned with struggles leading to World War II. Only with the revivification of Soviet power a decade after World War II was U.S. supremacy challenged. Precisely at that time, the United States began another series of imperialistic forays. The point is clear; real or imagined threats to U.S. control of the Western Hemisphere determine an imperialistic response by the United States.

The second "determinant" of United States imperialism is less specifically tangible, though no less important. A little earlier[73] a point was made concerning the revolution in thinking that was dramatized by the New Deal in the United States. That "backdrop of accomplished change in the United States" led to more sensitive hemispheric policies. It would have been impossible to pursue these policies earlier because the concepts informing the new departure were not accepted in the United States. In this sense, of course, imperialistic politics is determined by the values and attitudes of the time. Milton Eisenhower propounds the message in criticizing American policy during the first two decades of the century. "If, during the heyday of its intervention in Cuba," he says, "the United States had initiated even a reasonable degree of social justice, universal education, and true democracy . . . all succeeding developments in our relations with Latin America would have been far different than what they proved to be." But, he continues, the times were not ripe for such policies. "The leaders of those days were no doubt doing what they thought to be the proper thing. The concept of social justice was not then foremost in official or popular thinking."[74]

Ideas come of age at different periods. In one epoch men think that imperialism is, on the whole, not reprehensible and therefore are not hesitant to launch interventions and occupations. That was the case during the first two decades of the present century. If the actions of policy makers were not determined by the milieu of the time, they were at least partially justified by what seemed right and proper.

---

73. See p. 31.

74. Eisenhower, *The Wine Is Bitter*, p. 174.

Two

The Cold War and Communism

Introduction

Inter-American politics of the last 25 years must be studied in the context of the fear of Communist influence and Soviet power. The Cold War and communism theme has pervaded every aspect of hemispheric intercourse, dictating political and military policy, influencing the apportionment of economic aid, shaping the agenda of inter-American conferences, and motivating the establishment of the Alliance for Progress. Indeed, as the research into Latin American revolutionary predispositions encompassed in the ill-fated Project Camelot so poignantly exemplifies, fear of communism has even swayed American scholarship.

Many charge that the United States has exaggerated the importance of the Communist threat in Latin America, and that policy makers have failed to distinguish between authentic national revolutionaries and Communists. Furthermore, students deny that the Soviet Union has ever had serious intention of challenging U.S. hegemony in Latin America. These charges are discussed within this chapter. Whatever their validity, however, it is impossible to deny that the Cold War and communism have defined post-World War II hemispheric relations.

The fear of communism, of course, predates World War II. The Mexican revolution, during its more radical phases, was frequently characterized as "Bolshevistic." In 1926, U.S. military intervention in Nicaragua was justified on the grounds that Central America was a center of "Communist agitation." Ramon Grau San Martin was forced to resign the Cuban presidency in 1933 when United States Ambassador Sumner Welles charged him with propagating ideas that were "frankly communist."[1]

Understandably, U.S. opposition to the Soviet Union and communism receded during World War II. Both countries were locked in a struggle with Nazi Germany. The necessities of military cooperation gave rise to warmer relationships, and U.S. hostility to communism changed to "cooperation" and "apparent friendship." Indeed, some Latin American Communists "were welcomed with splendid receptions when they visited the United States." Even at the Rio Conference in 1947, the United States treated the Communist issue as a sensitive one in hopes of reaching a *modus vivendi* with the Soviet Union.[2]

The scenario for the Cold War, however, was completed by the late 1940's. The Soviet Union assumed an increasingly belligerent attitude toward the United States. Soviet belligerence became connected with the ideological appeal of communism. At that same time, the United States was forced to shoulder the burden of Western defense. Since that time, world politics has been dominated by dreary series of American – Soviet confrontations in Iran, China, Greece, Berlin, Malaya, Korea, the Congo, Vietnam, the Middle East, and Latin America. The entire world has become a theater of Cold War politics.

U.S. opposition to Communist influence and Soviet power in Latin America has been clearly set out on numerous occasions. Though the tone of pronouncements and responses has had some variations, the message is unequivocal. U.S. policy was announced as early as 1948, when Secretary of State George Marshall told delegates at the Bogotá Conference that the United States was compelled to counter the Soviet menace. The Organization of American States, which emerged from that conference, has been described in a little booklet issued by the State Department as "a bulwark against Communist subversion, infiltration, or armed aggression in the Western Hemisphere.[3] Even President Kennedy, usually not given to such rhetoric, made note of "alien forces which once again seek to impose the despotisms of the Old World on the people of the New."[4] Perhaps none have stated the position so bombastically and dramatically as Secretary of State John Foster Dulles. In an address to the nation in 1954, he described the CIA-assisted overthrow

---

1. See Kenneth J. Grieb, "The Role of the Mexican Revolution in Contemporary American Policy," paper presented at the Latin American Institute (Oshkosh: Wisconsin State University; 1967), p. 5, mimeo.; John Gerassi, *The Great Fear in Latin America*, rev. ed. (New York: Collier Books, 1965), p. 235; and John P. Powelson, *Latin America: Today's Economic and Social Revolution* (New York: McGraw – Hill Book Co., 1964), p. 29.

2. Robert J. Alexander, *Communism in Latin America* (New Brunswick, N.J.: Rutgers University Press, 1957), p. 27; and Jerome Slater, *A Reevaluation of Collective Security* (Colombus: Mershon National Security Program, Ohio State University Press, 1965), p. 28.

3. *Our Southern Partners* (Washington, D.C.: Department of State, 1962), p. 37.

4. *President Kennedy Speaks on the Alliance for Progress* (Washington, D.C.: Agency for International Development, n.d.), p. 3.

of the Communist-leaning Arbenz Guzmán regime in Guatemala. The events, he said,

> expose the evil purpose of the Kremlin to destroy the inter-American system. . . . The master plan of international communism is to gain a solid political base in this hemisphere, a base that can be used to extend Communist penetration to the other peoples of the other American governments. It was not the power of the Arbenz government that concerned us but the power behind it.
>
> If world communism captures any American state, however small, a new and perilous front is established which will increase the danger of the entire free world and require even greater sacrifices from the American people. . . . The need for vigilance is not past. Communism is still a menace everywhere.[5]

The tone and perhaps some implications of more "liberal" North American policy makers differ from Dulles's. The basic fear of Communist influence is shared, nonetheless. In pushing for U.S. assistance to the Latin American nations, President Kennedy called for "social progress and economic development." The alternative, he continued, was "a grave danger that desperate peoples will turn to communism or other forms of tyranny as their only hope for change. Well-organized, skillful, and strongly financed forces are constantly urging them to take that course."[6]

The Soviet Communist Intrusion

Though there may be some exaggeration to the rhetoric of U.S. politicos, Communist influence and Soviet power have intruded into the Western Hemisphere since the end of World War II. Soviet or Soviet-line challenges to U.S. hegemony in the hemisphere have taken three different guises. First, direct activity of the Soviet Union is shown by the Moscow-style Latin American Communist parties and the international policies of Soviet diplomacy. A second focus of Communist penetration is the Castro regime — sometimes as a vehicle of Soviet power and other times operating on its own initiative and pursuing its own causes.

Third, U.S. interests have been challenged by the emergence of the New Left in Latin America. As is true in the United States, the Latin American New Left is certainly not Communist in the traditional sense; that is, it is not necessarily guided by the Soviet Union. Rather, the movement is inspired by Castro, Che Guevara, Mao Tse Tung, Ho Chi Minh, and other ideologues. The

---

5. John Foster Dulles, "International Communism in Guatemala," in Donald M. Dozer, *The Monroe Doctrine, Its Modern Significance* (New York: Alfred A. Knopf, 1965), pp. 167–172.

6. John F. Kennedy, "Excerpts from Address to Congress, March 14, 1961," in *President Kennedy Speaks*, p. 19. For the same thesis, see Hubert H. Humphrey, "U.S. Policy in Latin America," *Foreign Affairs* 42 (July 1964), 593–594.

New Left assumes a militant revolutionary posture, launching guerrilla movements in the countryside and terrorist campaigns in the cities in an attempt to bring down the established governments. It is often intensely nationalistic and denies any intention of delivering the continent into the hands of the Soviets. The New Left charges that the present governments have sold out to the U.S. imperialists. Its triumph would be a repudiation of U.S. influence in Latin America. Although the New Left shares no long-range interests with the Soviet Union and Communist China, both nations would profit by a New Left victory. Thus, the triumph of the New Left would increase the hemispheric presence and influence of these two nations, at least for the short run.

There are a number of evidences of the strength and influence of the Moscow-directed campaign to wean the Latin American nations from the protection of the United States. Not all of these examples have the same meaning for the Soviet presence, but all contribute in one way or another to its increase. First, Moscow-style Communist parties have operated in a number of Latin American countries. At the end of World War II, the Latin American Communist movement was of some significance. In the Cuban elections of 1944, the party elected 3 senators and 7 deputies. In 1945, the Communist candidate for the Brazilian presidency polled 596,000 votes, almost 10 percent of the total votes cast. Two years later, the party counted 8.5 percent in the legislative elections and gained 1 senator, 14 deputies and 46 state legislators. In 1946, the Chilean party had 3 representatives in the president's cabinet. Immediately following the war, Communist parties counted members in the legislatures of Bolivia, Brazil, Chile, Colombia, Costa Rica, Cuba, Ecuador, Peru, and Uruguay.[7]

Second, Communists have been successful in the Latin American labor union movement. Like the political parties, Communist unions were most influential at the close of World War II. At that time

> They controlled or greatly influenced most of the important national trade-union organizations. At that time, also, they controlled the Confederación de Trabajadores de América Latina, which was until 1948 the only existing hemispheric labor confederation.[8]

Communist influence in both political parties and labor unions has diminished greatly since the immediate postwar period, but it is still significant in several countries. The victory of Dr. Salvador Allende in the 1970 presidential elections in Chile was interpreted by many as a Communist victory. It was not quite that—Allende is a Socialist and the Communist party is only one element of the victorious coalition. Still, the Allende triumph is a feather in the Soviet cap. The Chilean Communist party is a significant force in that country and Communists are the single most important force in the labor union movement.

---

7. Donald M. Dozer, *Are We Good Neighbors?* (Gainesville: University of Florida Press, 1959), p. 337.

8. Robert J. Alexander, *Organized Labor in Latin America* (New York: Free Press, 1965), p. 20.

The Communist movement also plays a significant role in other Latin American countries. From 1958 to 1963, for example, the Venezuelan party was represented by 7 of 133 deputies and 2 of 51 senators. In 1968, the Uruguayan Communists polled 6 percent of the vote. Communists have significant influence on labor unions in Brazil, Costa Rica, and Ecuador.

Most important Communist groups pay at least lip service to the mentorship of the Soviet Union in the international Communist movement. Nationalistic polycentrism has affected the relationship between Moscow and the Latin Communists, but Soviet influence continues in the hemisphere. Indeed, the rise of Castro's bastard communism has driven some groups to reaffirm their ties to the Soviet Union. Moscow, moreover, continues to assist the Latin American groups. In 1965, a Soviet shipment of $330,000, sent through the Italian Communist party, was intercepted by Venezuelan authorities before it reached the hands of the local Communist movement. As recently as 1967, the Mexicans uncovered an espionage operation. In the same year, the Argentines denied entrance to suspicious "diplomatic" materials sent by the Soviets.

The Soviet Union has also used more direct appeals to woo the Latin Americans and increase its political influence in the southern half of the hemisphere. During the 1950's and early 1960's the Soviets undertook a concentrated campaign throughout the Third World, including Latin America, to sell themselves as the leader of the anti-imperialist nations. The Third World countries were repudiating their Western ex-masters, and Soviet political strategists attempted to climb on the bandwagon. Though not completely successful in Latin America, or elsewhere, the Soviet ploy did have an impact. The value of that tactic has been reduced but not totally eradicated in recent years.

An American journalist charges that the Soviets have lately introduced the complementary appeal to racist feelings.

> As massive escalation of the war in Viet Nam began, strategists at Moscow's Latin American Political Institute came up with a different approach. Racism, frank and naked, is the watchword of the new appeal: colored peoples of the world, unite against the white aggressor.
>
> The campaign has had notably greater success in Latin America than the traditionalist tactic. Its effects are particularly apparent in the armed forces of the principal Andean nations — Peru, Colombia, Venezuela, Ecuador, Bolivia — where Indian and mixed-blood elements predominate.
>
> General Velasco (the military dictator of Peru who came to power in 1968) and his collaborators belong in this ethnic category. International Petroleum Company, the Standard Oil affiliate seized by Velasco's junta, has a history of covert discrimination in its employment and promotion practices, dating back half a century.[9]

A third appeal of the Soviet Union is the success of Soviet economic development. The Latin American nations are profoundly concerned with finding the magic of economic growth, and the appeal of the Communist

9. Thayer Waldo, "Nixon's New Latin Affairs Chief Must Face Soviet-Inspired Racism," *The Denver Post*, March 28, 1969.

economic model is widespread. The Soviets claim to have industrialized their country in less than 50 years. A poor, backward, agricultural society was transformed into the second most sophisticated industrial power in the world in only a fraction of the time taken by the capitalist West. Soviet technological growth and scientific achievements, particularly the launching of the first Sputnik in 1957, have been much admired in Latin America. Indeed, Latin American economic developmentalists have been impressed with the macroeconomics and national planning of the Soviet experience.

As a result of that economic success, the Soviets have recently launched a campaign to increase trade with Latin America. They posit two arguments to persuade the Latins of the advantage of increasing their trade. The economic advantages of large, expanding markets for many products exported by the Latin American nations are highlighted. The Soviet Union, a rich nation of nearly 250 million people, say the Soviets, is a ready consumer for the coffee, grains, meats, sugar, and other Latin American primary products. Further, Latin America resents U.S. political influence flowing from the role of the United States as the primary market for Latin exports. The political enticement of trade with the Soviet Union, Eastern Europe, and China is the lessening of U.S. pressure and the enhancement of the political independence of the Latin American states.

Though not an impressive success, the Soviet trade offensive has made economic inroads in Latin America. Trade has increased. Cuba accounts for much of that growth, and the figures are small in absolute amounts, but in relative terms the increase has been significant. Data published by the United Nations' Economic Commission for Latin America show that exports to the Soviet bloc grew from $10 million in 1950–52 to $344 million in the 1965–67 period. Imports evidenced a less dramatic, but still significant, growth from $17 million to $140 million.[10]

More important than economic gains, however, is the fact that the trade offensive seems to be achieving some political success. The Peruvian military regime characterized its new trade agreement with the Soviets as "the beginning of an end to economic dependence on the United States." The Costa Rican José Figueres, long a close ally of the United States, called for increased trade with the socialist bloc in his 1969 campaign for the presidency. In an article ranking the news of 1968, Chile's *La Nación* pointed to a number of missions from Soviet bloc countries as indicative of "the opening of Chile to the world."[11]

The same trend is evidenced by the increasing success of the Soviet Union in establishing or restoring diplomatic relations with Latin America. A number of the Latin American nations had never established diplomatic relations

---

10. See "CEPAL: el por qué del saldo negativo," *Visión*, 4 de julio de 1969, p. 32.

11. See "Costa Rica: Figueres Gains from a Third Front," *Latin America*, 3: 18 (May 2, 1969), p. 141; *News from Chile* (Washington, D.C.: Embassy of Chile, January 11, 1969).

with the socialist countries. Others, because of pressure from the United States, broke relations in the late 1940's and 50's. However, Colombia restored relations with the Soviet Union in 1968. In late 1968 through 1969, Peru established diplomatic relations for the first time with the Soviet Union, Hungary, and Bulgaria, and upgraded to full diplomatic status its consular relations with Czechoslovakia, Romania, and Yugoslavia. Bolivia and Ecuador announced resumption of diplomatic relations with Czechoslovakia. In 1969, Venezuela established diplomatic relations with Czechoslovakia and Hungary and seemed on the verge of exchanging ambassadors with the Soviet Union. Only three Latin American nations continue to have no official relations with any Soviet-bloc country — the Dominican Republic, Guatemala, and El Salvador.

The second, and even more dramatic, example of communism's intrusion into the Western Hemisphere is Fidel Castro's Cuba. The Castro regime has evolved an unprecedented working relationship with the Soviet Union, leading to a significant increase in Soviet hemispheric presence. Equally important, the Castro regime is a revolutionary base in the hemisphere designed to inspire, aid, and harbor anti-U.S. movements. Without analyzing the seriousness of that threat, it is clear that Fidel Castro has added a new significance to the inter-American responses to the Cold War and communism. Cold War battles are no longer limited to Europe and Asia but have been transferred to the doorstep of the United States.

Following the triumph of the Cuban revolution on January 1, 1959, the regime began an anti-Yankee policy buttressed by increasing ideological affinity and political friendship with the Soviet Union. Soviet First Deputy Premier Anastas I. Mikoyan's visit in early 1960 cemented economic accords; in mid-1960 Nikita Khrushchev claimed a political protectorate over Cuba and promised to use Soviet missiles to defend the island; Castro's famous "I am a Marxist-Leninist" speech in late 1961 tied the Communist ideological knot.

Meanwhile, the Cuban regime encouraged anti-Americanism throughout Latin America. As Soviet influence grew and Castro became increasingly bellicose in his anti-Yankee position, both American official policy and public opinion became disenchanted with the Cubans. The inevitable break of diplomatic relations came in early 1961.

The Cold War came perilously close to becoming hot with the crescendo of the Cuban missile crisis in October 1962. Soviet missiles, supposedly defensive in nature, had been secreted into Cuba. In addition to the missiles, 28,000 Soviet troops were on the island. The United States set up a blockade around Cuba to forestall the implacement of more weapons and ordered those already in place to be dismantled and returned to the Soviet Union. After several tense days, the crisis was resolved. Soviet ships carrying missiles turned back, and the Soviets promised to retrieve missiles already on the island. The immediate threat of Soviet power was erased from the hemisphere.

After the successful repulse of Soviet Russian military power, attention shifted to Castro's exportation of revolution to other American states. Although Castro's Cuba no longer seemed a direct menace to U.S. security, its inspiration of and aid to subversive guerrilla movements was depicted as a serious indirect threat, because of the intrinsic instability of many Latin American regimes and their susceptibility to overthrow by left-wing guerrillas. The Castro-aided groups all made it clear that they considered the United States as an imperialistic force must be expelled from the continent. Even though these groups were not necessarily tied to the Soviet Union, they would be much more receptive to Soviet penetration than the regimes they sought to replace.

The ideological and political inspiration of the New Left in Latin America is somewhat muddled and inconsistent, but four elements can be identified. The first two contributing forces, the Soviet Union and traditional Latin American Communist parties have now backed away from the movement, but both groups were involved at the outset and continue to exercise some influence. In the mid sixties, for example, the Soviet Union was actively engaged in training Latin American revolutionaries.

> Lumumba University in Moscow, according to a broadcast from the Soviet capital, is training thousands of Latin American students. The broadcast, beamed to Latin America in the Quechua language of the Indians of Peru, Bolivia, and Ecuador, said that when these students return to their homelands, "they will teach their brothers the modern techniques they have learned. But they will do more than teach. . . . They will fight alongside peasants and humble people to ensure that their countries have freedom."[12]

The traditional Communist parties at first embraced Castro and the New Left, although the relationship has become strained. In some cases, one group has repudiated the other. In Venezuela, the Soviet-style Communist party and the Castro-inspired Movimiento de Izquierda Revolucionaria (MIR) had a very close working relationship in the early 1960's. As the decade advanced, however, internal power struggles, nationalistic propensities within the Communist party, and the increasing radicalization of the MIR combined to cause a serious split. The abortive attempt of Che Guevara's guerrilla movement in Bolivia also dramatized the suspicion and animosity that poisoned cooperation between the two forces. Many Bolivian Communists thought the subversive attempt an imprudent adventure. Some suspect that the Communists may have assisted the government in tracking Che.

Castro's Cuba has been both ideological inspiration and material assister of the New Left. The contribution is probably best exemplified by Castro's leadership in the organization of a Third World New Left organization. In January 1966, the First Conference of the Solidarity of Peoples of Asia, Africa, and Latin America met in Havana. At that meeting, the Latin American

---

12. Paul D. Bethel, "The Havana Conference," *The Reporter*, March 24, 1966, p. 28.

Solidarity Organization was founded to map out, coordinate, and assist the anti-imperialist struggle in the Western Hemisphere.

The New Left has also borrowed heavily from the Chinese peasant-based revolutionary ideology, the mystique of Third World internationalism, burgeoning Latin American continentalism, and the more particular nationalisms of each Latin American country. The flying of the black flag in Paris during the student revolts of 1968 also introduced an anarchist flavor to the movement. Even this list of the components of the New Left, however, fails to capture the essence of the position. The New Left is more than the sum of its parts.

For this analysis, the most crucial characteristic of the New Left is its tendency to increase the intrusion of the Cold War into the Western Hemisphere. Though one cannot postulate profound unity of interest between the New Left and the Communist powers, it is nonetheless true that the success of the New Left would encourage the entry of Soviet power into the hemisphere and add another significant arena to the Cold War struggle. "The Generation of 1950," notes a scholar, "had neither the experiences of Soviet unsuitability nor of United States acceptance of reforms like the Mexican oil expropriation. To them, the problem of the times could be identified as Imperialism."[13] Their repudiation of that imperialism tends to increase confrontations with the Cold War and communism that have dominated inter-American politics for too long.

The United States' Response

As the introduction to this chapter noted, U.S. preoccupation with the Cold War and communism has colored every facet of inter-American politics since the termination of World War II. The issue has touched 25 years of political policy and infected everything from U.S. treatment of visiting intellectuals to U.S. treatment of resident dictators.

First, Washington has periodically issued ringing statements declaring the presence of the Communist evil and the U.S. resolve to withstand that threat. In 1970, reacting to rumors of a Soviet submarine base in Cuba, a "White House official" warned the Soviets that the United States "would view the establishment of a strategic base in the Caribbean with the utmost seriousness." A special study on the 1965 Dominican Republic intervention proposed that "trained Communist agents were on hand to exploit the chaotic situation." It continued that U.S. intervention "gave the Dominican people another chance to institute representative government in that troubled nation." Three administrations have declared that there are to be "no more Cubas." President Johnson pledged that "the American nations cannot, must not, and will not

13. Luigi Einaudi, *Changing Contexts of Revolution in Latin America* (Santa Monica, Calif.: The Rand Corporation, 1966), p. 21.

permit the establishment of another Communist government in the Western Hemisphere."[14]

Not satisfied with its own declarations, Washington has also sponsored a series of hemispheric organizations and resolutions aimed at identifying, damning, and mustering opposition to the Soviet and Communist threat. The foundation of the Rio Hemispheric Defense Pact in 1947 was supported by many in the United States because they interpreted it as an anti-Communist agreement. In 1951, during the Korean War, an inter-American meeting of foreign ministers looked to the "common defense of the Western Hemisphere against the aggressive activities of international communism." Only three years later, Secretary of State Dulles extracted another resolution, "The Declaration of Solidarity for the Preservation of the Political Integrity of the American States against the Intervention of International Communism." In 1960, Secretary of State Christian Herter sponsored another statement, the "Declaration of San José." In 1962, the American Foreign Ministers Conference reaffirmed the principle that the inter-American system is incompatible with the principles of communism.[15]

The United States also was instrumental in voting sanctions against Fidel Castro's Cuba. The stage was set in 1960, when the United States supported sanctions against the Trujillo right-wing dictatorship "in the hope that its Latin American neighbors would reciprocate by supporting the vigorous measures which the United States intended to propose against Castro's Cuba."[16] Two years later, the American foreign ministers conference voted limited sanctions against Cuba. In 1964 the United States was finally successful in having the Organization of American States impose drastic sanctions, which included severing diplomatic relations and stopping trade with Cuba.

In more positive moves, the United States has undertaken a number of programs designed to strengthen its own position. First, various foreign aid initiatives by the United States have been popularized as a way to combat communism. The Alliance for Progress is the best example, but only one of many. The Alliance is concerned with the redemption of the Latin American masses, but is equally motivated by the hope that economically secure, de-

---

14. Robert M. Smith, "U.S. Warns Soviets Not to Build Base for Subs in Cuba," *New York Times*, September 26, 1970; *Report of the Special Study Mission to the Dominican Republic, Guyana, Brazil, and Paraguay* of the House Committee on Foreign Affairs (Washington, D.C.: U.S. Government Printing Office, 1967), p. 2.; J. P. Morray, "The United States and Latin America," in James Petras and Maurice Zeitlin, ed., *Latin America: Reform or Revolution* (Greenwich, Conn.: Fawcett Publications, 1968), p. 114.

15. See George I. Blanksten, *Peron's Argentina,* reissued (New York: Russell & Russell, 1967), p. 425; Robert N. Burr, *Our Troubled Hemisphere* (Washington, D.C.: The Brookings Institution, 1967), p. 68; *Our Southern Partners*, p. 38; Pat M. Holt, *Survey of the Alliance for Progress: The Political Aspects*, a staff study prepared for a subcommittee of the Senate Committee on Foreign Relations (Washington, D.C.: U.S. Government Printing Office, 1967), p. 3.

16. J. Lloyd Mecham, *A Survey of United States-Latin American Relations* (Boston: Houghton Mifflin Co., 1965), p. 289.

cently housed, well-fed men will be less receptive to the allure of the Communist message.

At the same time, as the Alliance demonstrates, the United States has also pushed for political, social, and economic reform in Latin America. If the rising expectations of the people for political participation, social mobility, and economic opportunity are satisfied by their own political systems, they will not turn to communism. U.S. pressure has unquestionably led to reform that has both contributed to the well-being of the masses and empowered the governments to operate more effectively. However, the push for reform has also been a defense against Communist critiques. A U.S. scholar sets out the reasoning.

> Partially as a response to the Castro revolution, the United States sought to encourage a particular mode of reform — the gradual, peaceful, evolutionary variety. This stand, however, was designed as much to stave off violent upheavals as to promote reform. Thus, the American position still exhibited a negative aspect. For Washington contended that if change was indeed inevitable, it was imperative that it occur "the American way." Americans tend to view the situation through a Cold War mental set, and, therefore see only a choice between gradual reform under democracy and violent revolution under communism. Although Americans sincerely believed that the Latins would derive greater benefits from a gradual transformation than from sudden tumultuous change, the Americans also perceive that this evolutionary process would provide the least danger to their interests. The American assumption that violent revolution meant communism played a key role, and thus the United States' stand was influenced as much by the Communist threat and the Cold War as by the conditions in Latin America.[17]

The point is well made. U.S. aid and reform programs are mightily influenced by the fear of communism. That preoccupation too frequently leads to petty and indefensible measures. For example, a Latin American source ridicules a "Checklist of Statutory Criteria, Alliance for Progress," used by the Agency for International Development. The checklist sets out a number of criteria for evaluating a Latin American government's acceptability for economic assistance. "The Checklist," says the critic, "is little more than a child's report card. . . . Question 13, for example, reads: 'If assistance is to,a government, has the secretary of state determined that it is not controlled by the international Communist movement?' Other parts," concludes the comment, "are hardly more elevated."[18]

Another instance of the corruption of U.S. aid played a part in the 1962 expulsion of Cuba from the Organization of American States. The United States had great difficulty mustering the two-thirds vote necessary for expulsion. Finally, the United States bought the vote of Haiti's tyrant, François Duvalier, by promising monies to build a new airport in Port-au-Prince.[19]

---

17. Grieb, "The Role of the Mexican Revolution," p. 1.
18. *The Visión Letter*, April 2, 1969.
19. George W. Grayson, "SOS for the OAS," *The Reporter*, May 30, 1968, p. 32.

U.S. military aid to the Latin American armed forces is another element of its response to the Cold War and communism.[20] Between 1950 and 1964, the United States supplied over $500 million in military assistance; between 1950 and 1969, 21,000 Latin Americans were trained in military schools in the United States and 200,000 more in Panama. Other activities include a school for Latin Americans in the Canal Zone, regular U.S. training missions to the Latin American countries, anti-guerrilla training provided by the United States Special Forces, CIA and FBI collaboration with and training of Latin American police forces, and even, according to the Guatemalan vice president, sorties by U.S. planes, flying from Panama, against guerrillas hiding in Guatemalan mountains.[21]

The U.S. concept of the Latin American military's role changed in the early 1960's from an emphasis on defense against extra-hemispheric attacks to a concentration on defense against internal subversion. The basic rationale, nonetheless, remains: Whether aid is offered for conventional warfare or for internal security, the intention of the U.S. policy makers has been to buttress the Latin military in its struggle with the forces of communism. A second purpose of military aid, moreover, has been to cultivate the friendship of the military establishments. The military are important political policy makers in their respective countries, and the United States has been anxious to retain their friendship. Senator Margaret Chase Smith makes the point: "The greatest friends that the United States has in South America are the members of the military forces — and the greatest enemies of communism are the military."[22]

Another U.S. response to the problems of the Cold War and communism has been aid to dictatorships.[23] In its quest for stable regimes in Latin America, the United States has buttressed dictatorships on the grounds that Communist penetration is the only alternative. In a meeting of American foreign ministers in 1959, for example, Secretary of State Herter opposed any action against the Trujillo tyranny because "he feared that the overthrow of Trujillo would more likely promote chaos and disorder in the republic than democracy, and possibly open the door to Communist penetration."[24] The argument is based on the

---

20. The best general work is still Edwin Lieuwen, *Arms and Politics in Latin America*, rev. ed. (New York: Frederick A. Praeger, 1961).

21. For these and other examples, see Willard F. Barber and Neale Ronning, *Internal Security and Military Power* (Columbus: Ohio State University Press, 1966), p. 36; Editorial, "Aid to Latin Military Men Misfires," *The Denver Post,* December 19, 1968; Edwin Lieuwen, *Generals vs. Presidents* (New York: Frederick A. Praeger, 1964), pp. 147 – 148; Morray, in Petras and Zeitlin, *Latin America,* pp. 115 – 116. "Guatemala: Napalm on the Guerrillas," *Latin America* 1: 21 (September 15, 1967) 159.

22. Quoted in a footnote in James Petras, "The United States and the New Equilibrium in Latin America," *Public Policy*, 18: 1 (Fall 1969) 98. See Chapter IV for a more comprehensive discussion of military aid.

23. See Chapter IV for a comprehensive discussion of this theme.

24. Mecham, *A Survey*, p. 289. A puzzling question about Herter's stance appears in the fact

supposed inability of the United States to confront more than one problem at a time. In criticizing the U.S. rapprochement with Perón's Argentina in the late forties, a U.S. scholar outlines the policy makers' reasoning.

> The Soviet Union is now the greater evil; meanwhile, pick up Perón and dust him off. And suppose the power politics approach damages other elements of United States' policy in the Western Hemisphere, what then? The high priests have an answer for that question too: "A foreign policy which attempts simultaneously to solve two different and mutually exclusive problems will be vacillating, and will not, in the end, solve either. The most urgent and vital problem must be solved first. . . . Generally speaking, foreign policy can be effective only if it is directed at one major problem at any one time. If there are several problems to be solved at a given moment, compromise must clean the slate for the sake of the major problem's solution" Q.E.D. The Soviet Union and the "cold war" must come first. Meanwhile, compromise on other matters, including Perón.[25]

Finally, the Cold War and communism have been the basic motivation in several physical interventions since the end of World War II. (That theme is analyzed in detail in Chapter 3.) In Guatemala (1954) and Cuba (1961), the United States inspired, financed, and supported natively recruited military units in invasions of the two countries. In the Dominican Republic (1965), the United States undertook an intervention using its own troops. These interventions were all evoked by fear of the increased Soviet or Communist influence in the hemisphere. The U.S. position was that the dangers of Soviet power and Communist penetration were so compelling as to merit the ultimate response of intervention. Following the Dominican intervention, the House of Representatives passed a resolution declaring that the United States had the right to intervene in any country in Latin America threatened by communism.

The Latin American Position

Opposition

The Cold War and the Communist danger exist for Latin America, but with far less immediacy and importance than for the United States. The Latin American response, therefore, has varied. On some issues and at some times, the Latins have offered enthusiastic support to the United States; in other

---

that two years later, however, Trujillo was assassinated in what many charge was a CIA-supported plot. A left-wing analysis implicitly answers the question in proposing that Trujillo had to be removed because he had become an obstacle to U.S. domination of the Dominican Republic. See Fred Goff and Michael Locker, "The Violence of Domination: U.S. Power and the Dominican Republic," in Irving Louis Horowitz et al., *Latin American Radicalism* (New York: Random House, 1969), p. 261.

25. Blanksten, *Perón's Argentina,* pp. 433 – 434. Blanksten is quoting Robert Straz-Hupe and Stefan T. Possony, *International Relations* (New York: McGraw-Hill Book Co., 1950), p. 240.

instances, only grudging support has been forthcoming; in other situations, considerable pressure by the United States has been unable to enlist support from many of the nations.

Latin Americans have been profoundly angered by their relegation to a minor position in U.S. foreign policy. Latin America does not seem to exist in itself for U.S. policy makers, but only within the context of the Cold War. This situation became evident at the 1948 Bogotá Conference. Secretary of State George Marshall outlined the strategic world-wide necessities of American interests. The message was clear to the Latins — the confrontation with Soviet Russia meant that Latin America would take a back seat. A leading Latin American thinker sees Yankee policy as resting on the premise

> that Latin America had lost priority in relative terms because its wartime strategic importance had declined as a result of changing warfare concepts and of the displacement of the area of potential contamination.[26]

In other words, Latin America was safe from Soviet penetration and the United States could forget about it. Power politics demanded that the United States develop priorities; Latin America had a low priority. Until the late 1950's, then

> The Latin American policy of the United States was essentially one of postponement or, where unavoidable, placation — never of positive policies, promptly implemented. Washington, regarding Latin America as peripheral to the Cold War in comparison with other areas of the world, and believing that Latin America was already committed irrevocably to the Western cause, assigned it a low priority for attention.[27]

Only when the rise of Castro signaled the Soviet Union's intrusion into the hemisphere did the United States pay much attention to Latin American affairs. The Latins, understandably enough, feel that the United States has been far too concerned with the Communist issue and often take a cynical view of the increasing U.S. interest in their salvation. Many insist that the United States has been irrationally preoccupied with the vision of international communism. A Mexican leftist has used the term "hysterical" in describing the Yankee response to Fidel Castro. To "twice the ovation that Dulles received," Guatemala's foreign minister characterized the 1954 Caracas anti-Communist resolution as "the internationalization of McCarthyism, the burning of books, and the imposition of stereotyped thought."[28]

---

26. Roberto de Oliveira Campos, "Relations between the United States and Latin America" in Mildred Adams, ed., *Latin America: Evolution or Explosion?* (New York: Dodd, Mead & Co., 1963), p. 28.

27. Burr, *Our Troubled Hemisphere*, pp. 22 – 23.

28. Carlos Fuentes, *The Argument of Latin America* (Ann Arbor, Mich.: The Radical Education Project, n.d.), pp. 498 – 499; Philip B. Taylor, Jr., "The Guatemalan Affair; A Critique," in Harold A. Bierck, ed., *Latin American Civilization* (Boston: Allyn and Bacon, 1967),

Further, Latin Americans frequently charge that the United States promiscuously pins the Communist label on liberal reforms, genuine moves for social revolution, or programs of nationally inspired economic independence. These charges of communism are not only incorrect, say the Latin Americans, but work a hardship on the authentic Democratic Left's search for solutions to national problems. A Chilean outlines the argument.

> The United States cannot continue to consider movements in favor of just social recovery as communistically inspired. That attitude would be conducive to making the workers believe that only the Communists are capable of struggling for their interests.[29]

Many Latins also charge that the United States has failed to understand the nature of the threat. Even if there is danger in Communist activity, the correct solution lies in the economic development, social redemption, and political democratization of the Latin American countries. The Communist challenge can be defeated not by arms, but by eradicating the conditions that breed communism. While the United States has used military and political measures that only strengthen anti-democratic elements within the military, the Latin Americans point to economic and social programs designed to defeat the attraction of the Communist ideology.

Concomitantly, many Latin Americans have accused the United States of overstating the aggressive intentions of the Communist world. Strong opposition has always developed when North American policy makers attempt to define communism as "inherently aggressive." Many Latin Americans deny that proposition and refuse to adhere to pronouncements and declarations that make that interpretation of communism or of the foreign policies of Communist states.

The Latin American nations have frequently opposed U.S. Cold War policies because their own sovereignties are threatened when the principle of non-intervention is endangered. The tradition of non-intervention is almost sacred in Latin America, and provocations must be serious indeed to induce the Latin American countries to repudiate it. Mexico and Chile, particularly, have opposed numerous U.S. Cold War initiatives because they seemed to transgress the non-intervention principle.

Opposition to supporting the United States in its extra-hemispheric Cold War confrontations is almost unanimous. The Latin American nations have no intention of reacting to the Communist challenge until they are specifically threatened. A leading authority notes that "they have been moved by little or

---

p. 266. See also Daniel Goldrich and Edward W. Scott, "Developing Political Orientations of Panamanian Students," in John D. Martz, ed., *The Dynamics of Change in Latin American Politics* (Englewood Cliffs, N.J.: Prentice-Hall, 1965), p. 250.

29. Tomás Reyes in *Congresos Internacionales Demócrata-Cristianos* (Santiago de Chile: Editorial del Pacífico, 1957), p. 392.

no sense of obligation to resist Communist aggression before it reaches the Western Hemisphere."[30]

Immediately after World War II, the Latin American nations successfully defeated U.S. attempts to apply the Rio Treaty to extra-hemispheric aggression. The treaty becomes fully operable only if an armed attack is made within rigidly defined geographic limits of hemispheric territory or adjacent seaspace.

The Korean War again demonstrated Latin American lack of enthusiasm for the overseas adventures of the United States. One student observes that there was a "generally disappointing reaction to United States' attempts to involve the Latin Americans in the Korean War."[31] Another adds:

> Although the provisions of the Rio Treaty did not specifically cover the Communist attack in Korea, Latin America's apparent general acceptance of the principle of collective security led the United States to expect its military cooperation in fighting the Communists in Korea. Only Colombia responded, however. Despite the provisions of the bilateral MDA (Mutual Defense Assistance) agreements under which the countries receiving military aid are pledged to participate in missions important to the defense of the hemisphere, eleven of the twelve Latin American signatories chose not to join in the fighting abroad.[32]

Failing to entice Latin American troops to Korea, the United States then pressured the Latin Americans into limited economic assistance and military mobilization. These accords, consonant with the reigning Latin American attitude toward the Korean effort, were "largely ignored."[33]

In 1957 the United States again attempted to encourage the Latin Americans to cooperate with its containment policies. Secretary of State Dulles issued a "vague proposal" designed to effect a "closer interlocking" between the OAS and NATO. The initiative "met with such a chilly reaction that it had to be dropped."[34]

The Latin American nations have shown even less enthusiasm for the U.S. intervention in Vietnam. In an attempt to demonstrate hemispheric support, the State Department listed seven Latin American nations as having contributed to the anti-Communist struggle. The evidence, however, belies the claim of active support. Argentina contributed 5,000 tons of wheat flour; Brazil sent medical supplies and coffee; the Dominican Republic was listed as having made "an offer of cement;" the other nations' contributions were no more impressive.[35] More than lacking enthusiasm, Latin America has shown a strong current of opposition to the Vietnam War. The war is often depicted

---

30. Lieuwen, *Arms and Politics*, p. 209.
31. Slater, *A Revaluation*, p. 26.
32. Lieuwen, *Arms and Politics*, p. 209.
33. Slater, *A Revaluation*, p. 26.
34. Slater, pp. 26–27.
35. *New York Times*, March 12, 1957, quoted in *NACLA Newsletter*, March 1967, p. 7.

as another Yankee overreaction to the supposed threat of communism. The rejection of the United States position is buttressed by the image of the United States as an imperialistic power. Furthermore, many feel that the Alliance for Progress is suffering because of the shift in American interest to Southeast Asia and the high financial expenditures demanded by the Vietnam conflict. Moreover, a growing Latin American identification with the underdeveloped Third World has created a strong current of anti-colonialism and a genuine sympathy with the anti-colonial struggle of the North Vietnamese.[36]

Support

Despite considerable opposition to the U.S. response to the Cold War and communism, Latin America has frequently supported that response throughout the postwar period. Economic and political pressure has often been applied to elicit that assistance, but more often it has been motivated by the Latin Americans' interpretation of their own self-interest. Whatever the condition of the support, the Latin nations have stood with the United States on numerous issues. The specific contributions of the Latin American states have ranged from philosophic defense of the "Two Spheres" ideology to provision of national troops for the ad hoc inter-American peace keeping force in the Dominican Republic. They have also contributed voting support in the United Nations on Cold War issues, suppression of internal Communist movements, and the expulsion of Castro's Cuba from the Organization of American States.

On the most general philosophic level, Latin Americans have always thought of themselves as Western people adhering to the values of Western civilization and striving for the realization of Western ideals. Though challenged by the growing affiliation of Latin America with the Third World, the theme continues to be the dominant strain in Latin thought. Adherence to Western civilization implies a rejection of the philosophic values, cultural modes, and political institutions of the East, and the Soviet Union and the Communist bloc are frequently defined as Eastern cultures. Jose Mora, past Secretary General of the OAS, answers the question: "Will Latin America continue to adhere to the West?" in the affirmative and adds that "Latin America is one of the strongest influences for the preservation of the political beliefs and the democratic institutions of the West."[37]

The Latin American Christian Democratic movement also highlights this position in its thinking about the Cold War and communism. To the Christian Democrats, the Soviet Union represents an essentially alien, non-Western, non-Christian civilization. The western world, despite its imperfections, is presented as having achieved a higher stage of evolution. Soviet penetration,

---

36. For more discussion of this point, see pp. 133 – 136.

37. Jose A. Mora, "Will Latin America Continue to Adhere to the West?" *The Annals*, July 1961, p. 103.

in that sense, is degrading and endangers the advances made by the West in its struggle for personal emancipation. A Latin American Christian Democratic international conference, for example, declared that "neutralism cannot exist before the Soviet threat. Our peoples, because they belong to the Western World, have their most profound roots in the Christian civilization." José Rasco, a Cuban exile, proposes much the same idea in rejecting "a fence-sitting position between the Western World, essentially Christian, despite its lapses, and the Eastern World, essentially pagan. . . . If, in case of political conflict a choice must be made between Washington and Moscow, between Lincoln and Lenin, we must decide, despite risks, for the world where liberty does not perish."[38]

The Latin Americans have also been chary of Soviet imperialism. In a speech delivered in Havana during the third month of Castro's power, José Figueres damned the hemispheric ambitions of the Soviet Union and declared that "it's time that we remembered our friend, the United States, faces a grave problem with Soviet Russia, and that we align ourselves in a solid front in the Western Hemisphere against communism." Another source proclaims that "Soviet imperialism constitutes an even greater threat than capitalist imperialism" and denounces "the hypocritical anti-imperialism of the Communists and their allies which . . . opens up the field for the penetration of Soviet imperialism, whose oppression is already exercised in an asphyxiating form over the satellite countries."[39] Probably feeling some degree of empathy, the Latins have been especially critical of Soviet Russia's control of the Eastern European satellite nations. The 1954 Hungarian intervention was condemned throughout Latin America. In 1969, not only established governments but even Latin American Communist parties vehemently criticized the use of Soviet military forces against the liberal Czech regime.

Even in the days of lessened tensions between the Soviet Union and the United States, most Latin American nations seem suspicious of the ambitions of the Soviets. Soviet embassies are watched closely and Communist diplomatic personnel have been frequently declared *personae non gratae*. Twice within two years Uruguay expelled Soviet diplomats for interfering in domestic affairs. The lack of an enthusiastic response to the Soviet trade offensive may also indicate distrust. In listing reasons why the Soviet Union had not been as successful as anticipated in developing trade relations, a *Visión* article notes that many Latin American governments fear that the Soviets have political rather than economic intentions.[40]

The rejection, distrust, and suspicion of the Soviet Union has encouraged support of the United States in numerous Cold War moves. Although the

---

38. "El Congreso del Caribe," *Política y Espíritu,* 15 mayo de 1961, 53 – 56. Quoted in Leslie Dewart, *Christianity and Revolution: The Lesson of Cuba* (New York: Herder & Herder, 1963), p. 151.

39. "Congreso del Caribe," p. 53 – 56.

40. "Para ganar la América Latina," *Visión*, 10 de noviembre de 1967, 40.

contributions of the Latin American states have usually been of peripheral importance and their support has frequently been offered only after great urging and pressure, in practically every situation they have ultimately backed the United States in its ongoing struggle with the Soviet Union. The 1962 missile crisis is the extreme case, of course, but may also contain the ultimate lesson. The events of those portentous days are still beclouded. One North American critic notes that the United States "created enormous pressures on the Latin governments to fall into line,"[41] but Robert F. Kennedy, in his dramatic *Thirteen Days*, presents a different image.

> But the Latin American countries, demonstrating a unique sense of unity, unanimously supported the recommendations of the United States. In fact, a number contributed men, supplies, and ships during the several weeks that followed. . . .
>
> It was the vote of the OAS that gave a legal basis for the quarantine. Their willingness to follow the leadership of the United States was a heavy blow to Khrushchev. It had a major psychological and practical effect on the Russians and changed our position from that of an outlaw acting in violation of international law into a country acting in accordance with twenty allies legally protecting their position.[42]

There is little doubt that "enormous" pressure was indeed exerted on the Latin American countries. It is equally true, however, that the OAS unanimously supported the U.S. position, and that a number of the nations mobilized their defense forces and contributed military assistance.

Latin America has also supported the U.S. position on Fidel Castro's Cuba. At the outset, of course, most of the progressive forces in both Latin America and North America approved of the Cuban revolution. But approval soon gave way to hesitant criticism and finally to rejection and repudiation.

Opposition to the Castro regime has several bases. First, many Latin Americans oppose the domestic policies of the Cuban government. The summary trials and executions of people connected with the previous Batista regime soured many in Latin America. The purges of "counter-revolutionaries" that followed close on the heels of the executions also caused concern. The endless delay of promised elections and the personalistic, demagogic style of the regime elicited opposition. Many have interpreted the Castro regime as a totalitarian dictatorship that tramples on the liberties of the people.

Others oppose the international stance of the Cuban regime, pointing more directly to the Cold War and communism theme. Many hemispheric governments have censored the "interventionistic and aggressive" activities of Cuba. Venezuela has suffered much from Cuban bellicosity and has frequently initiated moves to condemn and counteract the Cuban threat. Speaking in mid-1964, Venezuelan President Raúl Leoni outlined his country's position.

41. Petras, "The United States and the New Equilibrium," p. 119.
42. Robert F. Kennedy, *Thirteen Days* (New York: W. W. Norton & Co., 1969), pp. 57, 121.

> We have contributed to the Meeting of Foreign Ministers with the end of trying to achieve the application of measures outlined in inter-American treaties against the acts of intervention and aggression proved to have been undertaken by the Cuban regime in Venezuela.
>
> It is well-known that this aggressive and interventionistic policy of the present Cuban regime, as demonstrated by the Report of the Investigatory Committee of the OAS, has for its object the subversion by means of force, through terrorism and other acts of violence, of the institutional order which has given Venezuela the exercise of the principle of free self-determination of peoples, legitimately expressed in irreproachable elections.[43]

The Latin Americans charge that Castro has introduced Soviet imperialism into the Western Hemisphere. In implicit support of the traditional Two Spheres concept, some of the opposition is based on the extra-hemispheric nature of the Soviet threat. The Colombian daily, *El Espectador*, has editorialized against readmitting Castro to the OAS. The editorial damns Castro's aggressions against several Latin American countries and concludes by depicting Cuba as the source of "communism's regional attack against Pan-Americanism."[44]

Latin Americans deplore Castro's subservience to the Soviet Union as much as they dislike Castro's domestic policies or his stance against the United States. One Latin critic, deploring Castro's submission to the designs of the Soviets, has seen the "tragic-comic lesson" of the 1962 missile crisis in Khrushchev's treating Cuba like a "miserable colony."[45]

To switch from the international to the domestic arena, many Latin American countries have also cooperated with the United States by outlawing and suppressing the traditional Communist parties and by subduing the guerrilla movements of the New Left. Immediately following World War II, the United States began to urge its hemispheric neighbors to suppress their domestic Communist parties as a necessary Cold War measure. Political risks were often involved. The parties were strong in several countries and counted considerable support and sympathy. Nonetheless, most of the Latin countries cooperated with the United States. By 1963, only six nations permitted formal Communist party organizations. Even in those countries, Communists were so frequently badgered by the police and military that normal activity was difficult to maintain. Uruguay is probably the only country where the local Communists have enjoyed continual, relatively free access to political militancy.

In addition to instigations by the United States, a strong current in

---

43. Raúl Leoni, *Documentos Presidenciales*, Tomo I (Caracas: Oficina Central de Informacion, 1965), p. 165.

44. Quoted in Virginia Prewett, "Hemisphere Sentiment Hardens against Castro," *Washington Daily News*, March 7, 1969.

45. Luis Alberto Monge, "Unas lecciones del bloqueo a Cuba," *Combate*, 3: 25, noviembre y diciembre de 1962, 58.

Latin America opposes the domestic Communist parties on nationalistic and democratic grounds. Many governments and influential politicos have repudiated the Communists because of their subservience to the Soviet Union or their anti-democratic stance. Rómulo Betancourt, for example, has refused to cooperate with the Communists because he sees them as "agents of Russian imperialism . . . whose methods (are) inimical to democratic processes." "The philosophy of communism," he has also charged, "is not compatible with the development of Venezuela." The Chilean Christian Democratic Party has taken a similar stance. In a debate over the acceptibility of the Alliance for Progress, the Christian Democrats damned the Communist party for the "'dogmatic, mechanical' application of the word 'imperialist' to anything which 'conflicts with the international interests of the Soviet Union.'" The Christian Democrats continued that the refutation of the Alliance as imperialistic would be "imbecilic" and "anti-Chileno."[46]

The Latin Americans have also cooperated closely with the United States in combating the New Left guerrilla movements. Beginning early in the Kennedy administration, the United States recognized the dangers of the guerrilla challenge and initiated new military assistance designed to increase the anti-subversive capabilities of the Latin American governments. The Latins responded eagerly, immediately establishing new priorities within their military establishments. The Latin American militaries successfully defeated the guerrilla movements in the countryside in every nation but Guatemala. The new offensive launched by the terrorists in the cities is much less important than the previous campaign. Despite widespread publicity emanating from urban terrorism and kidnappings, the threat to the established governments has been significantly lessened.

What appeared in the early 1960's as a serious challenge to Latin American stability and, of course, U.S. Cold War interests, has been effectively countered. The success of anti-guerrilla activity again attests to a community of interest between the two Americas that contributes to U.S. strength in the struggle with Soviet power and the allure of communism.

Some Analysis

An attempt to understand the meaning of the Cold War and communism for inter-American politics is fraught with problems. Although in 1970 the United States and the Soviet Union seemed to be creeping toward a rapprochement, the vagaries of international politics may well introduce disruptive elements leading to a reintensification of the Cold War conflict. Furthermore, complicating changes in Latin America have drastically affected the theme of the Cold War and communism. The rise of Latin American nationalism, for

---

46. Edwin Lieuwen, *Venezuela* (New York: Oxford University Press, 1961), p. 105; Romulo Betancourt, *Tres Años de Gobierno Democrático*, Tomo III (Caracas: Imprenta Nacional, 1962), p. 12; *Hispanic American Report* 16: 2 (April 1963), 162.

example, is only peripherally tied to the issue, yet has affected it greatly and will continue to condition inter-American politics in the future. Finally, the theme of the Cold War and communism has never completely dominated inter-American politics even in the most crucial periods of American-Soviet confrontation. However confusing, several points can be made, some context can be explained, and some trends can be noted to aid in understanding the past, present, and future of inter-American relations.

A Corrupted Policy

In the words of a diplomatic practitioner-scholar, "our Latin American policy has been marred by an awkward if unavoidable dualism" in the post-World War II era. On the one hand, the tradition of Pan-Americanism and the Good Neighbor has shaped United States policy vis-à-vis Latin America. On the other hand the U.S. perception of the strategic necessities of the Cold War has also played a major role in the formulation of positions and programs.[47] This dualism resulting from the two determining criteria has made a vacillating, unpredictable mess of U.S. policy. It has achieved neither goal. Castro's Cuba is evidence that the Soviets have made inroads into the U.S. sphere of influence. Growing anti-Americanism and increasing repudiation of U.S. leadership is equal evidence that the postwar period has witnessed the decline of Pan-Americanism.

While the political evolution of both Americas might be the same no matter what the policy, the plain fact is that no single policy is followed. Rather, there are two clashing, if not contradictory policies — neither pursued with complete dedication. Professor John Plank outlines the intrinsic ambiguity of the situation.

> Is military assistance to a despotic regime to be curtailed because it is known that the regime maintains itself in power only through the use or threat of force; or is such assistance to be continued because the despot and his armed henchmen have been ferocious, if frequently overzealous and unsophisticated, battlers against the Communists? Is economic aid to be given to a country because of the country's desire to develop and our recognition of the crying needs of its people; or is it to be withheld because of doubts about the depth of commitment of the country's political leaders to our side in the Cold War?[48]

Based on the history of U.S. policy following World War II, the responses to those questions would be ambiguous. The answers might be "yes" or "no," depending on the circumstances, or they might be "sometimes" or "perhaps."

47. John N. Plank, "Our Good Neighbors Should Come First," *New York Times Magazine,* reprinted in *Congressional Record*, June 7, 1965. The following several paragraphs borrow heavily from the article.

48. Plank, "Our Good Neighbors."

The indecisiveness of the responses, moreover, does not necessarily arise from the complexity of the problems, but emanates from the absence of a predictable policy. The injection of the Cold War and communism theme into inter-American relations, in short, has at least led to a befuddling dualism that has affected U.S. ability to think out any predictable, long-range posture vis-à-vis Latin America.

Alienation of the Latin Americans

A second major conclusion to be drawn from the preceding discussion concerns the alienation of many Latin Americans by U.S. policies on the Cold War and communism. Many factors have led to an increasing disaccord in hemispheric relations. The United States has little control over some elements; its blame for others has been frequently exaggerated. Perhaps just as frequently, however, the United States has perpetrated patent absurdities and insensitive stupidities in its concern with the menace of communism.

For example, in 1969 the Mexican intellectual Carlos Fuentes was temporarily jailed in Puerto Rico while his ship was in port. The reason for his internment was political, emanating from U.S. security concerns. The immigration law then in effect had a "mandatory custody requirement" for aliens who were barred from the United States for political reasons.[49] At some time, Fuentes had been dubbed a "Communist," a "Communist sympathizer," or a "Communist dupe," and as a result, one of Latin America's outstanding intellectuals was ingloriously thrown in jail while passing through Puerto Rico. The reason: the necessities of U.S. security dictated by the Cold War.

Only those fevered by irrational anti-communism can fail to see the absurdity of such measures. Two influential newspapers set out the arguments. It "makes the United States ridiculous rather than secure. Literary imprimaturs by the Immigration Service or any other governmental body are alien to the United States itself." It "contributes nothing to United States' security and often keeps out artists and intellectuals who might participate in constructive dialogue. Excluding such persons can be interpreted as an official admission that American democracy is not strong enough to withstand the onslaught of ideas. Any test of ideas in the marketplace ought to be welcomed."[50]

U.S. aid to dictatorships is another example of Cold War policies con-

---

49. That section of the law has since been eliminated.

50. Editorials in the *New York Times*, March 5, 1969, and *St. Louis Post–Dispatch*, March 12, 1969, respectively. See also "Treatment of Excluded Aliens to Be Eased under New Rules," *Arizona Daily Star*, June 20, 1969, which reports that the "mandatory custody requirement" has been dropped.

tributing to the alienation of Latin Americans. The U.S. position is that security requirements have compelled compromise with American ideals of democratic government. The Latin Americans have been quick to point out what they interpret as blatant hypocrisy by the United States. They are understandably angered by the U.S. blessing of Trujillo, Somoza, Batista, and other dictators. A North American scholar points up the disillusionment.

> Once upon a time, many North Americans and Latin Americans believed that the United States pursued an active interest in the progress of democracy in the American hemisphere. North Americans as well as Latin Americans have retreated from this belief since 1945, driven back by the newly heavy emphasis on power politics.[51]

U.S. response to the Cuban revolution has added to the alienation. Many Latin Americans charge that the United States overreacted to the revolution's supposed Communist ideology. Because of its "hysterical" preoccupation, the United States became even more afraid of social reform movements in Latin America. A leading Latin American statesman outlines the harmful implications of the Yankee response.

> But the major harm which it has worked on us, and of this there is no doubt, is that it has encouraged a reaction in favor of conservatism and of dictatorial government. It has stabilized several of the remaining dynasties of the old order which had been on the way out. In a continent that so badly needs reform, it has generated support for the status quo out of fear that reform might take the Cuban way.[52]

Another Cold War policy adding to the alienation has been the military aid programs of the United States. Although recent scholarship seems to indicate that no correlation exists between military assistance and military intrusion in politics,[53] it is obvious that most people think otherwise. Critics in both Americas have charged U.S. Cold War policies with increasing the influence of the anti-democratic Latin American military. Moreover, military aid is charged with fostering expensive, counter-productive arms races in Latin America.[54] Finally, the military assistance programs are accused of encourag-

---

51. Blanksten, *Peron's Argentina*, p. 434.

52. Jose Figueres, "Unity and Solidarity in the Hemisphere," in William Manger, ed., *The Two Americas: Dialogue on Progress and Problems* (New York: P. J. Kenedy & Sons, 1965), p. 49.

53. See Samuel P. Huntington, *Political Order in Changing Societies* (New Haven, Conn.: Yale University Press, 1968), pp. 193 – 194.

54. For a rejoinder, see Edward B. Glick, "The Feasibility of Arms Control and Disarmament in Latin America," *SP, a professional paper* (Santa Monica, Calif.: Systems Development Corporation, 1964), esp. p. 3.

ing an unsophisticated, promiscuous anti-communism among the Latin military that leads them to depict even moderate reformers as Communists.[55]

Besides the several examples discussed, the Latin Americans resent being treated as pawns in the grand strategy of U.S. world politics.

> What must be stressed is that the Latin Americans think of themselves as people, not as objects at stake in global conflict. They think of their states as societies in search of individual identities and destinies, not as pieces of inhabited territory to be allocated to one side or the other in the cold war.[56]

More examples of alienating policies and programs could be mustered, but the message is clear. The theme of the Cold War and communism has led to a serious decline in the small store of good will and trust that was so arduously built up between about 1925 and 1954. Inter-American relations have been poisoned by the issue and its influences are likely to be a cogent consideration in hemispheric politics for many years to come.

The Invalidity of the Communist Threat

The third conclusion concerning the Cold War and communism theme is that the United States exaggerated the threat to its security and, therefore, overresponded. U.S. policy makers have failed to understand or correctly weigh the elements of Latin American reality, the ambitions of the Soviet Union, and the facts of international politics. U.S. postwar policy seems to be based on false assumptions about Latin America. True to form, the Yankees assumed that Latins were either too naive to know their own best interests or too incompetent to pursue them. The tone of relations within the hemisphere was not much different from that of the first two decades of this century, when Presidents Roosevelt and Wilson were imposing Yankee wisdom on Latin America.

Contrary to the direction of American policy, the Latin American nations are not about to fall into the Soviet orbit either intentionally or accidentally. (As will be discussed below, the Castro phenomenon is only a temporary aberration.) There are strong movements in the southern half of the hemisphere to launch more independent foreign policies, but this independence does not mean that the Latin Americans intend to sever ties with the United States and deliver themselves to the Soviets. The Latins are cautious and wise

---

55. Martin C. Needler, "The Latin American Military: Predatory Reactionaries or Modernizing Patriots?" *Journal of Inter-American Studies*, 11: 2 (April 1969), 240–241. On the same general topic, see Jeremiah O'Leary, "Latin Military Missions Hit as Costly U.S. 'Boondoggle'," *Washington Evening Star*, January 8, 1969.

56. Plank, "Our Good Neighbors."

enough to realize the difficulties of attempting to develop their countries without U.S. cooperation and assistance. Even Fidel Castro has put forth feelers for the resumption of diplomatic and trade relations.[57]

As with the rest of the underdeveloped Third World, the most important fact about Latin America is burgeoning nationalism. The Soviets attempted to turn Third World nationalism to their advantage but failed. Although nationalism has frequently taken on an anti-Yankee flavor in Latin America, it is also a solid bulwark against Communist penetration.

The fear of internal revolution that prompted U.S. intervention in the postwar period is equally groundless. The Latin American situation is not so ripe for revolution as the scarce literature proposes. The failure of the New Left guerrillas is only partly explained by a United States-trained military. Equally important is the nonreceptivity of the Latin masses — especially to revolutionary appeals invented in foreign lands and launched by foreign nationals. "Soviet writers" themselves, according to an expert on Russian-Latin American affairs, "are hardly sanguine about the prospects for revolution on the continent." A study on "Insurgency in Latin America" contracted by a Senate committee concludes that the "record implies that revolution is not the facile, advantageous method that Castro has suggested it is." Another study of Che Guevara's failure in Bolivia is even more specific.

> Che's death at age 39 at the hands of the ragged Bolivian army, after less than six months of guerrilla combat, testifies less to one man's failure than to the profound weakness and incompetence of the current wave of "Marxist" revolution in Latin America. . . . The chronicle of guerilla disasters so far is a tale of hardship, failure, and wasted idealism.[58]

As noted earlier, the shift of the revolutionary activity to the cities is an implicit admission of the movement's failure. The New Left opposition was driven from the countryside to the urban areas; it did not originally see urban terrorism as effective strategy. Urban terrorism is a step backward, not just a new tactic in the overall struggle. If the New Left guerrillas have been unable to swing the revolution, the "Old Left," the traditional Communists, are both unwilling and unable, because they are too weak and incompetent. Their incompetence is dramatically exemplified by the Brazilian military coup of 1964. Many, including the Brazilian military, feared a strong Communist-led defense of the João Goulart regime. Surprisingly, the defense did not material-

---

57. On this point, see "Review and Outlook," *The Wall Street Journal*, March 18, 1969.

58. Herbert S. Dinerstein, "Soviet Policy in Latin America," *American Political Science Review* 61: 1 (March 1967), 85; David D. Burks, *Insurgency in Latin America*, a study prepared for a subcommittee of the Committee on Foreign Relations of the United States Senate (Washington, D.C.: U.S. Government Printing Office, 1968), p. 1; Norman Gall, "The Legacy of Che Guevara," A *Commentary* Report with Study Guide, n.d., p. 2.

ize. A postmortem analysis revealed the lack of preparation, disorganization, and factionalism among Communist ranks.[59]

In areas where the old-line Communists are relatively strong, moreover, revisionistic polycentrism has eroded their revolutionary verve. They still count some strength in the Latin American labor union movement; the party in Chile is also significant. Neither the Chilean party nor the labor unions, however, seem to be potentially revolutionary. They have been engulfed by reformist ideology and are not much more radical than the United States-backed Democratic Left.[60]

Finally, the competition between the Old Left and the New Left has probably weakened both and resulted in a decline in their trouble-making potential. Analysis of Castro's stance in forming the Organization of Latin American Solidarity (OLAS) makes the point.

> Yet, in the long run, Castro's victory at the OLAS will prove to be costly for him. His steadfast insistence on his viewpoint and his unwillingness to compromise... gives the Soviet orthodox party group in Latin America no real alternative but to move away from Cuba. Rumor has it that the orthodox parties are now planning their own meeting to condemn Castro for interference in the affairs of other parties and his denial of the peaceful path to power. The Soviets may well concur to salvage what they can from the wreckage of the OLAS. Luis Corvalán, leader of the prestigious Chilean Communist Party, laid the groundwork for this by warning Castro to behave in a *Pravda* article published the day before the OLAS conference began. The article demanded that Castro cease imposing his viewpoint on the other parties and interfering in their affairs .... Thus Castro has split western hemispheric communism even more deeply than it was before 1964. The net effect has been, in the short run, to lessen the Communist danger confronting the hemisphere.[61]

To carry the argument one step further, even if revolutions were successful in Latin America, the fear that they will "go Communist" is not substantiated. There have been three major social revolutions in the hemisphere in this century: Mexico (1910), Bolivia (1952), and Cuba (1959). Despite the misguided fears of the United States, the Mexican revolution has produced one of the most stable, economically successful regimes in Latin America. It is, beyond question, the sort of bulwark against communism and Soviet penetration that the United States seeks. The Bolivian revolution, though less successful economically, is intensely nationalistic and has never manifested the slightest evidence of "going Communist." Indeed, the United States has been a major supporter of the Bolivian experiment to the point that some have charged U.S. assistance with corrupting it.[62]

---

59. See Timothy F. Harding, "Revolution Tomorrow: The Failure of the Left in Brazil," *Studies on the Left*, 4 (Fall 1964), 30–54.

60. For a short description of the moderation of the Chilean Communists, see Donald W. Bray, "Chile: The Dark Side of Stability," *Studies on the Left*, 4 (Fall 1964), 90–92.

61. Burks, *Insurgency in Latin America*, pp. 12–13.

62. See Grieb, "The Role of the Mexican Revolution"; Richard W. Patch, "Peasant and

The implications of the Castro revolution are set out below.[63] Suffice it here to note that the regime is only ten years old and is already showing strong signs of willingness to come to terms with the United States. Castro's closeness with the Soviet Union has been of valid concern to the United States, but the Cold War implications of that relationship are also passing away.

The second aspect of the invalidity of the Communist threat is even more basic. Latin America does not, and cannot, make much of a damn in the Cold War. Therefore, policies and programs based on the importance of Latin America are ultimately misguided rhetoric. Good reasons exist for assisting the Latin American states to become viable, economically stable political systems, but their significance in the Cold War must be assigned a very low priority among those reasons. In a study on the No-Transfer principle, a scholar posits the proposition:

> The No-Transfer principle and its sister hemispheric defense policies have been preserved, but one might almost say preserved as fossilized relics of an earlier era of American foreign policy. Under the tensions of the Cold War and in the day of nuclear weapons, with its emphasis on massive retaliation as a deterent to aggression, the Western Hemisphere has lost its traditional significance in United States defense planning. If any hemisphere is of outstanding strategic importance in a struggle that involves the entire planet, it is the Northern: Strategic Air Command maps look at the world from a polar projection which emphasizes the adjacency of North America to the Eurasian land mass across the North Pole rather than the old Mercator projection of the seafarers, which emphasized the contiguity of North and South America and their separation from the rest of the world by ocean barriers.[64]

Though there has been some recognition of that position throughout the postwar period,[65] it has never become official policy, and the United States has continued to operate under a questionable theory. The Cold War and communism played a substantial role in the formulation of U.S. policy toward Latin America. If the premise that Latin America is important in the Cold War is wrong, the policy conclusions that flow from the premise are equally wrong. A more fruitful policy would have rejected Cold War considerations at the outset and attempted to contribute to the democratic growth of Latin America. That policy would have led to a more harmonious relationship between the two Americas.

By 1970, it seemed that the Soviet Union was forsaking any ambitions to

---

National Revolution: Bolivia," in K. H. Slivert, ed., *Expectant Peoples: Nationalism and Development* (New York: Random House, 1963), pp. 95 – 126; Héctor Charry Samper, "La beligerancia de interamericanismo," *Combate*, 16, enero y febrero de 1961, 33; Huntington, *Political Order,* pp. 333 – 334.

63. See pp. 64 – 65.

64. John A. Logan, *No Transfer, An American Security Principle* (New Haven, Conn.: Yale University Press, 1961), pp. 394 – 395.

65. Lieuwen, *Arms and Politics*, p. 226 ff.

seriously prosecute the Cold War in the Western Hemisphere. Though U.S. resolve in the Cuban missile crisis has certainly buttressed Soviet reluctance, the nature of Soviet imperialism and evolving trends in Latin America are equally influential. Probably only for a short time in the early 1960's did the Soviets entertain any hopes of significant intrusion in the hemisphere. Both before and after that time, Soviet policy was informed by "geographic fatalism." Writing in 1954, a Latin American interpreted Soviet intentions.

> The Communist version of United States imperialism seems to accept the idea that Latin America is a *politically secure zone* (for the United States) . . . as may be judged by the fact that Communist propaganda and activities do not strike directly at the adversary which they de facto repute invincible on his own grounds, and are rather limited to secondary maneuvers designed to support the Soviet cause as the center of opposition to the United States.[66]

Premier Khrushchev's position on Cuba lends credence to this interpretation. He once proposed that the Soviet Union was prepared to defend Cuban sovereignty to the point of using intercontinental missiles. Later, however, in an interview with a Cuban journalist, he backed down, saying that he had thought only of a "symbolic defense" of the country. His response, in the words of a Latin American critic, would be "to set off lovely roman candles in Moscow's Red Square."[67] In 1969, a North American scholar came to essentially the same conclusion.

> The Soviet Union views Latin America as lying within the sphere of influence of the United States. At the maximum, therefore, the Soviets would like to see Latin governments which are independent enough from State Department policy so that they will establish diplomatic and commercial ties with Russia and perhaps offer some resistance to United States military intervention. At the same time Soviet policy makers hope these independent governments do not become too identified with the Soviet Union, thereby imposing heavy economic and political obligations on the USSR's economy and government. The Soviets are not interested in becoming involved in another Cuban type situation.[68]

The U.S. attitude toward Castro introduces still another analytical puzzle in the theme of the Cold War and communism. The olive branches offered Fidel Castro usually include two conditions. First, the United States wants Castro to sever his close relationship with the Soviet Union — especially military ties. Second, the United States demands that Castro cease fomenting and

---

66. Gonzalo Barrios quoted in Einaudi, *Changing Contexts*, p. 10. Emphasis in Einaudi. Dinerstein uses the term "geographic fatalism" in "Soviet Policy in Latin America," p. 84.

67. Daniel Cosío Villegas, *Change in Latin America: The Mexican and Cuban Revolutions* (Lincoln: University of Nebraska Press, 1961), p. 50.

68. Petras, "The United States and the New Equilibrium," p. 108. In support of the thesis presented here, see also Dinerstein, "Soviet Policy in Latin America."

assisting revolutionary guerrilla movements in Latin America. Not long after the missile crisis, President Kennedy outlined the policy.

> As for our part, if all offensive weapons are removed from Cuba and kept out of the Hemisphere in the future, and if Cuba is not used for the export of aggressive Communist purposes, there will be peace in the Caribbean.[69]

The conditions mention nothing of Castro forswearing communism or altering his domestic totalitarianism. They seem to imply that the Communist government can stay. If this conjecture is correct, the implication follows that "Communist dictatorship" has little to do with our objections to Castro; at least, it is not a crucial concern. The historical context of American foreign policy seems to bear out this supposition. The United States has been living with and aiding dictatorships for some years. The domestic Left points to U.S. relationships with traditional right-wing regimes in Latin America and elsewhere; the domestic Right damns economic aid and trade with Poland and Yugoslavia.

When the situation merits, moreover, the United States has worked closely with the Soviet Communists. The United States encouraged Latin American communism during World War II. At present, the United States has official relations with every Communist nation in the world except Albania, China, East Germany, North Korea, North Vietnam and, of course, Cuba. Relations with the Soviet Union get better yearly. In sum, the record indicates that the United States would not necessarily object to either the political totalitarianism or the Communist ideology of Cuba.

Opposition to Castro is based on other considerations. Two relate to the Cold War — the possibility of increased Soviet power in the Western Hemisphere — but none relate to communism as a threat.

President Kennedy assured "peace in the Caribbean" if Soviet offensive power were kept out of the hemisphere and if the export of aggressive communism were stopped. Soviet offensive power could obviously threaten American security. The export of aggressive communism is not so apparently a direct challenge to American security, but some have interpreted it as an indirect threat.[70] Again, however, the indirect threat does not necessarily derive from the existence of Communist governments, but rather from the popularly held opinion that Communist-controlled governments will be bellicose agents of Soviet power.

The evidence seems to belie both these rationales for U.S. preoccupation with the Cold War and communism theme in the Western Hemisphere. First, most agree that the Soviet Union does not intend to press its political or military power in the hemisphere. It is interested in trade and some degree of

---

69. Quoted in Benjamin Keen, ed., *Americans All* (New York: Dell Publishing Co., 1966), p. 247.

70. See Theodore Draper, *Castroism: Theory and Practice* (New York: Frederick A. Praeger, 1965), pp. 223–253.

independence of action for the Latin American countries. Second, the historical evidence shows that Communist-dominated governments are not necessarily belligerent agents of Soviet power. Albania, China, Yugoslavia, and perhaps Romania are not conduits of Soviet imperialism. With the exception of China, whose belligerence may be more rhetoric than action, none of the Communist nations seems bellicose. The Castro government, moreover, is decreasingly bellicose and decreasingly tied to the Soviet Union. The failure of the guerrilla movements in Latin America and Castro's economic problems seem to have limited his attempts to foment revolution in Latin America.[71] The natural evolution of the Cuban nationalistic revolution has taken its toll on Cuban-Soviet relations. American demands, in short, seem close to being met.

The third reason for U.S. opposition to Castro and communism can be summarily put to rest. U.S. dignity has been wounded; its sphere of influence has been transgressed. If the above argument is valid, a Communist Cuba has no meaning for national security, but only for national pride.

It seems that the theme of the Cold War and communism has been one gigantic mistake on the part of the United States, save for a short period in the early 1960's. As the "Rockefeller Report," issued in late 1969, indicates, however, that mistake will probably be continued into the foreseeable future and will continue to work its negative effect on inter-American politics.

The Positive Effects of the Cold War for Latin America

The foregoing analysis suggests that the preoccupation with the Cold War and communism has been damaging to inter-American relations. Given its harmful effects, however, a few positive effects should also be noted.

The competition implicit in the Cold War struggle has sometimes worked to Latin America's advantage. U.S. aid programs and general concern with Latin America have been in direct proportion to the intensity of the Soviet challenge. Before the mid-fifties, Latin America was considered a safe area and elicited little interest on the part of the United States. A Communist-leaning Guatemalan government, coupled with the growth of Soviet power, triggered increased concern that led to U.S. agreement on the Inter-American Bank and modification of policies toward dictatorships and financial assistance. Fidel Castro's success in 1959 profoundly frightened the United States and evoked the entire panopoly of U.S. economic assistance featured in the Alliance for Progress.

Had Soviet power never penetrated into the Western Hemisphere, U.S. policies probably would not have changed. The Cold War, however, played on

71. The "Rockefeller Report" disagrees with this analysis. See *Quality of Life in the Americas,* report of a U.S. presidential mission for the Western Hemisphere (Washington, D.C.: Agency for International Development, 1969), pp. 20–21.

the fears of the United States. When U.S. policy makers perceived a threat to their interests and security in Latin America, they responded by initiating programs and policies advantageous to the Latins.

Both Latin Americans and friends of the Latins have obviously played on that fear. The dictators in Latin America used the Communist spectre to extract funds and diplomatic recognition from the United States. Though less often discussed, the same is true of democratic governments. The Frei administration in Chile is only one case of the Democratic Left's use of the fear of Communist control to extract sympathy and aid from the United States.[72] The Communist scare is also used by North Americans in their attempt to catalyze more generous assistance to Latin America. Robert Kennedy, for example, played on fear of communism to persuade Congress to increase its contributions to Latin American development. An analysis of Kennedy's plea implies the double-edged character of the Communist issue.

> You don't, the experience of 20 years of aid suggests, dig money for Latin America out of the Congress of the United States except by waving the bloody shirt of Communism, and Senator Kennedy wants more money, among other things.[73]

The allure of successful Soviet economic development has also contributed to a change in North American policy concerning the style of Latin American development. In the immediate postwar period, the United States advertized the advantages of the free enterprise capitalist road to development. Official policy placed primary emphasis on private loans and private investment as the U.S. contribution to Latin America's capital needs. In recent years policy has changed, however, and the United States now foresees a more significant place for public aid to Latin America. A well-known Brazilian economist elaborates on this point in noting that the Latin American countries

> view the Cold War from a different perspective and are readier to accept the competitive coexistence of the two systems. This is not only because coexistance seems the only viable alternative to global holocaust or to a rigid partition of the world into ideological compartments, but also because they believe that the competition with socialism will render democratic capitalism more humane and socially conscious and may prod the West into greater efforts in helping underdeveloped areas.[74]

Finally, some Latin Americans say that the coming of Fidel Castro has added a new dynamic quality to domestic politics in Latin America. The internal oligarchy has been frightened. The democratic reformers have been

---

72. See "News in Brief," *Latin America* 3: 17 (April 25, 1969), 136. See also Edward J. Williams, *Latin American Christian Democratic Parties* (Knoxville: University of Tennessee Press, 1967), pp. 279–281.

73. "Kennedy's Prescription for Latin America," *New Republic*, May 28, 1966, p. 9.

74. Campos, in Adams, *Latin America*, p. 38.

struck by an increased sense of urgency. Thus, receptivity to change may be increasing in Latin America, and possibilities for the growth of economic stability and democracy may be strengthening.

Three

Intervention

Introduction

Although other political and economic themes have challenged it in recent times, the issue of U.S. intervention is the most important ongoing problem in inter-American relations. Apart from "imperialism," the cry of "intervention" is the most frequently heard complaint of the Latin Americans.

The first U.S. intervention in Latin America was the promulgation of the Monroe Doctrine in 1823. The doctrine was at first well-received in the southern half of the hemisphere, but favorable reactions soon gave way to suspicion and distrust. The blatant intervention of the United States in Mexican affairs leading to the Mexican War (1846) fanned the flames of Latin American apprehension. Throughout the middle part of the century, moreover, the United States developed a keen interest in the nations of the Caribbean and Central America. William Walker's seizure of the Nicaraguan government during the early 1850's and the attempts of President Grant to annex the Dominican Republic added to the fears of the Latins. Their growing anxiety was voiced at the Washington inter-American conference of 1889, when they first raised the question of Yankee intervention. From that time to the present the problem has either dominated or seriously conditioned inter-American relations.

From 1895 to the 1930's, the theme of intervention was clearly the most important element of hemispheric politics. Motivated by Theodore Roosevelt's police power and Woodrow Wilson's crusading democratic idealism, the

United States intervened more than 60 times in Latin America,[1] eliciting the condemnation, fear, and hatred of the Latins. By the outbreak of World War I, notes one author, the Latin Americans' "main objective was to restrain their powerful neighbor," and by 1928 intervention had become "the most critical issue in United States-Latin American relations."[2]

The United States began a retreat from its interventionistic policies in the late 1920's, and the theme of intervention gave way to an era of good feeling characterized by the philosophy of the Good Neighbor. But by the mid-1950's the charge of Yankee intervention had again attained a prominent role in hemispheric intercourse. In the present era the intensity of the intervention theme is equaled by others, but it has taken on more comprehensive nuances than before. Latin American charges of intervention have multiplied.

The Meaning of Intervention: Some Definitions and Gradations

Yankee ingenuity and power combined with Latin sensitivity and paranoia have spawned a bewildering array of definitions, gradations, and nuances of the intervention theme. The United States intervenes when it acts and when it does not act; intervention is charged when money is given and when money is withheld; transgressions of sovereignty encompass everything from landing marines in the Dominican Republic to launching debates on the Senate floor. Intervention may occur, to quote the Organization of American States' Charter,[3] "directly or indirectly," in the "internal or external" sphere. It might be characterized by "armed force," "attempted threat(s)," or merely "interference." Intervention may be either "economic or political," directed against the "personality" of a Latin American nation, or perhaps at one of its "political, economic, and cultural elements." Intervention is defined as the "use" of "coercive measures," and also the "encourage(ment)" of them. Intervention may be charged if the United States seeks "special advantages" or "advantages of any kind." The possibilities for intervention, in short, are myriad; Latin American charges of intervention are, if anything, "extra-myriad."

Some examples of intervention are obvious enough. The use of armed forces against another country is intervention. Theodore Roosevelt transgressed Colombian sovereignty when he dispatched naval forces to prohibit Colombia from suppressing a revolt on its own territory in Panama in 1903. The occupation of the Dominican Republic in 1965 was intervention. North

---

1. John Gerassi, *The Great Fear in Latin America,* rev. ed. (New York: Collier Books, 1965), p. 231. In 1962, the House Committee on Foreign Affairs compiled a list of over 100 interventions from 1798 to 1945. See C. Neal Ronning, ed., *Intervention in Latin America* (New York: Alfred A. Knopf, 1970), pp. 25–32.

2. Gordon Connell-Smith, *The Inter-American System* (New York: Oxford University Press, 1966), p. 53; J. Lloyd Mecham, *A Survey of United States-Latin American Relations* (Boston: Houghton-Mifflin Co., 1965), p. 106.

3. Articles 15, 16, and 17, quoted on p. 78.

American policy makers have attempted to justify these interventions,[4] but they have not denied them.

Direct intervention is also exemplified by particular treaty rights which the powerful United States extracted from the weak Latin American countries. In 1855 the United States compelled Nicaragua to accede to the Cass-Irisarri Treaty, which gave the United States free passage on Nicaraguan soil and the right to intervene in the country.[5] After the turn of the century, the United States similarly took over customs operations and forced budgetary limitations on several Central American and Caribbean nations via formal treaty. The occupation of Haiti (1915 – 1934) was sanctioned by treaty rights thrust upon the sovereign will of the Haitian state. The United States compelled Cuba to permit intervention by adding the Platt Amendment to the Cuban constitution.

The definition of intervention, however, becomes less clear beyond these obvious cases. "Threat of force," for example, is certainly intervention, but the specification of the threat and the intentions of the threatener are not so easily defined. Nonetheless, it seems that there are sufficient instances in inter-American relations to prove that the threat of force is also a method of U.S. intervention. Throughout the first third of the present century, the threat of intervention was constant. Latin American nations were forced to follow U.S. preferences lest marines impose even more onerous Yankee presence. For instance, President Taft's Secretary of State Philander Knox pronounced a "preventive policy" to the Cuban government designed to "prevent the development of conditions conducive to intervention."[6] Later, a show of naval force brought about the resignation of Grau San Martín from the Cuban presidency. A recent incident occurred in 1961 when the United States put on a naval demonstration to discourage the "wicked uncles" (Trujillo's brothers) from their ambitions to reinstitute the family dynasty in the Dominican Republic.

The use of diplomatic recognition has been another weapon of indirect intervention. Especially in earlier times, U.S. recognition was so important for Latin American states that it was a powerful lever. Recognition by other nations was often dependent on the attitude of the United States. The ability to effect treaties, negotiate economic and political arrangements, and contract loans was affected by recognition from the Colossus of the North.[7] President Wilson's refusal to recognize the Victoriano Huerta government in Mexico contributed to its demise. The policy was also pursued in the 1960's. When the Peruvian military assumed power by a coup d'etat in 1962, the United States

---

4. See below, pp. 79 – 86.

5. Gerassi, *The Great Fear,* p. 228.

6. Mecham, *A Survey,* p. 300.

7. Martin Needler contends that even in these times "the mildest deterrent threat, such as a firmly stated nonrecognition policy on the part of the United States, may still be effective." He bases his conclusions on the nature of military coup coalitions. See *Political Development in Latin America* (New York: Random House, 1968) p. 76. See pp. 66 – 76 for the argument.

withheld recognition until the military restored civil liberties and promised elections. Nonrecognition was again used, though with less success, against the Dominican Republic in 1963. The following year the United States refused recognition to the military government of General Rene Barrientos in Bolivia until it received an "ideological clarification" of the nature of the military regime.[8]

Now, the most widely used form of indirect intervention is the withholding of U.S. financial assistance. Aid programs are conditioned by a series of amendments (including those named for Pelly, Conte, Hickenlooper, Symington, and Roess) designed to dissuade the Latins from buying weapons, seizing fishing boats, and nationalizing property owned by U.S. investors. Besides these specifically listed transgressions, the policy makers also use suspension of financial aid to encourage conformity in other ways that limit the sovereignty of the Latin American states. In the 1960's the United States has withheld aid from Argentina, Bolivia, Brazil, Colombia, the Dominican Republic, Ecuador, Haiti, Panama, and Peru to encourage the regimes in those nations to undertake fiscal and monetary reforms, hold elections, restore civil liberties, or simply to act more in keeping with U.S. policies and prejudices.

In other situations, financial aid has been given rather than taken away. In 1962 the United States bought Haiti's vote to expel Castro's Cuba from the OAS. At about the same time, many charged that a loan issued to Argentina was payment for its breaking of diplomatic relations with Cuba. More benignly, the United States awarded a loan to the Dominican government of Juan Bosch in 1963 for economic and social development, but also "in recognition of the valiant efforts of the Dominican government and people to establish a viable, democratic state."[9]

U.S. attempts to influence the sovereign will of the Latin governments through economic measures also include the refusal to buy, sell, and trade. Traditionally, the sale of arms to governments or counter-governments in Latin America was used to extract certain promises. A revolution often succeeded or failed on the basis of which side was successful in buying American produced and exported weapons. More recently, the United States has suspended arms sales to Latin American nations to punish them or to encourage them to pursue different armament policies. In the late 1950's the United States suspended arms shipments to both Cuba and the Dominican Republic as a means of expressing opposition to the Batista and Trujillo regimes. In the late 1960's, the Pelly Amendment, prohibiting arms sales to nations interfering with U.S. fishermen, was imposed on Ecuador and Peru because they had seized American fishing boats. At the time, Ecuador's volatile president, José María Velasco Ibarra, charged the United States with intervention contrary

---

8. See Robert N. Burr, *Our Troubled Hemisphere* (Washington, D.C.: The Brookings Institution, 1967), p. 45.

9. Quoted in Burr, *Our Troubled Hemisphere,* p. 45.

to the norms spelled out in the charter of the Organization of American States. The action was an act of " 'external coercion' against decisions taken by his country in the use of its sovereignty."[10]

The United States has also refused to sell sophisticated weaponry to the Latins on rather more noble grounds. The policy makers disapprove of these purchases because they encourage arms races detrimental to hemispheric peace and because they employ funds that the United States thinks could be better spent for social and economic development. However benevolent in its intent, the Latins look on such U.S. policy as a transgression of their rights as sovereign nations.

Besides refusing to sell arms, the United States has also denied access to its domestic market. Through a bewildering array of tariffs, quotas, and commodity agreements, the United States has been able to reward and punish the Latins by expanding, restricting, lowering, raising, and otherwise manipulating the importation of coffee, meat, oil, sugar, and other products.[11] U.S. policy concerning the importation of Venezuelan oil, for example, profoundly affects Venezuelan domestic politics and lessens the sovereign will of that nation. Argentina has accused the United States of discriminating against Argentine beef on political grounds, not on hygienic grounds as the United States claims.

Sugar quotas particularly have been used by the United States to reward friends and punish wrongdoers. The suspension of the Cuban sugar quota was political intervention, and the subsequent distribution of that quota to other nations was politically determined. The United States gave a slice of the sugar business to the Dominican Republic for instance, because it approved of the government. When the Peruvian military came to power in 1968 and nationalized the Standard Oil-owned International Petroleum Company, the United States threatened to cut off the Peruvian sugar quota. The Peruvian Foreign Ministry raised the intervention issue by accusing the United States of "economic aggression" counter to Article 16 of the OAS Charter.[12]

Finally, the cry of intervention has been raised on a number of occasions because the United States has attempted to influence public opinion in the Latin American nations against their governments. One of the most spectacular attempts (a failure) was the campaign of Spurille Braden, U.S. ambassador to Argentina, against Argentina's Juan Domingo Perón. Braden set out to engineer the defeat of Perón in the 1946 elections by speaking and campaigning against him within Argentina. The State Department issued the famous "Blue Book," officially called *Consultation among the American Republics with Respect to the Argentine Situation*, which, in the words of a student, "was frankly addressed to two publics — to the governments of all the American

---

10. "Lanza en triste," *Visión,* 14 de marzo de 1969, 12.

11. For discussion and recommendations on this problem, see the "Rockefeller Report," *Quality of Life in the Americas* (Washington, D.C.: Agency for International Development, n.d.), pp. 56–77.

12. See "Peru Warns U.S. against Aid Cut," *Arizona Daily Star,* February 1, 1969.

nations, and to the voters of Argentina."[13] It condemned Perón as fascist and tyrant.

The Braden episode was an extreme case of Yankee intervention, but the Latin Americans are very sensitive to U.S. pressures in their domestic politics. Newspaper editorials, speeches by both public and private citizens, or even mention of a nation's politics elicit the charge of intervention. In 1962, for example, Hubert Humphrey was charged with "intolerable meddling" in Peruvian domestic affairs because of almost casual observations on their elections.[14]

The Latin American Position

Opposition

The Latin American position on intervention is clear. Interference that in any way restricts the exercise of the nation's sovereign will is unequivocally opposed. The Latins have mustered countless legal, philosophical, and political arguments against Yankee intervention. They have sought out countless measures to ward off the interventionistic power of the United States. The Latins have pleaded, harrangued, and threatened; they have petitioned international law and international organizations for protection; they have pushed for the foundation of a unique hemispheric international law designed to frustrate Yankee intervention; most recently, they have sought Soviet and Afro-Asian help to increase their bargaining power.

Even the one possible exception to this opposition to intervention proves the rule. A long strain of Latin American thought looks to the establishment of mechanisms for collective intervention.[15] One purpose of collective action is to bring pressure against dictatorial regimes, but it is also designed to obviate the possibility of U.S. unilateral intervention. The Latin Americans, in short, have displayed what one Latin calls a "morbid sensitiveness"[16] to intervention and have been preoccupied in a search for ways to counter the power of the United States.

The Latin Americans have frequently seen international law as a bulwark against intervention. They have stressed the doctrine of the sovereign equality of nations and attempted to reinforce it at conferences and in international

---

13. George I. Blanksten, *Perón's Argentina*, reissued (New York: Russell & Russell, 1967), p. 413. See pp. 409–413 for the discussion.

14. *Hispanic American Report*, 15: 6 (1962), 541.

15. See pp. 86–95.

16. Roberto de Oliveira Campos, "Relations between the United States and Latin America," in Mildred Adams, ed., *Latin America: Evolution or Explosion?* (New York: Dodd, Mead & Co., 1963), p. 34.

organizations. They have frequently charged the United States with transgression of international law.

The Latin American nations have also seen general international organization as a possible counter to U.S. intervention. When the League of Nations was founded in 1919, the Latins rallied to it in hopes that it might provide some protection against the United States. The establishment of the League occurred during one of the worst periods of U.S. intervention, and there was a special urgency to Latin American problems. They were particularly concerned with the efficacy of Article 10 of the League Covenant, which spelled out the right of political and territorial integrity. "The Members of the League undertake to respect and preserve as against external aggression the territorial integrity and existing political independence of all Members of the League."

Hemispheric tensions were low when the United Nations was founded in 1945, and the intervention issue did not draw so much attention from the Latins. Indeed, the Latin nations pushed for arrangements giving the inter-American system primary rights within the Western Hemisphere that weakened the role of the United Nations. Nonetheless, the Latin delegations fought for more influence for small powers, and Latin Americans now look to increased UN jurisdiction in the Americas. Guatemala, Cuba, Mexico, Panama, and some elements in the Dominican Republic have attempted to call in the United Nations to stave off U.S. interventions in the postwar period.

Though the Latin Americans have searched outside the hemisphere for assistance in countering U.S. power, most of the effort (and some minimal success) has been within the inter-American system. Inter-American diplomatic intercourse, hemispheric conferences, and inter-American treaties have all reflected the insistence of the Latins on the intervention theme. The confrontations began with the First International Conference of American States in 1889. The meeting, in the words of a scholar, was an "event of considerable importance (because) it reveal(ed) at the outset the differences limiting effective international organization in the hemisphere."[17] The Latin Americans pressed for a resolution barring intervention to protect foreigners. All the Latin American states except Haiti approved the principle and urged the United States to accede. The United States refused.

Although the battle was lost, the war continued; and the Latins badgered and pressured the United States at almost every inter-American meeting. In 1901, the Second International Conference of American States again urged the United States to accept non-intervention. Again the United States opposed the principle. The United States then countered by pushing the intervention issue off the agenda of the conferences. The increasing bitterness of the Latins finally exploded at the Sixth Conference in Havana in 1928. The United States again opposed the surrender of its rights to unilateral intervention, offering a spirited defense based on international law.

---

17. Connell-Smith, *The Inter-American System,* p. 42.

The Havana Conference proved, however, to be a turning point. Subsequent conferences were primarily concerned with intervention, but the United States began to accede to the virulent criticism of its southern neighbors. At the following conference in Montevideo (1933), the United States repudiated all special rights of intervention, retaining only those "by the law of nations as generally recognized." Latin American fears were not put to rest, however, but three years later at Buenos Aires, the United States seemed to go even further in repudiating its right to intervene, coming close to completely forsaking the intervention prerogative.[18]

Though intervention was no longer the first theme of inter-American relations after 1936, it continued to play a major role. Fear of U.S. interference was (and is) never far from the Latin American mind. Following the war, for example, the Latin Americans raised the issue at the Bogotá Conference in 1948, and forced the United States to accept an OAS Charter that included "the most sweeping prohibition of intervention ever written into an international treaty."[19] The Latins have also been careful to limit the OAS itself because of their fear that Yankee influence might corrupt the activities of the organization. A student of the OAS outlines the argument.

> The majority of the Latin American states have strongly resisted any centralization of political authority in the OAS beyond the bare minimum necessary for the keeping of the peace. The non-intervention principle, considered by the Latin Americans to be the "cornerstone" of the inter-American system, symbolized their firm intention to keep the OAS from developing into a "superstate."[20]

U.S. interventions motivated by Cold War politics began to add a new cogency to the theme in the mid-1960's. Interventions in Guatemala, Cuba, and the Dominican Republic rekindled the flame of Latin American fear. Pronouncements against Yankee intervention became more frequent and more intense. In fact, the 1967 Buenos Aires Protocol amended the OAS Charter and weakened the authority of the organization in matters that might lead to intervention. The revision was clearly influenced by renewed Latin American fear of U.S. intervention.

Legal Blocks to Intervention

The stated intention of the Latin American nations has been the creation of a series of legal blocks to U.S. intervention. The strategy involves a special

---

18. The meaning of U.S. policy announced at the Buenos Aires meeting is not too clear. Obviously, there remained differences in what the Latins thought was meant and what the United States thought was meant. See below, p. 96 for the discussion.

19. Jerome Slater, *A Revaluation of Collective Security: The OAS in Action* (Columbus: Mershon National Security Program, Ohio State University Press, 1965), p. 39.

20. Slater, *A Revaluation,* pp. 38–39.

hemispheric international law that supplements and modifies general international law. As implied by the U.S. reservation to the 1933 Montevideo resolution, traditional international law permits intervention in some circumstances. The Latin Americans have attempted to plug those gaps in traditional international law.

In 1868 an Argentine jurist, Carlos Calvo, promulgated the Calvo Clause (or Doctrine) in an attempt to revise international law. At that time, the supposed inferiority of Latin American domestic justice was a favorite excuse for intervention (mostly European during that period). The Latin Americans were considered either too primitive or too wicked to administer justice to North Americans and Europeans residing in their countries. The Great Powers felt compelled to intervene to insure that civilized levels of justice were maintained. Calvo denied that principle. He repudiated the accepted rules of international law by positing that sovereignty was absolutely inviolable.

> *Under no circumstances* does the resident alien enjoy the right to have his own government interpose in his behalf. Not even a denial of justice could warrant intervention, for it would convey a privileged status to aliens not enjoyed by the nationals.[21]

Another innovation was proposed by Luis Drago, a countryman of Calvo's, just before the turn of the century. Drago's Doctrine attempted to create a second principle of hemispheric law to forestall another favorite justification for Great Power intervention. The Latin American governments often defaulted on debts contracted in Europe and the United States, so the lending institutions in those countries called on their governments to press for collection of the debts. During the latter part of the nineteenth century, European powers intervened frequently to force payment of the obligations.

Beginning about the turn of the century, the United States began a program of "defensive imperialism"[22] in which it intervened to forestall European intervention. The Roosevelt Corollary establishing the United States as policeman of the Western Hemisphere was in large part motivated by this problem. The United States became hemispheric debt collector to prevent the European nations from using debt collection to establish permanent influence in the hemisphere. The Drago Doctrine was directed against both Europe and the United States, although application of the Roosevelt Corollary meant that its prohibitions were primarily pointed at U.S. intervention.

Like the Calvo Clause, Drago's contribution to hemispheric law stressed the absolute sovereignty of the nation state. It too attempted to modify existing international law by specifically obviating one of the justifications used by the United States in its intervention practices.

Still a third attempt to transform international law emanated from Mex-

---

21. Mecham, *A Survey,* p. 95. His emphasis.
22. See pp. 21–25.

ico. Again, it was aimed at U.S. intervention. Recognition had been one tool of United States policy makers to encourage Latin American governments to conform. In Mexico, President Wilson had used it to good effect against Huerta, and later American presidents employed it to discourage the Mexican government from implementing particular sections of the revolutionary constitution of 1917. Genaro Estrada, the Mexican foreign minister, pronounced the Estrada Doctrine (or *Doctrina Mexicana*)[23] in 1930. It called for the automatic and immediate recognition of new governments. Although the doctrine was primarily a statement of Mexican policy, it was also urged upon other hemispheric and world governments. The Estrada Doctrine was also an effort to obviate a situation that frequently led to U.S. intervention.

Attempts to append these several doctrines to international law or to establish them as the foundation of a special hemispheric law have been made throughout the history of inter-American relations, and the Latin Americans eventually did succeed in effectively creating a special legal relationship between themselves and the United States. The Calvo Clause and the Drago Doctrine are incorporated in the more comprehensive prohibition to intervention contained in the Additional Protocol Relative to Non-Intervention signed at Buenos Aires in 1936.

> The High Contracting Parties declare inadmissible the intervention of any one of them, directly or indirectly, for whatever reason, in the internal or external affairs of any other of the Parties.[24]

Furthermore, the Charter of the Organization of American States, ratified by the United States in 1951, contains a sweeping prohibition of intervention in Articles 15, 16, 17, and 18.

> *Article 15.* No State or group of States has the right to intervene, directly or indirectly, for any reason whatever, in the internal or external affairs of any other State. The foregoing principle prohibits not only armed force, but also any other form of interference or attempted threat against the personality of the State or against its political, economic and cultural elements.

> *Article 16.* No State may use or encourage the use of coercive measures of an economic or political character in order to force the sovereign will of another State and obtain from it advantages of any kind.

> *Article 17.* The territory of a State is inviolable, it may not be the object, even temporarily, of military occupation or of other measures of force taken by another State, directly or indirectly, on any grounds what-

23. See Graham H. Stuart, *Latin America and the United States,* 5th ed. (New York: Appleton-Century-Crofts, 1955), p. 173. For the Estrada Doctrine, see Ronning, *Intervention in Latin America*, pp. 154–155.

24. Quoted in Connell-Smith, *The Inter-American System,* p. 97.

ever. No territorial acquisitions or special advantages obtained either by force or by other means of coercion shall be recognized.

Article 18. The American States bind themselves in their international relations not to have recourse to the use of force, except in the case of self-defense in accordance with existing treaties or in fulfillment thereof.[25]

The United States' Position: A Defense of Intervention

If the Latin Americans have seemed preoccupied with ways to combat Yankee intervention, U.S. policy makers and apologists have been equally ingenious finding justifications for it. Although the OAS Charter denies intervention "for any reason whatever," and "on any grounds whatever," the United States has posited countless "reasons" and "grounds." At times, the U.S. position has been cogent and rational; at other times it has been far fetched or so broad as to encompass all. The 1855 Cass-Irisarri Treaty (between the United States and Nicaragua), for example, is described as giving the United States intervention rights "for whatever purpose we saw fit." About a century later, not long after the 1965 Dominican intervention, the United States announced that it would intervene if "circumstances warrant."[26]

Generally, the United States appeals to the precepts of international law to justify intervention. International law, of course, can be interpreted in several ways, and the United States has made full use of its many implications. International law permitted intervention to collect debts and to maintain internationally approved levels of justice. International law sanctioned intervention to protect U.S. lives and property and to maintain treaty rights. Most important, international law justified intervention in pursuit of the right of national self-defense. In 1914, speaking as the president of the American Society of International Law, former Secretary of State Elihu Root outlined the position and the implications of intervention.

> Self-protection is recognized by international law. The right is a necessary corollary of independent sovereignty. It is well understood that the exercise of the right of self-protection may and frequently does extend in its effect beyond the limits of the territorial jurisdiction of the state exercising it.[27]

Besides its own security, however, the United States has frequently assumed the right to protect the entire hemisphere. When Theodore Roosevelt

25. Articles 18 and 19 do outline some exceptions to the otherwise comprehensive prohibition. These instances are discussed below.

26. Gerassi, *The Great Fear*, p. 228; Burr, *Our Troubled Hemisphere*, p. 233.

27. Elihu Root, "The Real Monroe Doctrine," in Donald Marquand Dozer, ed., *The Monroe Doctrine: Its Modern Significance* (New York: Alfred A. Knopf, 1965), p. 55.

barred European interference in the Americas, he was partially motivated by a paternal interest in protecting the sovereignty of the Latin nations. During World War II, the Axis-supporting Argentine government was characterized as "a menace to the security of the American nations,"[28] and the United States led attempts to force it into line by withholding recognition and urging other American nations to join in hemisphere-wide diplomatic isolation. Intervention against Guatemala, Cuba, and the Dominican Republic in the postwar period has also been defended on the grounds that the United States was acting to protect the entire hemisphere and not simply in its own self-interest.

U.S. intervention has been elicited because of two major threats. Throughout the nineteenth century and the first third of the present century, the major devils were the traditional European powers — the Austrian Empire, France, Germany, Great Britain, Italy, Russia, and Spain. The interventionist implications of the Monroe Doctrine were to protect nation and hemisphere against the supposed ambitions of the Holy Alliance. The Polk Corollary, Olney's declaration of paramount interest, and the Roosevelt Corollary were also written in response to threats to national and hemispheric security from the traditional powers of Europe.

Since World War II, the major threat has been Soviet communism, and U.S. claims to an interventionist prerogative have become more expansive than ever. Point Two of a House of Representatives resolution passed in 1965 declares a Communist threat in the hemisphere and outlines its opinion of what the response should be.

> In any such situation any *one* or more of the high contracting parties to the Inter-American Treaty of Reciprocal Assistance may, in the exercise of individual or collective self-defense, *which could go so far as resort to armed force,* . . . take steps to forestall or combat intervention, domination, control, and colonization in whatever form, by the subversive forces known as international communism and its agencies in the Western Hemisphere.[29]

In the words of the *Washington Post*, this resolution, "in effect, authoriz(es) the President to intervene with armed forces whenever and wherever in the Western Hemisphere he deems this necessary to forestall Communist subversion."[30] The policy pronouncements of both presidents Kennedy and Johnson support the *Post's* position. President Kennedy stated his readiness to employ forceful intervention against any hemispheric nation that was "becoming" or "acting like" a Soviet agent. President Johnson resolved that intervention was to be used whenever there was a possibility that communism might assume power in the Americas.[31] As early as 1953, Spurille Braden anticipated the

28. Blanksten, *Perón's Argentina*, p. 403.
29. Quoted in *NACLA Newsletter* 1: 7 (September 1967), 2. Emphasis in the newsletter.
30. Editorial, *Washington Post*, September 18, 1965.
31. See Burr, *Our Troubled Hemisphere*, p. 36.

policies of the sixties in noting that "to act with arms against a foreign country representing a Communist threat does not constitute intervention."[32] The policy, in short, seems unequivocal. The United States posits that a Communist threat to the hemisphere justifies intervention.

A somewhat similar, though older, apology for intervention centers on the United States as the guardian of hemispheric conduct. This justification proposes that it is the right and the duty of the United States to intervene in the hemisphere to maintain civilized decorum in both the internal and external affairs of its southern neighbors.

After Olney's proclamation of hemispheric hegemony in 1895, it became clear that the United States would have to police the Americas if it was to prevent the European powers from entering. Indeed, Europe urged the United States to undertake that charge, and in 1904 the Roosevelt Corollary officially promulgated the United States as keeper of hemispheric morals. The United States not only had the "right," but the "duty" of intervention in the Americas.[33] Partly on these grounds, of course, the United States rejected the Calvo Clause and the Drago Doctrine that would have limited its right to care for its less civilized neighbors. In 1889, its vote against the Calvo Clause was cast because it was "eager to maintain high standards of international conduct." Later, in 1928, Secretary of State Hughes opposed curbs on intervention because he sought to achieve a "hemisphere of international justice."[34]

A related apology for intervention is the insistence by the United States of the necessity to protect the rights, lives, and property of its citizens. The "high standards of international conduct" pursued by the United States have almost always implied the protection of the rights of Americans dwelling or dealing in Latin America. Theodore Roosevelt's manipulation of the Drago Doctrine is a case in point. The United States championed the doctrine at the Second Hague Conference in 1907, but with the important proviso that the Latins employ certain arbitration procedures in disputes over debts. If they failed to adhere to the procedures, they were liable to international law. Thus, the final document "actually recognized the right to use armed force"[35] for the collection of debts. Drago himself repudiated the declaration and few Latin American nations ever ratified it.

Later, of course, intervention to protect the lives and property of American citizens became a major factor in the "Big Stick" policy of intervention throughout the Caribbean and Central America. A 1912 intervention in Nicaragua listed among its motivations the necessity to "protect American lives and property." In 1915, forces landed at Port-au-Prince, Haiti, "to protect foreign lives and property." When President Coolidge sent troops to

32. Gerassi, *The Great Fear*, p. 241.

33. Connell-Smith, *The Inter-American System*, pp. 48–49.

34. Mecham, *A Survey*, pp. 95, 107.

35. Connell-Smith, *The Inter-American System,* p. 51.

Nicaragua in 1925, he explained to the Congress that "the person and property of a citizen are a part of the general domain even when abroad."[36] To mounting Latin American fury, Secretary Hughes offered the same defense at Havana in 1928.

> What are we to do when government breaks down and American citizens are in danger of their lives? Are we to stand by and see them killed because a government in circumstances which it cannot control and for which it may not be responsible can no longer afford reasonable protection? . . . Of course, the United States cannot forego its right to protect its citizens. International law cannot be changed by the resolutions of this Conference.[37]

The "lives and property" argument is still broached from time to time. One of the many excuses for the Dominican action in 1965 was that the United States was intervening to protect the lives of Americans and citizens of other nations who were endangered by the revolutionary upheaval.

The protection of American property, moreover, continues to be a significant motivation informing less dramatic, indirect methods of intervention. Since the end of World War II, the United States has attempted to discourage the Latin nations from interfering with or nationalizing American-owned business. In 1948, the United States objected to a Latin American-sponsored article included in the Pact of Bogotá which would have limited the right to protect citizens doing business in Latin America. The United States issued a reservation to its adherence to the document and eventually refused to ratify it. Beginning in the 1960's, the threat to American property became even more apparent, and intervention in behalf of property holders became more pronounced. The Pelly and Hickenlooper Amendments were promulgated to dissuade the Latins from measures detrimental to the preservation of American property. The Hickenlooper Amendment, directed against the nationalization of American-owned business, called for the suspension of aid when prompt and adequate compensation was not forthcoming. Though not yet employed in Latin America, Peru was threatened with it throughout 1969 because the new government had failed to compensate for the nationalization of the International Petroleum Company.

The Pelly Amendment was designed to counter Latin American seizures of American fishing boats operating in what the Latins claimed were territorial waters. Pelly's punishment was the revocation of military aid. Both Ecuador and Peru were sanctioned with the amendment, and both raised the charge of Yankee intervention.

---

36. Mecham, *A Survey*, p. 326; Dana G. Munro, "The American Withdrawal from Haiti, 1929 – 1934," *Hispanic-American Historical Review* 49: 19 (February 1969) 2; Milton S. Eisenhower, *The Wine Is Bitter: The United States and Latin America* (New York: Doubleday & Co., 1963), p. 176. See also Howard J. Wiarda, *Dictatorship and Development* (Gainesville: University of Florida Press, 1968).

37. Quoted in Mecham, *A Survey*, p. 107.

The defenses of intervention thus far discussed have been largely negative in connotation. The United States has intervened to rectify some wrong perpetrated by the Latin American nations; to prevent the Latins from falling prey to their own weakness or incompetence; or to dissuade them from undertaking measures prejudicial to hemispheric or United States interests or security. However, U.S. action has often been pursued from the most benign motive. The United States has intervened in the Latin American nations to promote democracy and to further economic and social development. A large dose of narrowly defined, selfish national interest has been a significant ingredient in Yankee intervention, but the United States has also been partially guided by the pursuit of more noble goals.

On the international level, the United States has intervened to counter extra-hemispheric imperialism on the grounds that the Latin American interests and well-being would be seriously jeopardized by Germanic or Soviet imperialism. U.S. hegemony has compromised the sovereign will of the hemispheric nations, but in the formal sense, the United States has not implanted colonial regimes as the European powers did during their own period of imperialist intervention. American intervention was undertaken to avoid other intervention and to preserve the independence of some of the Latin American nations.

Moreover, the United States was frequently motivated by its desire to improve the economic and social lot of the Latins. Americans pushed economic infrastructural improvements in all the nations they ruled. Roads, harbors, and dams were constructed. In the social sphere, occupation governments improved education, public health, and other social services. In the postwar period, the United States has used its intervention power to press for reforms outlined in the Alliance for Progress. It has encouraged agrarian reform, national planning, military civic action, and birth control. Again, American pressure for economic reforms to combat inflation or encourage private investment was well intentioned. Americans believe that these measures will promote economic growth.

The United States has a long record of intervening against dictators. A Latin American testifies:

> Most of the armed interventions to 'restore civil order' in the Central American republics and the Caribbean area from 1912 to 1934 had an implied objective of discouraging the implantation of dictatorial regimes.[38]

President Wilson's campaign against the reactionary Huerta, and Sumner Welles' contribution to the unseating of the Cuban tyrant Gerardo Machado, had redeeming qualities. These were the actions of honest democrats who were repelled by reaction and tyranny. U.S. postwar interventions were frequently

38. Campos in Adams, *Latin America*, p. 41.

guided by the same motives. President Harry Truman tried to bring down Nicaragua's Somoza in 1947 by withholding recognition. Spruille Braden's intervention against Perón was an attempt to counter what became a ruinous dictatorship.

Although in the sixties U.S. interventions against dictatorships were seldom dramatic, the list of proximate successes is impressive. Recognition was withheld or aid suspended in a number of the Latin American countries including Argentina, Bolivia, Brazil, the Dominican Republic, Ecuador, Guatemala, Panama, Peru, and El Salvador.

Beyond opposing dictatorships, the United States has intervened in even more positive and specific ways to encourage democratic processes. The United States "practically sustained" the Bolivian revolution of 1952, which started that nation on the road to democratic government and social redemption.[39] In 1961, intervention to counter Trujillo's brothers gave a new lease on life to the floundering Dominican democracy. (CIA complicity in Trujillo's assassination has also been alleged.) A year later, intervention forced the Peruvian junta to set a date for elections. In 1964, pressure on the Bolivian military junta led to some revision of the regime, and, finally, in 1968 – 70 the United States was engaged in a struggle with the Brazilian dictatorship in an attempt to pressure it to restore some democratic processes.

Two other variations on the apologies and provocations for intervention seem to lessen its burden of guilt. First, as is true of the entire panorama of inter-American relations, the United States is frequently caught in a dilemma vis-à-vis intervention. The Yankee is assuredly damned if he does, but sadly enough, he is also damned if he doesn't. That is, the Latin Americans have frequently urged the United States to intervene in the hemisphere to combat various evils. The strong anti-dictatorial and anti-Communist groups in Latin America are quite prepared to sacrifice their anti-intervention demands to other considerations. Intervention against Castro and Trujillo, for example, was not only approved by many in Latin America, but some groups petitioned and pressured the United States to exercise its intervention power. The case of Nicaragua's Somoza is another example. A student of the hemisphere describes the situation:

> Moreover, in circumstances of instability and civil conflict, there were groups in Latin American countries urging the United States to interfere, and accusing her of consciously aiding their rival by not doing so. Nicaragua provided the Roosevelt administration with experience of such difficulties; it was much criticized by some Latin Americans for not preventing the seizure of power by General Somoza.[40]

---

39. On the United States' role in the Bolivian revolution, see Héctor Charry Samper, "La beligerancia del inter-americanismo," *Combate*, 3: 14, enero y febrero de 1961, 33; and Samuel P. Huntington, *Political Order in Changing Societies* (New Haven, Conn.: Yale University Press, 1968), pp. 333 – 334.

40. Connell-Smith, *The Inter-American System,* p. 103.

A second benign apology for intervention is presented by Hubert Humphrey. He sees hidden virtue in bilateral intervention based on the nature of domestic political forces operating in Latin America.

> There may be instances where it is actually preferable to take bilateral action to meet a Communist threat rather than require the participation of the OAS. An effective response to Communist subversion does not always require that all Latin American governments publicly and officially take a strong positive position. Undue pressure to do so may sometimes be counter-productive, by weakening the political position of a government which is fundamentally anti-Communist but whose freedom of action is restricted by a delicate balance of internal political forces.[41]

Also, attempting to discern the motivations of intervention, it is impossible to discount the influences of internal politics in the United States. Politicos are ever cognizant of domestic pressures or of issues that may jeopardize their political ambitions. "The hot breath of American domestic politics invariably scorches the neck of American foreign policy," says one author in explaining the 1965 Dominican intervention. Lyndon Johnson, he continues, was in "deep trouble over Vietnam" and President Kennedy's "Bay of Pigs fiasco" was "seared in the memory" of the American electorate. "It is difficult to imagine," he concludes, that President Johnson "would jeopardize his political fortunes and those of his party by handing the loyal opposition a made-to-order campaign issue: who lost the Dominican Republic?"[42]

Finally, there is some reason to believe that intervention has sometimes been informed by a repudiation of chaos and social revolution. Misgovernment, anarchy, and social upheaval lead to the specific evils that the United States has used as justifications for intervention. In the traditional situation at the turn of the century, for example, Latin disorder threatened American lives and property. In the contemporary era, the confusion attending social revolution has also endangered lives and property, and, many charge, has created a situation conducive to Communist subversion, thereby threatening the United States. A further extrapolation of the same argument proposes that the United States is concerned with any change in the status quo because it is now powerful. Change may be for the worse and shake it from the top of the heap. These explanations for intervention are more or less understandable, if not always valid.

The point proposed here, however, is rather different. It suggests that the U.S. penchant for order triggers intervention simply because it is disturbed by the Latins thrashing chaotically about. The response is only secondarily motivated by political calculation, but is primarily informed by a cultural

---

41. Hubert H. Humphrey, "United States Policy in Latin America," *Foreign Affairs*, July 1964, 595.

42. Peter Nehemkis, *Latin America: Myth and Reality*, rev. ed. (New York: Mentor Press, 1966), p. 291.

tradition that repudiates disorder. Latin disorder demands the genius of the Yankee to set things aright; intervention is only the political tool used by the United States to exorcise its psychological and cultural hangups.

Collective Intervention

The Position

Despite the more general repudiation of intervention, a long strain of Latin American thought favors collective intervention. The United States in early periods opposed collective intervention; during the middle third of the present century, the United States was its major proponent; at present, official policy seems to favor it, but a strong undercurrent of rejection is developing.[43]

The century-long debate concerning the multilateralization of the Monroe Doctrine had real implications for collective intervention. A strong, if not dominant, sector in Latin America looked to the modification of the Monroe Doctrine from the outset. Latin Americans have always wanted to change the doctrine into a hemispheric policy against European intrusion backed and implemented by the entire American community. The United States originally defined the doctrine as its own policy in pursuit of its own security and has resisted a broadening of the concept.[44]

Beginning in the late 1920's and early 1930's, the Latin Americans began to apply the concept of collective intervention to intra-hemispheric relations, also. They began to think about the necessities or possibilities of collective intervention against hemispheric nations. At the present time, at least on a theoretical level, there is a strong inclination to approve multilateral intervention in Latin America.

The leading advocate of collective intervention has been the Aprista Social Democratic (or Popular Party) movement, which has considerable influence in several Latin American nations. In recent times, the Apristas have been joined by the equally influential Christian Democrats. Both defend the theory of multilateral intervention and both have spoken out emphatically to advocate it. Among the Apristas, Venezuela's Rómulo Betancourt has frequently argued for the necessity of unseating hemispheric dictatorships by multilateral intervention. "We are," he has said, "partisans of collective intervention of the democratically ruled countries in order to impede the persist-

---

43. For discussion of the present policy, see "Analysis" below.

44. For a discussion of Latin American multilateralism vs. U.S. unilateralism during that period, see Arthur P. Whitaker, *The Western Hemisphere Idea: Its Rise and Decline* (Ithaca, N.Y.: Cornell University Press, 1965), pp. 86 – 107.

ence of dictatorial or despotic American governments."[45] The Christian Democratic movement assumes a similar position.[46] The movement, in official international conclave as well as through national parties and individual spokesmen, has often cried for a rethinking or revision of the traditional policy of non-intervention in Latin America.

In one specific contemporary situation, moreover, many Latin Americans left, right, and center see the probability and desirability of intervention. The impending chaos of post-Duvalier Haiti elicits the approval of intervention throughout Latin America. In an article entitled "Are We Ready to Intervene in Haiti?" published in 1966, the author reported that "every Latin American diplomat with whom I talked thought it would be necessary to intervene when Duvalier fell." In the same article, the response of Dominican former president Juan Bosch is described.

> When I talked last June to the Dominican leader, he fulminated at length against American intervention in the affairs of other nations. "But intervention will be necessary in Haiti when Duvalier goes?" I interjected. "Yes," he replied, "of course."[47]

The Organization of American States is usually the intervening agency envisaged by the advocates of collective intervention. The debate continues concerning the intricacies of the OAS machinery and its domination by the United States, but, for want of a viable alternative, most settle on it as the appropriate tool of collective action.[48]

The basic motivation for the advocacy of collective measures among the Latins stems from their opposition to despotic regimes. Latin American despots, say the critics, have used the doctrine of non-intervention to obstruct the progress of democracy and trample the rights of their citizens. Speaking against the dictatorship of Venezuelan Marcos Pérez Jiménez (1948 – 1958), an Uruguayan posits the charge:

> The idea of non-intervention, which began as a defense of weak Latin America against Yankee imperialism, has now been transformed into a perfect guarantee for military dictatorships to the effect that it can convert the international protection of the rights of man into the international protection of tyrants.[49]

The Costa Rican delegate to the OAS, Gonzalo J. Facio, reiterated the message

---

45. Rómulo Betancourt, *Interpretación de su Doctrina Popular y Democrática* (Caracas: Editorial Suma, 1958), p. 107.

46. See Edward J. Williams, *Latin American Christian Democratic Parties* (Knoxville: University of Tennessee Press, 1967), pp. 143 – 146.

47. Robert Debs Heinl, Jr., *The Reporter,* June 2, 1966, 28.

48. See below for some examples, discussion, and analysis of OAS intervention.

49. Dardo Regules quoted in Williams, *Latin American Christian Democratic Parties*, p. 145.

and added other reasons when he pleaded for an inter-American force during the 1965 Dominican intervention.

> Until now we have heard talk with impressionable insistence of a single principle of the inter-American system: the principle of non-intervention. It would appear as if this were the only principle that governs inter-American relations. The Costa Rican delegation does not share that criterion. It believes that the system is ruled by a series of principles of great importance, without it being possible to subordinate their validity to the principle of non-intervention. There is, for example, the principle of respect for human rights, the principle of the effective exercise of representative democracy as a sine qua non condition of continental solidarity, there is the principle of the peaceful settlement of controversies, and furthermore there is the fundamental proposition of the (OAS) Charter of offering the American man a land of liberty and an atmosphere favorable for the development of his personality and the realization of his just aspirations.
>
> All those principles, and much more, are at stake in the tragic situation which the Dominican Republic today lives — not only that on non-intervention.[50]

Collective procedure is envisaged, then, as a negative tool against despotic government, and, more positively, it looks to the protection of human rights within a democratic political system. An Uruguayan proposal for multilateral intervention promulgated in 1945 sought to protect "the elementary rights of man." Betancourt would launch intervention against governments that "oppress or humiliate their people." Former Secretary of Defense Robert McNamara sees collective intervention directed to the "development of democracy." A leading Social Christian explains the position in constitutional terms, urging that the prohibitions to intervention contained in Article 15 of the OAS Charter be interpreted in relation to Article 5, paragraphs "d" and "j," which define the principle of representative democracy.[51]

Many North and Latin Americans see a close, if not intrinsic, connection between despotism and transgression of hemispheric peace. A scholar has noted that "President Bosch saw a close relationship between the violation of human rights and the disturbance of international peace, and believed that this interrelationship should be a major concern of the OAS." As early as 1933, President Franklin Roosevelt was advocating the same principle and, more recently, McNamara has envisioned collective action as a means to "help keep internal situations from spilling over and disrupting the peace of the hemisphere."[52]

---

50. Quoted in Jay Mallin, *Caribbean Crisis: Subversion Fails in the Dominican Republic* (New York: Doubleday & Co., 1965), pp. 83 – 84.

51. Burr, *Our Troubled Hemisphere*, p. 83: Betancourt, *Interpretación de su Doctrina*, p. 107; Robert McNamara quoted in James Petras, "The United States and the New Equilibrium in Latin America," *Public Policy*, 18:1 (Fall 1969), 118; Rafael Caldera, *El Bloque Latino-Americano* (Santiago de Chile: Editorial del Pacífico, 1961), p. 23.

52. Robert D. Tomasek, "The Haitian-Dominican Republic Controversy of 1963 and the

President Johnson hinted at still another advantage of multilateral intervention in a speech delivered at Baylor University not long after the Dominican intervention. Referring to the image of the Western Hemisphere as mentor to the world in democratic procedures and international organization, he depicted the multilateral peacekeeping force then in the Dominican Republic as a step in peaceful settlement of disputes. He called for "a new thrust forward to show the world the way to true international cooperation in the cause of peace and in the struggle to win a better life for all of us."[53]

Critics in both Americas have frequently rejected the U.S. claims of benevolence in collective intervention, however, and assigned less laudatory motives to it. One writer postulates an ulterior design in U.S. emphasis on an inter-American peacekeeping force. He sees the idea as based on the "hope that an OAS insignia on the uniform and the name 'inter-American' in the mass media will prove to be diplomatic and psychological assets, even if most of the troops speak nothing but English." Another commentator is even more critical.

> From the United States' government's point of view the necessity and value of an inter-American force is clear: it generalizes responsibility and legitimizes the use of force to defend United States' corporate domination of the hemisphere. Secondly, it permits the United States to continue reaping benefits of control at a minimum of external costs (dead United States soldiers) which might have unsettling effects in the United States.[54]

Whether collective intervention is informed by the best of motives, as characterized by Rómulo Betancourt, or by baser determinants, as charged by critics of the United States, a Chilean argues that it can be consistent with hemispheric legal norms. Multilateral intervention, he says, can be undertaken by

> international organizations to which nations have freely adhered. In the measure in which a country has accepted a determined scheme of international organization and has inserted itself in it, in this measure it is subject to the agreements acquired, and it accepts that this organization is collectively able, in some measure, to rectify its own internal acts. This decision to participate in international determinations also represents a renunciation of part of the concept of sovereignty.[55]

Organization of American States," *Orbis*, 12: 1 (Spring 1968), 303; Franklin D. Roosevelt quoted in Benjamin Keen, ed., *Americans All* (New York: Dell Publishing Co., 1966), p. 235; Petras, "The United States and the New Equilibrium," p. 118.

53. Quoted in Petras, "The United States and the New Equilibrium," p. 122.

54. J. P. Morray, "The United States and Latin America," in James Petras and Maurice Zeitlin, eds., *Latin America: Reform or Revolution?* (Greenwich, Conn.: Fawcett Publications, 1968), p.116; Petras, "The United States and the New Equilibrium," p.118.

55. Tomás Reyes Vicuña, *Planificación en la Libertad*, lecture prepared for El Instituto de Formación Demócrata Cristiana, n.d., p. 29, mimeo.

Collective Initiatives

As might be expected, the long-lived concern with collective intervention has given rise to a number of initiatives and a few undertakings that could be called multilateral intervention. As early as the War of the Pacific (Chile against Bolivia and Peru, 1879 – 1884), Secretary of State James Blaine called for something that was close to collective intervention. In 1916, Woodrow Wilson proposed an inter-American pact designed to facilitate multilateral action. Writing in *Foreign Affairs* in 1928, Franklin Roosevelt also hinted at the possibility of joint intervention. Finally, the Betancourt Doctrine, which refuses recognition to governments coming to power unconstitutionally, was practiced by Venezuela for ten years (1959 – 1969). It has also been sometimes followed by Costa Rica as well as Juan Bosch's Dominican Republic. The Betancourt Doctrine can be interpreted as an example of collective intervention.

Not until after World War II, however, were there any real attempts at multilateral interventions. The stage was set by two developments in 1945. First, the American nations met in Mexico City during February and March of that year and issued the Act of Chapultepec. The document laid the foundations for an inter-American collective security system and licensed collective action to counter a threat to the peace and security of the hemispheric states. The same principle was later included in the Rio Treaty.

In November of the same year Uruguay's foreign minister, Eduardo Rodríguez Larreta, circulated a note calling for the establishment of machinery for collective intervention against dictatorships in order to protect human rights. Peace, said Rodríguez Larreta, was impossible without democracy. The Uruguayan minister was particularly concerned with Perón's Argentina, traditionally a threat to Uruguayan independence. The United States supported the declaration, but it was opposed by other American states. Nonetheless, the principle, in modified form, was incorporated into the Inter-American Treaty of Reciprocal Assistance signed at Rio de Janeiro in 1947, and is now operable through the machinery of the Organization of American States.

Since that time, the OAS has pursued several gradations of collective intervention in the hemisphere. At the least controversial and least effective level is the Inter-American Commission on Human Rights. The foundation of the commission was authorized at a foreign minister's meeting in Santiago de Chile in 1959. Three years later the commission was strengthened somewhat, but interventionist potential is limited. Its functions consist of "exchanging information with governments and making proposals for measures of cooperation." It is permitted to receive complaints from individuals, but "not permitted to make individual decisions on them."[56] It may travel to specific nations only at the invitation of the host government.

---

56. Connell-Smith, *The Inter-American System*, pp. 290 – 291.

A second group, the Inter-American Peace Committee, was rather more effective as an agency of collective intervention during the late 1940's and 50's, but its influence waned considerably in the 1960's. The Peace Committee was originally established in 1940, but was dormant until 1948 when it was called into action to investigate a Cuban-Dominican controversy. The committee has undertaken a series of investigations and inquiries that at one time or another have involved every Caribbean and Central American nation in addition to Colombia, Ecuador, Peru, Venezuela, and the United States (concerning its dispute with Panama in 1964). From 1948 to 1956, the committee was particularly effective. Its investigations and recommendations frequently came close to intervention. Undoubtedly for that reason, the committee's competence was cut back in 1956; it was allowed to function only at the request of the parties in a dispute. Previously it could undertake investigations at the request of any hemispheric nation that considered a controversy as a possible threat to peace.

In 1959, the Peace Committee was granted temporary authorization to investigate the Trujillo dictatorship. The committee issued a strongly worded report damning the Dominican Republic as a threat to hemispheric peace.

> The Committee stresses the fact that international tensions in the Caribbean area, far from diminishing, have been increased and that, in its view, these tensions will continue to increase so long as the flagrant violations of human rights in the Dominican Republic persist.[57]

The committee's report was a cogent factor in the eventual moves undertaken by the OAS against Trujillo. Still, the Trujillo dictatorship was a special case in Latin America. Only the hemisphere-wide hatred of that regime permitted the committee to temporarily regain its intervention power. Since that time, the Peace Committee's influence has drastically receded. The record indicates, however, that it did operate as a force for collective intervention for the first ten years following World War II.

In hopes of creating a really effective agency for collective intervention, the United States has recently pushed for the establishment of a third group, an inter-American peacekeeping force. The formation of such a group has been a policy goal of the United States for some years. During a foreign ministers' meeting in 1951, for instance, the Argentine, Guatemalan, and Mexican delegates strongly protested the idea of a "Pan-American" army, which they thought implicit in a resolution offered by the United States.[58] The ad hoc military group formed to police the Dominican Republic after the U.S. occupation in 1965 was touted as such a group, and at that time the United States began a concentrated campaign to establish an inter-American peacekeeping force on a permanent basis. The U.S. position is that the Dominican Republic dramatized a glaring weakness in inter-American machinery for peacekeeping.

---

57. Quoted in Connell-Smith, *The Inter-American System*, p. 244.

58. Blanksten, *Perón's Argentina*, p. 425.

The organization of a peacekeeping force would remedy that deficiency and counter charges of Yankee intervention by sharing the responsibility for the maintenance of hemispheric peace. Haiti is often cited as the next nation where action may be necessary. The United States is anxious to have a collective intervenor at hand when the situation arises.

The United States first officially introduced a resolution looking to its establishment in May, 1965, but the proposition met with widespread opposition. A number of Latin American countries including Argentina, Bolivia, and Brazil seemed at first to support the idea, but even those military-ruled nations soon retreated. The United States seems to have forsaken the idea for the time being.

Though these three groups (the Inter-American Commission on Human Rights, the Inter-American Peace Committee, and an inter-American peacekeeping force) have had some meaning for collective intervention in the hemisphere, the only examples of effective multilateral intervention have derived from the OAS Foreign Ministers' action to counter threats to the peace and security of the hemisphere. In the 1960's, collective intervention was launched against Trujillo's Dominican Republic and Castro's Cuba. Both were dictators, but the legal grounds for multilateral intervention were only secondarily the protection of human rights or the promotion of democracy. Intervention was grounded on the stipulation in the Inter-American Treaty of Reciprocal Assistance that authorizes the American nations to vote sanctions by a two-thirds majority against nations threatening the peace and security of the hemisphere.

No matter how the sanctions against Cuba and the Dominican Republic were justified, they resemble collective intervention designed to pressure governments into revising their conduct. The sanctions were designed to limit the sovereign independence of the offending nations in their internal and external acts. These two instances are the closest to multilateral intervention ever undertaken in the entire history of the inter-American system.

In 1960, the foreign ministers intervened against Trujillo by voting diplomatic and economic sanctions against the Dominican Republic. The sanctions contributed to the eventual downfall of the tyranny and may be the only example of effective collective intervention ever pursued in the hemisphere. The 1965 OAS approval of the U.S. occupation is a postscript to 1960 action, but hardly merits the title of authentic multilateral action.

The collective measures taken against Castro were equally comprehensive, but less successful. Between 1962 and 1964, the OAS acted three different times against Cuba in barring the Castro government from the organization, voting diplomatic and economic sanctions, and backing the U.S. position in the missile crisis. Hemispheric accord and intensity of commitment on the expulsion and sanctions were much less than in the Trujillo action. The case for calling these measures genuine collective intervention is, therefore, much weaker. If they are multilateral action, they are less convincing instances than those invoked against the Dominican Republic.

Hemispheric support during the 1962 missile crisis may come close to authentic collective intervention, though the argument would surely be disputed by some. Unanimous support was forthcoming, of course, but the crisis was an extraordinary situation, to say the least. The immediacy, catastrophic implications, and U.S. pressure may vitiate its credibility as an example of hemispheric collective intervention.

Opposition

During the nineteenth and early twentieth centuries, Latin Americans fought a long campaign to nurture collective hemispheric opposition to European intervention, but the rise of aggressive U.S. power in the twentieth century modified the situation. Since then, the dominant position has opposed multilateral action. The opposition to collective intervention is based on many of the same grounds as rejection of unilateral action by the United States, although there are some variations.

The loudest and most frequent response to suggested collective action is the principle of non-intervention, based on the sovereign independence of nations within the international political system. Collective intervention may seem different from Yankee intervention, but most Latin Americans reject the distinction. The non-intervention principles of the Organization of American States, indeed, bar that organization from intervention just as they bar unilateral intervention (except in situations which threaten hemispheric peace.) The Latins, furthermore, have been on their guard lest the OAS attempt to increase its power. The Latin Americans have fought attempts to strengthen the multilateral capabilities of the OAS. The "cornerstone" of the inter-American system, for the Latins, has always been the non-intervention principle. They are adamantly opposed to any ambitions of the OAS to intrude upon their sovereignty.[59]

The 1967 Buenos Aires Protocol modifying the OAS structure mirrors the growing concern of the Latins that the OAS was becoming too powerful. The protocol, motivated largely by OAS action in Cuba and the Dominican Republic, reduces the potential of the OAS for collective intervention. An article on the significance of the protocol laments that "the spirit of collective responsibility and collective action is less strong today than at any time in recent decades. As a political institution, an effective medium for the solution of international differences," the commentator continues, "the Organization is reduced to the status of an international post office."[60]

Much Latin American mistrust of the OAS is a reflection of the fear of Yankee intervention power. The OAS is only the United States in another

---

59. Slater, *A Revaluation*, pp. 38 – 39.

60. William Manger, "Reform of the OAS: An Appraisal," *Journal of Inter-American Studies*, 10:1 (January 1968), 13.

guise. U.S. influence in the OAS is not far from absolute, and the United States has been very successful in manipulating the organization to buttress the goals of American foreign policy. With the possible exception of the Dominican and the Cuban interventions, the so-called collective measures of the OAS in the postwar period have been essentially U.S. actions. Formal multilateral legitimacy has been given to the United States to carry out its work, but that formality has never disguised the fact that the collectivity has not functioned.

Though fear of U.S. power is certainly the major block to effective hemispheric multilateralism, it should be noted that rivalries among the Latin American nations also have significance. Latin America's record of international conflict is far better than most, but the continent is far from free of mistrust and suspicion. Argentina has long nurtured ambitions to continental hegemony. Its sobriquet, the Yankee of the South, is enough to suggest how other Latin American nations see Argentina. Brazil is also viewed with mistrust by many in Latin America. It has managed to annex territory from almost all neighboring states over the last 150 years. Historical wars and conflicts have engendered mistrust and animosity between numerous other Latin American states including Argentina with Chile, Chile with Peru, Peru with Ecuador, Costa Rica with Nicaragua, Nicaragua with Honduras, and Honduras with El Salvador. These nations and others with similar problems visualize a powerful OAS as a threat to their sovereign independence. Fear of the United States may outweigh these internal considerations, but they certainly contribute to Latin opposition to collective intervention.

Underlying these specific grounds for opposition to the OAS is what one writer has called the "mood of the times." In discussing the Buenos Aires Protocol to the OAS, he notes that the organization was founded when inter-American amity was at an historical high. The Good Neighbor policy had healed old wounds, and the Allies' triumph in World War II had created cooperative good will. The ensuing two decades, however, had witnessed the resumption of U.S. imperialism and the rise of Latin American nationalism leading to distrust of international organization.

> The current mood is not toward more internationalism but toward more nationalism, not to a strengthening of international organization but to a lessening of the authority of international agencies and a reaffirmation of national individuality and sovereignty.[61]

Finally, the United States is not clearly in favor of collective intervention. Traditionally, the United States opposed any multilateralization of its self-proclaimed rights under the Monroe Doctrine and its corollaries. That opposition shifted in the second third of the present century, and the United States emerged as an advocate of collective action. Really effective collective competence has never developed in the OAS, however, and it may well be that U.S.

---

61. Manger, "Reform of the OAS," p. 13

policy makers are now having second thoughts. The failure of the OAS to respond to the threat of Castro as enthusiastically as the United States had wished may mark the beginning of U.S. disaffection with the OAS.

> The feeling developed in Washington that the United States had relinquished the use of its own overwhelming force in hemispheric relations in exchange for a system of collective security that could not deal effectively with the new problems created by insurgency and subversion within individual Latin American countries.[62]

The subsequent rejection of a United States-backed hemispheric peace-keeping force has also added to disillusion. The post-1965 period has witnessed several strong U.S. declarations affirming its intention to intervene when necessary. There are strong indications, in short, that the United States has at least temporarily forsaken its attempts to strengthen the collective capabilities of the inter-American system and has reasserted its historic position of unilateral intervention.

Some Analysis

As proposed at the beginning of this chapter, the intervention theme has probably been the most important ongoing issue in inter-American relations. The future importance of the issue is not clear. On the one hand, the cry of intervention will probably be heard as much in the future as it was in the past. Latin American nationalism has added a new sensitivity to inter-American relations that will elicit the charge of Yankee intervention on many occasions. On the other hand, the most overt, direct forms of intervention will probably decline in the years ahead because of developments in the Cold War, in inter-American relations, and in U.S. foreign policy.

The "Right" to Intervene

Before proceeding to that analysis, however, one crucial point should be made. The major determinant of any decline or increase in intervention is how the United States perceives its security and interests, and not how the Latin Americans construct, design, or manipulate inter-American resolutions, accords, or treaties.

The history of the intervention theme outlined in this chapter records many Latin American attempts to extract U.S. promises to forswear intervention. Estrada, Drago, and Calvo all proposed new international law. Later, the conferences at Havana, Montevideo, and Buenos Aires seemed to make some headway. Those accomplishments were pushed further by the OAS Charter, which seemed to be a foolproof legal prohibition forever outlawing interven-

62. Burr, *Our Troubled Hemisphere*, p. 70.

tion. But the series of direct and indirect interventions in the postwar period seem to put the lie to Latin American hopes for the OAS. Whether those interventions or any others were legal or not is beside the point.

In defense of the United States, however, a solid case can be proposed that the Latin Americans misunderstood U.S. pledges from the outset. The United States never intended to forsake its rights to intervene in Latin America, and the history of the intervention theme buttresses the point. First, the United States never acceded to the principles promulgated by the Calvo, Drago, or Estrada doctrines. The minimal exception was some degree of U.S. adherence to the Drago Doctrine after Theodore Roosevelt had stripped it of the qualities the United States would not accept. The Drago Doctrine accepted by the United States at the Hague in 1907 permitted intervention rather than outlawing it.

U.S. reservations to the series of accords and protocols negotiated during the 1920's and 30's tell the same story. Though Secretary of State Hughes seemed to back off from some of the more egregious implications of intervention in 1923, he was careful to uphold the right of "temporary interposition." Five years later he reiterated the government's stand on the necessity of "interposition of a temporary character." In that same year the Clark Memorandum on the Monroe Doctrine was issued. It took a conciliatory tone, but nowhere did it forswear intervention.

Secretary Hull advanced another step in 1933 at Montevideo, but held on to intervention rights "by the law of nations as generally recognized." Indeed, a telegram that Hull dispatched at the time seems almost to hint at intimidation. He noted that he had affirmed the non-intervention declaration after a debate in which "the demand for unanimous affirmation was very vociferous and more or less wild and unreasonable."[63] To set the record straight, President Franklin Roosevelt declared only two days after the Conference ended that the "definite policy of the United States from now on is opposed to *armed* intervention,"[64] obviously asserting that the United States intended to maintain its rights to use other intervention measures.

The United States also differed from the Latin Americans in its interpretation of the 1936 non-intervention pledges offered at Buenos Aires. The Latins, it seems, thought that the United States had finally forsworn all intervention, but although the United States may have disavowed armed intervention, it retained the right and will to use other forms of intervention.[65]

The legal intricacies of the postwar intervention turmoil make the same point. The Charter of the OAS outlaws intervention in Articles 15, 16, and 17, but Articles 18 and 19 have provided the United States with its formal loophole.

---

63. Quoted in Connell-Smith, *The Inter-American System*, p. 90.

64. Connell-Smith, *The Inter-American System*, p. 90. His emphasis.

65. See Eisenhower, *The Wine Is Bitter*, p.181; Connell-Smith, *The Inter-American System*, p. 103; and Mecham, *A Survey*, p. 119.

> *Article 18.* The American States bind themselves in their international relations not to have recourse to the use of force, except in the case of self-defense in accordance with existing treaties or in fulfillment thereof.

> *Article 19.* Measures adopted for the maintenance of peace and security in accordance with existing treaties do not constitute a violation of the principles set forth in Articles 15 and 17.

The future implied for the intervention theme is clear enough. The United States, or any other nation in its position, will not repudiate intervention. The United States has intervened in the past when it thought necessary; it will do so in the future. The security interests of the United States are not necessarily bound to lead to more intervention in the future. Indeed, exactly the opposite argument is made below. However, the power of the United States permits it to intervene at will. Recent declarations by presidents Johnson and Kennedy, as well as the House of Representatives, have reaffirmed the U.S. intention to use that power when it deems necessary. The intervention theme, in short, will continue to be a possible issue in inter-American relations.

Influences for Continued Intervention

Several developments in inter-American affairs point to the increased cogency of the intervention theme in coming years. First, and most important, the rise of Latin American nationalism has created increased sensitivity to the theme of intervention among Latins. Examples of direct and indirect intervention that went unnoticed or unheralded in the past will not escape condemnation in the future. The Latin Americans are bent on creating their own nations characterized by their own personalities. Their striving for definition of their personality will assuredly make them more sensitive than before. This means they will be looking even more closely into U.S. actions and motivations.

Beyond the subjective perceptions of the Latin Americans, the objective reality of increased hemispheric intercourse will provide a second focus for the charge of intervention. The commitment of the Alliance for Progress will probably be continued far beyond the original ten-year program. Although the Nixon administration's policy, announced in late 1969, promised less meddling in Latin American affairs, it also implied added U.S. efforts to assist the Latin Americans. No matter how well intentioned, those efforts spell more aid agreements, more trade negotiations, more technical missions, and an increased U.S. presence in Latin American affairs. Combined with growing Latin American sensitivity, these initiatives will lead to further accusations of intervention.

The last decade has also witnessed an astonishing growth of private efforts in Latin America, further compounding the opportunities for inter-American disagreement. U.S. labor unions are more active than ever in Latin

America; the U.S. Roman Catholic Church has significantly increased its aid to its Latin coreligionists; U.S. research scholars have come in increasing numbers to Latin America; even private investment continues to grow (though not so rapidly as in previous years). These private initiatives have already brought charges of Yankee interference. In the labor field, the AFL-CIO backed Organización Regional Interamericana de Trabajadores (ORIT) has long been a center of controversy, and Latin American charges against it seem to be growing. The U.S. Roman Catholic Church has been criticized in Latin America for attempting to intrude on the Latin Church. Yankee business, of course, has long been the butt of intervention charges. Even U.S. scholars have been suspected of late as agents of Yankee interventionistic imperialism.

In a more speculative and less confident vein, the 1965 Dominican action may be a third factor in the rise of the intervention theme in the coming years. Many policy makers have depicted the Dominican adventure as a "remarkable success."[66] Although vehement criticism issued from Latin America at the outset, apologists propose that U.S. intervention strategy and tactics were vindicated by the subsequent evolution of events in the Dominican Republic and Latin America more generally. It is difficult to say whether this analysis is dominant, but many policy makers agree with it. If this group's opinion becomes accepted, the supposed success of the Dominican intervention may entice the United States into other similar actions in the years to come.

Influences for Decreased Intervention

Despite the appearance and growth of some factors leading to an increase in the intervention theme, this analysis takes the position that they are outweighed by developments contributing to an objective decline in U.S. intervention, if not in Latin American charges.

First, the costs of wielding intervention power are on the increase. It will become more and more difficult to justify the costs on the grounds of political profit. The Latin Americans have preached that intervention is bad political business. They are probably correct.

In analyzing the 1965 Dominican intervention, a scholar has refuted those who called it a success by pointing out the broader implications of the venture.[67] Over 35,000 U.S. troops participated in the intervention. At least 44 American troops died and almost 300 were wounded. Besides the specific financial costs of the military expedition, moreover, emergency relief and

---

66. See Abraham F. Lowenthal, "The Dominican Intervention in Retrospect," *Public Policy*, 18: 1, (Fall 1966), 134. Lowenthal disagrees that the action was a success.

67. Lowenthal, "The Dominican Intervention" pp. 139–143.

assistance amounted to over $100 million. The stepped-up aid program that is still pouring relatively large sums into the Dominican Republic adds to the financial cost.

Among the less tangible costs was an upsurge of anti-Americanism in world and Latin American public opinion. Furthermore, the Alliance for Progress suffered a severe loss of image at the time. U.S. moves to strengthen the OAS's collective capabilities were reversed, leading to its weakening at Buenos Aires in 1967. The hopes for an inter-American peacekeeping force were obviated for the foreseeable future. The entire inter-American system was called into question and U.S. self-interest in pursuit of its continued viability set back at least a decade. Further attempts at intervention may destroy what is left of the fragile institution of hemispheric unity.

The inter-American system is worth saving. It pays diplomatic, economic, and political dividends for the United States, and calculating policy makers may well conclude that its preservation demands a retreat from the posture of hegemonic intervention. The 1969 Rockefeller Report cried for the retention of the special relationship between the northern and southern halves of the hemisphere on the grounds of national self-interest. It further warned that "the kind of paternalistic relationship the United States has had in the past with other hemispheric nations will be increasingly costly and counter-productive in the years ahead."[68] The report offered recommendations designed to reduce paternalism and obviate a number of sensitive interventionistic issues concerning aid, trade, economic integration, regional organization, the OAS, and recognition policies.[69] Although the subsequent policy speech by President Nixon did not include all of the report's recommendations, it did in both letter and spirit approve of the points looking to reduced interventionistic pressures.

The second trend that will lessen U.S. intervention (again, not necessarily Latin American charges) centers on international and inter-American developments leading to a reduction in threats to North American security. The supposed threat of the Cold War and communism is grossly exaggerated, if not basically invalid. The Soviet Union may have had ambitions in the Western Hemisphere in the early 1960's, but those ambitions have been put to rest. Castro and the New Left indirectly challenged U.S. security in the mid-1960's, but that challenge has passed. Most important, policy makers seem to realize that the Soviets and Castro no longer threaten hemispheric security. Most agree that the 1962 missile crisis was the last direct Soviet attempt to penetrate the Americas. International trends, moreover, point clearly to Soviet-American rapprochement. Recognition of spheres of influence has been more obvious in recent years. The Soviets have played down revolution in Latin America, and the United States reacted rather quietly to Russian repression of Czechoslovakia. Direct Soviet threats to U.S. security and interests in the Western

---

68. *Quality of Life in the Americas*, p. 29.
69. *Quality of Life in the Americas*, pp. 40, 42–44, 47, 66, 70–71, 79, 85–86.

Hemisphere have shown every evidence of steady decline. Thus, the necessity for intervention will also recede.

Indirect threats from Castro and the New Left guerrillas have also passed their peak. Anti-status quo and anti-Yankee guerrilla movements will not vanish, but it appears that the worst is over. Equally important, again, is growing sophistication among policy makers in their interpretations of those movements. Washington is beginning to realize that they are not necessarily a threat to U.S. security. This growing sophistication and confidence is manifested by two recent developments. First, military aid to Latin America has been cut back dramatically. Second, President Nixon's policy speech rejected the Rockefeller Report's exaggeration of the Communist threat. The lessening of the Castro and New Left challenges will decrease the propensity to intervene and lessen the impact of the intervention theme in inter-American relations.

Third, intervention may also be reduced as a result of growing disaffection with foreign adventures. The Vietnam debacle has eroded the U.S. will, resulting in what the first chapter of this study called "contemporary pessimism." The United States is clearly retreating from the world scene; it has turned inward in hopes of solving domestic problems. The United States is no longer so sure of itself and will probably be increasingly reluctant to intervene in the future.

The contemporary situation is analogous to the period in the 1930's when the United States last forsook intervention. As in the thirties, the hemisphere is relatively safe from external challenge. At the same time, postwar interventions, combined with rising Latin nationalism, have elicited vociferous opposition by the Latins as happened in the 1920's and 30's when Latin American opposition to the United States reached a fever pitch. Finally, the Great Depression forced the Roosevelt administration to look inward just as internal difficulties today have compelled the present administration to concentrate on domestic problems. If this study has interpreted history correctly, U.S. intervention should decrease in the years to come.

Before ending this analysis, something should be said about the future of collective intervention. Obviously, the OAS has fallen on bad times. The Human Rights Commission was never a good collective tool; the Peace Committee has been stripped of its competence by the jealous Latins; the peacekeeping force was aborted by the Dominican intervention, which heightened the fear of Yankee intervention. The coup de grace was administered by the ratification of the 1967 Buenos Aires Protocol, further weakening what little collective competence the OAS possessed. Beyond the constitutional modifications, there is no question that Latin American nationalism will steal what resolve the Latins have ever had for collective action.

The only possible countervailing influence may emanate from the Latins' increasing sensitivity to democratic government. A long tradition of Latin American thought has advocated collective intervention against dictatorships, and that inclination has grown in recent years. The OAS action taken against Trujillo's intervention in Venezuela attests to some Latin American commitment against dictatorships. Democratic sensitivities may catalyze the Latins again, but, in all candor, other developments in Latin America are probably too strong to be overcome. The Latin Americans, moreover, could probably expect little encouragement from the United States to intervene against dictatorships. The Nixon administration has pronounced unequivocally that it plans to live with regimes as they are. The United States will not move against military dictatorships.

The power of the United States in the OAS may be able to swing a so-called collective intervention in the future. Central American and Caribbean votes can always be recruited by fair means or foul, and some South American nations can be coerced into supporting the U.S. line. Still, any prognostication based on current trends must propose the decline of collective action along with unilateral intervention.

One possible exception to these conclusions demands discussion. Duvalier's Haiti was mentioned as one area where many foresee the possibility of intervention in the immediate future. Despite his mastery of the powers of voodoo, Duvalier can not live forever. Although no one really knows much about Haiti, most analysts agree that the death of Duvalier could initiate a period of chaos in that unhappy land. Disorder is bound to raise the spectre of communism for the United States. Even if it does not, both the United States and Latin America may agree to intervene on humanitarian grounds to save the Haitians from slaughtering one another. Whatever the motivations, Haiti must be posited as an exception to the previous analysis. The possibilities for either unilateral U.S. or multilateral hemispheric intervention are very real. Only half jokingly, Haiti is an exception to the entire universe; it is not surprising that it should be an exception to trends in the theme of intervention.[70]

In summary, the United States, no matter what the legal arguments, will not forsake intervention in Latin America. If the policy makers in Washington decide that U.S. security is threatened, they will dispatch naval forces, airborne troops, and marines just as they have in the past. More optimistically, trends indicate that both direct and indirect intervention will decline in the years ahead. Except for security threats, U.S. interests will not be so vigorously protected by interventionist measures. Despite the objective decline of U.S. interference, however, Latin charges of intervention will not decline because of the growing Latin American nationalist sensitivities. In that sense, the intervention theme will continue to play a major role in hemispheric affairs.

---

70. Lowenthal has discussed the possible ramifications of a Haitian intervention. He paints a sad picture featuring a costly, long-range U.S. commitment. See "The Dominican Intervention," pp. 146 – 147.

Four

Aid to Dictatorships

Introduction

The aid-to-dictatorships theme is essentially a post-World War II controversy in inter-American relations. Though many traditional policies pursued by the United States could be defined as aiding Latin American authoritarian regimes, the issue did not gain currency until the first third of the present century, when widespread overt intervention characterized U. S. policy. By the 1950's it had become a major issue in hemispheric affairs.

Several developments explain its emergence as an important controversy at that time. First, Latin American democracy is a relatively recent phenomenon. The so-called democracies of the 19th century were restricted to small groups of the upper classes. By the turn of the century the democratic credo began to spread, and after 1930 something approaching popular democracy catalyzed elements of the lower classes.

Second, the democratic credo was popularized in Latin America by World War II. The war was popularly conceived as a struggle for the preservation and propagation of representative government. The rhetoric of the war depicted the forces of democracy locked in a life-and-death struggle against those determined to destroy popular government. The immediate postwar period actually witnessed a short-lived flowering of democracy in Latin America. The euphoria of democratic victory contributed to the demise of long-established authoritarian regimes throughout the continent. Democrats assumed political control and launched campaigns against the dictatorships remaining in the hemisphere.

The intensification of democratic propaganda by the Cold War added another significant dimension to the aid-to-dictatorships theme. The United

States emerged as the self-styled defender of the "free world," battling the forces of Communist totalitarianism. The free world, of course, should logically have been composed of democratic governments, but the reality was much different from the image. Latin American democrats realized that fact and soon began to attack the United States for its apparent hypocrisy. The United States advertised itself as the head of a democratic alliance, but frequently its supporters were authoritarian despots. Furthermore, the United States, in the name of anti-Communist democracy, was actively engaged in assisting those tyrannies to maintain themselves.

Peron's Argentina, the nemesis of the United States throughtout World War II, played a major role in establishing the aid-to-dictatorship's theme after the war. The United States wanted an anti-Communist hemispheric defense treaty, but the Latin Americans were reluctant to frame one without including Argentina. U. S. perceptions of Cold War necessities overcame opposition to Peron's semi-fascist tyranny, and the United States made its peace with the Argentine dictatorship. Good relations were restored; the Rio Defense Treaty was duly negotiated and ratified; and the aid-to-dictatorship's theme was launched.

From the late forties to the mid-fifties, as Cold War tensions mounted, the United States continued its aid to dictatorships. Concomitantly, Latin American disaffection expanded and Latin damnation of the United States increased. U. S. actions became most blatant during the middle years of the Eisenhower administration with the bemedaling of some Latin American tyrants. Latin American reaction to Vice President Nixon during his 1958 tour was in no small part motivated by U. S. aid to dictatorships.

In the late fifties and early sixties, policy changes were initiated in Washington. Many hemispheric dictatorships fell or were pushed from power (there were few left to aid). Perhaps most important, the United States threw its support to the ouster of the hated Trujillo, who had become a symbol of the theme. The middle and late sixties, however, witnessed renewed cogency in the dictatorship theme. It is now an important element in inter-American politics, though it has receded from the primary role it played a decade earlier.

Accompanying the aid-to-dictatorships theme, military assistance emerged in the early sixties as an important issue in hemispheric political intercourse. This study posits that aid to dictatorships and military assistance to Latin America are separate issues. Military assistance is not necessarily aid to a dictatorship. Military subventions are granted to despot and democrat alike in Latin America. Moreover, there seems to be no substantial validation that military aid encourages the foundation of authoritarian government. These points, and others, will be discussed more comprehensively as the chapter proceeds.

Methods of Aiding Dictatorships

The United States has employed its vast power and resources in numerous ways to demonstrate its approval of dictators, to maintain them in power, and perhaps even to encourage their seizure of the reins of government. The specific methods range from a posture of sympathy to military assistance.

Latin American dictatorships have been assisted by both unofficial and official U. S. approval of their regimes. In the first decade of the century, President Theodore Roosevelt referred to Porfirio Díaz, the Mexican dictator, as the greatest statesman of his time. Franklin Roosevelt was not so effusive in his comments concerning the tyrant Trujillo; still, the import of the observation must have made the Dominican dictator a little more secure. "I know he's an SOB," allowed Roosevelt, "but at least he is *our* SOB." The same Trujillo was defended on the floor of the House of Representatives as being "on the side of God and Christianity," and Cardinal Spellman commended him as a battler against communism. The Perón dictatorship was defended by the American ambassador to Argentina. The Somoza "boys" were adjudged as "all right" by the United States Ambassador in Nicaragua.[1]

Beyond these unofficial or semi-official declarations, the official foreign policy of the United States has frequently approved Latin American dictatorships. In the late 1940's and early 1950's, U. S. policy looked sympathetically on Latin American authoritarian governments. Though the policy shifted later, it swung back in the mid-1960's to what many charged was a pro-dictator emphasis. In 1964 the Mann Doctrine seemed to indicate that the United States was ready once again to offer its blessing to Latin American despotism. Two years later Inter-American Affairs Secretary Lincoln Gordon, supported aid to dictatorships by crying for a "realistic" policy.[2]

The "Rockefeller Report" and President Nixon's subsequent policy speech in late 1969 evidenced continuing official sympathy with dictators—or at least an official willingness to live with them. In one section, the report was enthusiastic about "new military leaders who are deeply motivated by the need for social and economic progress." A little earlier, the report outlined North American disapproval of some types of Latin American regimes, but recommended "maintaining at least minimal diplomatic relations with other governments of the hemisphere."[3]

---

1. For the allusions noted above, see Martin Needler, *Political Development in Latin America* (New York: Random House, 1968), p. 33; Alexander T. Edelmann, *Latin American Government and Politics*, rev. ed. (Homewood, Ill.: Dorsey Press, 1969), p. 139; John Gerassi, *The Great Fear in Latin America*, rev. ed. (New York: Collier Books, 1965), pp.144–145, 243, 245; George I. Blanksten,*Peron's Argentina*, reissued (New York: Russell & Russell, 1967), p. 417.

2. See Edwin Lieuwen, *Generals vs. Presidents* (New York: Frederick A. Praeger, 1964), p. 143; and James Petras, "The United States and the New Equilibrium in Latin America," *Public Policy,* 18: 1 (Fall 1969) 113.

3. The "Rockefeller Report," *Quality of Life in the Americas* (Washington, D.C.): Agency

President Nixon's speech was also interpreted by many as officially defining U.S. policy in favor of dictatorial regimes. The president noted U. S. preference for democratic government, but then qualified that preference.

> Nevertheless, we recognize that enormous, sometimes explosive, forces for change are operating in Latin America. These create instabilities, and bring changes in governments. On the diplomatic level, we must deal realistically with governments in the inter-American system as they are.[4]

The general policy, of course, has specifically encouraged and succored Latin American despots. First, North American diplomatic recognition has been employed to assist tyrants.[5]

When Fulgencio Batista administered his second coup in 1952, one commentator charged that "it was only American recognition that saved the day for him." More recently, the Johnson Administration recognized the Brazilian military coup of 1964 much more rapidly than normal diplomatic practice seemed to merit. Furthermore, Secretary of State Dean Rusk angered many in both Americas when he praised the military usurpers for having redeemed the Brazilian democracy.[6]

In addition to recognition and praise, the Eisenhower administration presented medals to two Latin American dictators. The U.S. Order of Merit was granted to General Manuel Odría of Peru, and to General Marcos Pérez Jiménez of Venezuela. There may have been some benevolence about Odria's regime, but Pérez Jiménez was clearly a brutal, corrupt tyrant. Both were certainly dictators, and the event has become a symbol in Latin America of the official policy of the United States toward dictatorships.

The United States has also issued material aid to dictatorships. "Aid to dictatorships" means that the United States has sent sums of money to non-democratic regimes. The division and allocation of "aid" monies is always difficult to calculate, but one critic claims that the United States has "allocated over two thirds of Alliance for Progress funds to military dictatorships or to military-controlled civilian governments."[7]Whatever the exact amounts, it is

---

for International Development, 1969), pp. 51, 46.

4. "Text of President Nixon's address to the Inter-American Association," *New York Times.* November 1, 1969. For comments typifying it as pro-dictatorial, see Virginia Prewett, "An Opening for Latin Coups," *Washington Post.* November 5, 1969; *Latin American Digest.* 4: 2 (November 1969), 9 – 10; and *Los Angeles Times.* November 30, 1969.

5. Martin Needler claims that "in a coup situation, even the mildest deterrant threat, such as a firmly stated nonrecognition policy on the part of the United States, may still be effective because of the structure of the pre-coup balance of forces." See Needler, *Political Development.* p. 76. See pp. 66 – 76 for the argument.

6. Sidney Lens, "Revolution or Reform," paper prepared for the 1969 Inter-American Forum, p. 5, mimeo; Robert N. Burr, *Our Troubled Hemisphere: Perspectives on United States-Latin American Relations* (Washington, D.C.: The Brookings Institute, 1967), p. 32.

7. Petras, "The United States and the New Equilibrium," p. 102.

obvious that much money has been sent to Latin American despots. Besides regular aid disbursements, furthermore, the United States has issued special allotments to hemispheric dictatorships. A special aid grant was promised Haiti in payment for Duvalier's vote to expel Castro from the OAS. The Brazilian military government was also favored by an extraordinary grant in 1964, as was the Ecuadorean "caretaker" dictatorship of Clemente Yerovi Indaburo in mid-1966.

Many have charged the United States with favoring dictators in its foreign trade policies. Allocation of large shares of the U.S. sugar quota to Cuba and the Dominican Republic were seen as helping Batista and Trujillo maintain their despotisms. The same charge is made today about Brazilian coffee quotas.

Finally, military assistance has become a major controversy within the aid-to-dictatorships theme. Many in both Americas point to military subventions as a serious offense in U.S. policies favoring Latin American despotism. Because it has become so important, an attempt to understand the political controversies of hemispheric relations would be incomplete without some organized discussion of the issue. Therefore, military assistance will be handled as a subtheme of this description and analysis of the aid-to-dictatorships theme.

Whether or not military assistance can be equated with aid to dictatorships, the United States has been involved in the military aid business for some time. The United States has trained many Latin military men and has sent rather large sums of money and materials to the Latin American military establishments. One major feature of the occupations in the Caribbean and Central America, for example, was the training of the local military. A U.S. naval training mission was established in Brazil as early as 1918. Beginning in the early thirties, the United States launched a concentrated effort to supplant German and Italian influence by offering military aid, and a large-scale program was operating by 1938. Military aid continued during World War II. It trailed off in the immediate postwar period, but in 1951 a new program was initiated that continues today. Since World War II, the United States has given $1.1 billion in direct military aid to Latin America and has trained almost a quarter million Latin military men in the United States and Panama.[8]

The U.S. Defense of Aid to Analysis

The explanations and motivations of the U.S. position vis-a-vis dictatorships are numerous, complex, and varying in validity. Some explanations do credit to the United States, but many do not. Some are easily understood, others are rather far-fetched.

To begin with the most general point, Latin American dictators have

---

8. Robert Dietsch, "President to Reject Latin Military Hike," *Washington Daily News*, November 11, 1969.

traditionally advertised themselves as friends of the United States. They have facilitated U.S. influence in Latin America. They have said the things the United States wanted to hear; they have acted in accordance with U.S. policies and prejudices; they have praised the United States and damned its enemies. Franklin Roosevelt's characterization of Trujillo as "*our* SOB" tells the story.

A Latin American cleric-social scientist points out another reason for U.S. friendship with despots.

> In order to understand why foreign governments and businesses have sometimes favored dictators, one can begin with the simplest of explanations: Affairs are expedited if you deal with one man. You don't have to wait until things are approved by a congress. To a foreign country operating in Latin America, it is of primary importance to have a stable government — stable at least in the sense that business can be carried on safely and with no disruptions.[9]

More substantial advantages of dictatorships are implied in their traditional friendly posture.[10] Until most recent times, dictators have looked kindly on U.S. business ventures. They have protected Yankee lives and property with more zeal than their democratic counterparts have. Foreign investments have been secure under tyrants, while democrats have frequently restricted business activity or nationalized property.

For the last generation, security considerations have been even more important in explaining the affinity for despotic regimes. U.S. policy makers concluded that security was best served by the supposed stability imposed by dictatorial governments. Friendly dictatorships (until most recent times, one term equaled the other) meant that the unpredictable forces of democracy would not interfere in U.S. hot and cold wars against Germany or the Soviet Union. During World War II, the United States had a pro-dictatorship policy because those governments provided the stability that permitted the most reliable economic and political contributions to the war effort. They delivered the necessary raw materials, suppressed the local Nazis, broke relations with the Axis powers, played down anti-Soviet Communist propaganda, and in general conducted themselves as the best of allies.

Not long after the end of World War II, the rise of Soviet belligerence introduced another threat to U.S. security and the pro-dictatorship policy continued. Stability in Latin America remained a key U.S. policy objective. Dictatorships meant stability, and stability implied the exclusion of communism and Soviet power from the hemisphere. The major criterion for recognizing and supporting Latin American governments was anti-communism.

---

9. Renato Poblete, S.J., "The Phenomenon of Dictatorship," in John J. Considine, ed., *Social Revolution in the New Latin America* (Notre Dame, Ind.: Fides Publishers, 1965), p. 52.

10. The term "traditional" has already been twice used in a conscious attempt to imply that some contemporary dictatorships are very different. See below, p. 113.

Dictatorships advertised themselves as the first anti-Communists, and, therefore, were first in the hearts of U.S. policy makers.

Aid was provided, decorations bestowed, and praise given to dictators because they seemed committed to the U.S. side in the Cold War and followed the anti-Communist line. General Odría's Order of Merit citation praised his "fight against the Communists and other subversive elements." Perón was "picked up" and "dusted off" because he was needed in the anti-Communist struggle. Trujillo was heralded as being on the side of "God and Christianity" because he was "against the encroachments of atheistic communism." A U.S. Secretary of State opposed action against the Dominican tyrant because he feared that Trujillo's fall would "promote chaos and disorder possibly opening the door to Communist penetration."[11]

Not only were dictators aided because they were anti-Communist, but, constitutional regimes and democratic forces were opposed because they were not. The Betancourt-Gallegos Venezuelan regime (1945 – 1948) was damned by many because it was thought to be soft on communism. The Peruvian oligarchy's long suppression of Haya de la Torre's Aprista party was approved for the same reason. The fall of the first Bosch government in the Dominican Republic was welcomed in the United States because he too was thought to be soft on communism. As recently as mid-1964, Inter-American Affairs Secretary Thomas C. Mann made the argument. He noted that the United States could not "put itself in a doctrinaire strait-jacket of automatic application of sanctions to every unconstitutional regime in the hemisphere." He then related the story of the CIA-supported 1954 overthrow of the regularly elected Arbenz Guzmán government in Guatemala. His conclusion:

> Had we been unconditionally committed to the support of all constitutional governments under all circumstances, we would have been obliged to do everything within our power to bring about the overthrow of Castillo (the military man who overthrew Arbenz), and to restore a Marxist-Leninist power against the will of the Guatemalan people.[12]

The pervasiveness of Cold War considerations in the policy of aid to dictatorships can also be seen in the changing U.S. position vis-à-vis Castro's Cuba. Castro's dictatorship has received neither praise nor succor from official United States policy makers. It has, of course, been praised by many from the New Left and the Old Left in the United States. However, there are solid signs that the United States may be willing to come to terms with Castro if he reduces his ties with the Soviet Union and ceases his exportation of revolution

---

11. See Charles O. Porter and Robert J. Alexander, *The Struggle for Democracy in Latin America* (New York: Macmillan Co., 1961), p. 192: Blanksten, *Perón's Argentina*, p. 433; Gerassi, *The Great Fear*, p. 245; J. Lloyd Mecham, *A Survey of United States – Latin American Relations* (Boston: Houghton Mifflin Co., 1965), p. 289.

12. Thomas C. Mann, "The Democratic Ideal in Our Policy toward Latin America," *Department of State Bulletin,* June 29, 1964, p. 999.

to the South American mainland.[13] If Castro fulfills these conditions, Soviet hemispheric presence would be expelled and a threat to Latin American stability reduced.

The most important implication is that the United States seems prepared to aid a Communist dictatorship (assuming the price is right) just as it has aided other dictators. Trade with Cuba would be resumed, the sugar quota probably renewed, and perhaps some special inducements offered. The United States, in short, might well aid a Communist dictatorship in the not too distant future for the same reasons that it has assisted other despotic regimes—calculating self-interest defined in terms of security. In passing, it should be noted that aid to Castro's Communist Cuba would hardly be a startling new departure in U.S. policy: Poland and Yugoslavia have been receiving U.S. aid for many years.

Although security interests informed by Cold War considerations may be the major defense for aid to dictatorships, Washington has also mustered other arguments to fend off Latin charges of callousness and hypocrisy. Among these secondary apologies, perhaps the most important has been the argument from realism. The Rockefeller Report, for example, rejects discriminating against dictatorships in Latin America and pronounces that "we, in the United States, cannot determine the internal political structure of any other nation, except by example." Elsewhere, the report urges policy makers to "recognize that diplomatic relations are merely practical conveniences and not measures of moral judgment."[14] A concomitant of the "realism" argument is the supposed adherence of the United States to its non-intervention pledges. In responding to the aid-to-dictatorship charge, Washington has countered that suspension of aid or other opposition to tyrants would violate non-intervention accords. That is, "the United States is not entitled to determine another nation's type of government."[15]

Underlying the realism argument is a more profound defense of U.S. assistance to despotic governments. This explanation centers on the nature of democracy and charges that it is not realistic to expect the Latins to evolve representative institutions. In 1950, for instance, U. S. Ambassador Stanton Griffis praised and defended the Peron tyranny. "There is some absence of freedom of the press, . . . there is some absence of personal liberty in Argentina," he noted, "but it is perhaps true that Argentina is not completely prepared for what is known as integral democracy." In supporting dictatorial takeovers in Latin America, the same apology was offered by Ambassador and Inter-American Affairs Secretary Lincoln Gordon. "Constitutional democracy is the desirable norm everywhere," he said, "but there are only approximations of it around the world. . . . It is more realistic to view democracy as

---

13. See pp. 63–65 for the discussion.

14. "Rockefeller Report," pp. 27, 46. ("Text of President Nixon's Address.")

15. Burr, *Our Troubled Hemisphere*, pp. 24, 295.

a process in time and place." In commenting on the Alliance for Progress, Ambassador John Moors Cabot argued the same point by proposing that "it is not realistic to expect the Alliance for Progress to create, in the forseeable future, democracy in Latin America." Finally, the Rockefeller Report posited that

> Democracy is a very subtle and difficult problem for most of the other countries of the hemisphere. The authoritarian and hierarchical tradition which has conditioned those societies does not lend itself to the particular kind of popular government we are used to. Few of the countries, moreover, have achieved the sufficiently advanced economic and social systems required to support a consistently democratic system. For many of these societies, therefore, the question is less one of democracy or a lack of it, than it is simply of orderly ways of getting along.[16]

Another interesting variant on the realism defense has recently evolved as a result of Latin America's new form of military dictatorship. It emphasizes economic and social reform and advertises a nationalistic ideology. Nationalism, naturally enough, frequently takes on anti-Yankee connotations. Anti-Americanism has been used by military dictators in some cases to bolster their regimes. The Peruvian military has been most skillful in forcing the United States to accede to their dictatorial regime and to renew assistance lest the United States be completely repudiated. The Brazilian military has also threatened the United States. One commentator charged that Washington has been reluctant to move against the Brazilian dictators because "they don't want to take any action that would rebound by a severe anti-American reaction in Brazil."[17]

Other secondary defenses of aid to dictatorships include the "lines of communication" and the "humanitarian" positions. The "lines of communication" apology defends recognition and friendship with authoritarian regimes as necessary if the United States wishes to encourage dictatorships to modify their practices. That is, Washington proposes that it is interested in reforming despots, and that it must maintain communication if it hopes to be effective. Any possible benign influence would be lost if the United States severed relations or repudiated the government. Therefore, it must continue to seek good relationships by maintaining assistance programs.

The "humanitarian" explanation in a sense denies the whole charge. It proposes that U.S. aid is offered to relieve the suffering of people in Latin America. Economic aid is not given to a dictatorship, but rather to a people who happen to be governed by authoritarian rulers. The Rockefeller Report insisted that the United States should continue to help people despite their

---

16. Blanksten, *Perón's Argentina* p. 417; Petras, "The United States and the New Equilibrium," p. 113; Lewis H. Diuquid, "Alliance: Tilt to the Right?" *Washington Post,* January 23, 1969; "Rockefeller Report," p. 46.

17. "Dilemma for U.S. in Brazil," *Miami Herald,* December 21, 1968.

government. Admitting the fact that there are governments in Latin America that the United States does not like, the report continues:

> However, the fundamental question for the United States is how it can cooperate to help meet the basic needs of the people of the hemisphere, despite the philosophical disagreements it may have with the nature of particular regimes. It must seek pragmatic ways to help people without necessarily embracing their governments.[18]

In some of its implications, the humanitarian argument shades into the explanation of dictatorships as agents of socio-economic development leading to political democracy. U.S. policy makers increasingly defend aid to dictatorships on the grounds that they are (or can be) effective modernizers. In a sense, this defense of authoritarian regimes is an extension of the security apology presented earlier. In the period immediately following World War II, the United States posited that the greatest threats to Latin American governments and to its own hegemonic position were communism and Soviet power. Hence, aid to dictatorships was offered to counter local Communists and to keep Soviet influence from invading the hemisphere.

The rise of Fidel Castro and the New Left guerrillas presented a new dimension to the problem, however. Neither Castro nor the New Left were Communist in the sense that the United States had previously understood. But their opposition to the United States seemed as great a menace as the more traditional challenges, and the definition of security threats shifted to include so-called subversive elements of all kinds. Beginning in 1962, President Kennedy outlined the new policy by proposing that socio-economic underdevelopment was the major cause for the rise of the New Left guerrillas. Hence underdevelopment was the most important challenge to Latin American stability and to U.S. security.

As the definition of the menace shifted, so did the response. First, the Alliance for Progress was launched to save the Latin masses. Second, military training policy changed from a concentration on external threats to an emphasis on teaching the Latin American military to counter guerrilla movements. Finally, aid to dictatorships began to be defended on the ground that authoritarian governments were the long-range answer to the problem of development. This new justification has become Washington's favorite defense of its assistance to authoritarian regimes. In the words of a critic of the new departure, military dictatorship has been defined as "the midwife of constitutional democracy."[19]

The most important elements of the art of "democratic midwifery" are "stability" and "direction." The argument from stability states simply enough that economic growth demands political stability, which is conducive to

18. "Rockefeller Report," p. 46.

19. Petras, "The United States and the New Equilibrium," pp. 113–114.

long-range planning, unencumbered internal development, the attraction of domestic and foreign capital, and overall predictability. Referring to anti-subversive aid to Latin American governments, former Secretary of Defense McNamara has said, "Economic and social progress requires an environment free from internal disorder and internal conflict. It is our policy to help our American neighbors maintain such an environment and protect the peace and security of the hemisphere."[20]

The "direction" half of the argument focuses on the new trends among Latin American military dictatorships. In recent years, the military posture has changed. Military officers are increasingly recruited from the middle sectors. They are better educated, and, say many in the United States, they have become the leading agents of the social and economic development necessary for the eventual establishment of viable democracies. The Rockefeller Report posits the proposition.

> We will have to give increasing recognition to the fact that many new military leaders are deeply motivated by the need for social and economic progress. They are searching for ways to bring education and better standards of living to their people while avoiding anarchy or violent revolution. In many cases, it will be more useful for the United States to try to work with them in these efforts, rather than abandon or insult them because we are conditioned by arbitrary ideological stereotypes.[21]

The justifications for military aid to Latin America are both similar and disparate from those of aid to dictatorships more generally conceived. In this discussion, arguments that reproduce positions already set out will be mentioned only by way of context. Apologies that differ from the general ones will be explained a little more comprehensively.

Military aid has been defended as a necessary Cold War measure. The Latin American military were supposed to play a role in hemispheric defense. Later, they were equipped to subdue internal threats to stability from the New Left guerrilla movements. Defenders of military aid point with special pride to the astonishing success of the anti-guerrilla activities of the Latin Americans as evidence of the efficacy of the program.

Military aid is also seen as contributing to the developmental process in Latin America. Its role in encouraging stability is obvious, but many also tout military civic action as a significant developmental program. Civic action involves the military in programs like road building, public health projects, school construction, and agricultural extension work. These important contributions to socio-economic growth, say the apologists, would not be accomplished save for the utilization of military skills and manpower. Civic action

---

20. "United States Department of Defense Estimate of the Latin American Situation," *Inter-American Economic Affairs,* 19 September 1966, 80.

21. "Rockefeller Report," p. 51.

also delivers the dividend of occupying the military in some capacity, thereby lessening the possibility that it will become politically involved.

The realism argument has been especially important in defending military aid. One leading work proposes that the major reason for military assistance has always been the cultivation of the Latin military.[22] The armed forces are influential throughout Latin America and the most important domestic political group in many nations. If the United States wished to maintain its influence in Latin America and the friendship and support of the Latin governments, then it was imperative to support the military establishments. A sympathetic military, in short, was solid insurance that the government would be friendly to the United States.

Two other arguments apply specifically to military programs. First, the refusal of the United States to provide military assistance or to sell military hardware will force the Latin Americans to go elsewhere. Indeed, U.S. prohibition of sales to Latin American nations has already caused that result. Peru has purchased French fighters, Brazil has announced that it intends to buy jets from Italy, and several other countries have announced their intention to follow suit. The defenders of military programs to Latin America point out that the U.S. economy is suffering the consequences of the policy makers' shortsightedness. Moreover, the hopes of standardizing arms in the Western hemisphere have suffered a significant blow because the Latins are buying and looking elsewhere. The receipt of European arms may also mean the resumption of European military missions in Latin America, thereby challenging the U.S. monopoly in the southern half of the hemisphere.

Second, many charge that the whole problem of Latin American militarism and U.S. military assistance has been exaggerated and misconstrued. Contrary to the critics, the Latin American military establishments are not gobbling up much-needed developmental capital. Indeed, defense expenditures are lower in Latin America than anywhere in the world except sub-Saharan Africa. Furthermore, spending on defense is decreasing in Latin America. On the United States side of the ledger, military assistance has rarely exceeded 5 percent of the total aid package. The 1969 military aid budget for Latin America, moreover, was the lowest since 1950.[23]The defenders also charge that the military assistance program has been confused with aid to dictatorships. Although military assistance is granted to authoritarian governments, it is also given to democratic regimes. There seems to be no correlation between dictatorship and military assistance. Indeed, military assistance may be conducive to the evolution of representative government.[24]

---

22. Edwin Lieuwen, *Arms and Politics in Latin America,* rev. ed. (New York: Frederick A. Praeger, 1961), pp. 218–225.

23. Joseph E. Loftus, *Latin American Defense Expenditures* (Santa Monica, Calif. :The Rand Corporation, 1968), p. 37; "Rockefeller Report," p. 51; United States House of Representatives, *Foreign Assistance Act of 1969,* Part III, p. 664.

24. For more discussion of this problem, see "Analysis" in this chapter.

Opposition and Response

The response to the aid-to-dictatorships policy is composed of moral outrage and reasoned argument. The Latins combine angry denunciation with reasoned appeals to U.S. self-interest. They charge the United States with being both sinful and stupid for having supported Latin American despots. One of the leading figures of the Latin American Democratic Left censures the Eisenhower administration for "aid, backing, and sympathy for the dictatorships of Latin America" compounded by "disdain and disinterest in the problems of economic and social development in Latin America." A representative of the Christian Democratic movement notes that he is "dismayed" and "confused" by the assistance offered to dictatorships, which does nothing but "strengthen their tyrannies." In defending the Cuban revolution, a Mexican Leftist harangues the United States for having been "so calm, so thoughtful and so indifferent" to dictators who have "exploited, tyrannized, and debased" the people of Latin America. He continues:

> Why did you not start press campaigns against Somoza, why did you not invade Venezuela when Pérez Jiménez was in power, why did you support Trujillo for 30 years, why have you not declared yourselves against Stroessner? What do you want us to think when you have supported and still support regimes of corruption and crime.[25]

Finally, a North American critic notes that "our partners, co-signers" of the 1954 anti-Communist Caracas declaration included "some of the most vicious and bloody dictators Latin America has ever known"—Cuba's Fulgencio Batista, Nicaragua's Anastasio Somoza, Venezuela's Marcos Pérez Jiménez, Colombia's Gustavo Rojas Pinilla, Paraguay's Alfredo Stroessner, Peru's Manuel Odría, and the Dominican Republic's Rafael Trujillo.[26]

The Latin Americans charge the United States with moral hypocrisy. In the name of democracy, the United States maintains right-wing dictatorships in power. A Costa Rican notes that the United States fought the "supercriminals" in Europe during World War II, but supported the power of "little tyrants" in the Caribbean. An Ecuadoran proposes the hypocrisy of fighting the fascists in Europe, but blessing the government of Peron in the name of anti-communism.[27] While the United States sings of the rights of man, say the

25. Rómulo Betancourt, *Tres Años de Gobierno Democrático,* Tomo II (Caracas: Imprenta Nacional, 1962), p. 173; *Congresos Internacionales Demócrata-Cristianos* (Santiago de Chile: Editorial del Pacifico, 1957), p. 228; Carlos Fuentes, "The Argument of Latin America" (Ann Arbor, Mich.: The Radical Education Project, n.d.), pp. 498-499.

26. Gerassi, *The Great Fear*, pp. 241-242.

27. Clodomiro Picado and Pío Jaramillo Alvarado, quoted in Donald M. Dozer, *Are We Good Neighbors? Three Decades of Inter-American Relations, 1930-1960* (Gainesville: University of Florida Press, 1959), p. 212.

Latins, it consciously abets the suppression of those liberties by its aid to Latin American dictatorships.

Beyond the indignity of assisting dictatorships, critics charge that the United States has actually encouraged their implantation. That is, the United States not only supports dictatorships already established, but by its policies actually rallies anti-democratic forces to seize power. The U. S. emphasis on anti-communism encourages the Latin American military to see communism in authentic reform proposals. The increasing U.S. emphasis on the military as agents of development emboldens them to assume the reins of power. Moreover, assistance to despotic governments incites groups in other countries to overthrow regularly elected regimes. It has been charged, for example, that U.S. recognition and praise of the Brazilian military coup in 1964 "had a stimulating effect" on the military in Argentina and Bolivia, where coups were undertaken not long after the U.S. commendation of the Brazilian usurpers. The Venezuelan military were reported to have been encouraged by President Nixon's speech in late 1969. The military in that country were said to have interpreted the speech as "all but suggest(ing) a military takeover."[28] The United States was also charged with rallying right-wing opposition to the 1965 pro-Bosch coup in the Dominican Republic.

> The evidence is now overwhelming that the '65 pro-Bosch bid for power would have been a bloodless success in the first 36 hours but for the subsequent realization by the Dominican military leaders that the United States government did not want them to submit or the revolt to succeed. . . . There is every reason to believe that a major, if not a decisive, role in rallying the armed forces' leaders against the revolt was played by the United States military attaches who frantically called upon them to resist.[29]

In addition to these charges of moral wrongdoing, the critics of U.S. aid to dictatorships have also attempted to show the United States the lack of wisdom in its policies. Not only is assistance to tyrants wrong, say these commentators, but it does not serve the best interests of the United States. It does not encourage stability, it does not bring about peace, it does not contribute to either hemispheric or U.S. security.

Many charge that dictatorships are a threat to hemispheric peace in that there is a close, if not intrinsic, relationship between domestic violation of human rights and international disturbance of peace. If the United States sees a tranquil hemisphere as being in its national interest, it must recognize that

---

28. For a discussion of the general charge and some of the examples noted, see John Saxe-Fernández, "The Central American Defense Council and Pax Americana," in Irving Louis Horowitz et al., ed. *Latin American Radicalism* (New York: Vintage Books, 1969), pp. 75 – 101; Howard J. Wiarda, "The Politics of Civil-Military Relations in the Dominican Republic," *Journal Inter-American Studies* (October 1965), 478; Petras, "The United States and the New Equilibrium," p. 121; *Los Angeles Times,* November 30, 1969.

29. Theodore Draper, "A Case of Defamation," *New Republic,* February 26, 1966, 16.

dictatorships are in direct opposition to that policy aim. International peace will be assured only by the installation of democratic regimes throughout the hemisphere. Aid to dictatorships increases the opportunities for international conflict and the chances that major problems will be created for the United States.

Furthermore, the American goal of domestic stability is not served by its support for authoritarian government. Though tyrants may insure temporary quiescence, the long run result is frequently extreme instability leading to serious problems for American policy makers. Authoritarian governments breed popular frustration and fail to nurture the evolution of responsible political institutions. When the tyrant falls or is unseated, unleashed popular passions combined with the lack of viable political institutions often create a situation of grave disorder. The chaotic instability of post-Perón Argentina or post-Trujillo Dominican Republic are partly attributable to the failure of those dictators to develop regular political processes. Responsible parties are lacking, the bureaucracy has been corrupted by political favoritism, and mature labor unions have never developed. Political chaos frequently follows the demise of a dictatorial regime.

The post-dictatorial frustrations, moreover, have often taken on an anti-Yankee flavor. Anti-U.S. sources are quick to inform the people that their former oppressors had the blessing and support of the United States. One scholar, for example, explains the demonstrations against Nixon on exactly those grounds.

> It should have occasioned no surprise when, on the recent collapse of those dictatorships, resurgent popular elements demonstrated their resentment against Vice President Nixon during his visits to Peru and Venezuela. In these cases the strategic and political advantages obtained by the United States military policies were temporary only. They were quickly undone, and in the process the psychological and moral position of the United States suffered severely.[30]

Even more serious than anti-Yankee riots and demonstrations was Castro's use of U.S. aid to Fulgencio Batista. Castro capitalized on the fact that the tyrant had been blessed by the United States and that Batista's arms had been supplied by the United States. Writing in 1960, John. F. Kennedy suggested that Castro's revolution might have "taken a more rational course. . . had the United States government not backed the Batista dictatorship so long and so uncritically."[31] It may be too much to name aid to Batista as the basis of Castro's repudiation of the United States, but it was at least an effective issue to rally the Cuban people to his anti-Yankee policy.

In sum, the Latins warn the United States that the temporary advantage

---

30. Lieuwen, *Arms and Politics*, p. 236.
31. John F. Kennedy, *The Strategy of Peace* (New York: Harper & Row, 1960), p. 133.

of its pro-dictator policies are far outweighed by the long-range costs of increased anti-Americanism. A Chilean senator posits the argument.

> It is equally necessary for the United States to understand that Latin American dictatorships, even when they are condescending to its immediate commercial interest, lead to the destruction of good understanding between the two Americas; and, therefore, it commits a great error when it accords them its backing, or still worse, preferential treatment.[32]

Within the context of the Cold War, anti-U.S. feelings that result from its sympathy with dictatorships benefit the Soviet Union. A U.S. scholar argues that the Communists point to support of dictatorships as "evidence" of the U. S. responsibility for the persecution of the Democratic Left and the suffering of the Latin masses. A leading Latin American statesman adds to the argument by highlighting the hypocrisy of the position.

> It would seem reasonable to expect the conflict between the United States and Russia to shift progressively towards spheres other than competition in armaments. The controversy will turn more on issues of doctrine and principles, and in such an ideological competition, the Soviets will have a solid arsenal of arguments if the governments of the Western camp continue to publish the speeches of Khrushchev to prove that Stalin was a leader of criminal conduct, and at the same time continue to offer assistance and support to Latin American governments with repressive traits similar to those of the Stalin regime.[33]

Even on the issue of domestic anti-communism, the critics charge that the United States is often duped by its despotic friends. While the United States commended and assisted anti-Communist dictators the tyrants were often cooperating with the local Communists. Batista, Trujillo, and Pérez Jiménez all cooperated with the Communists in their nations. Communist parties were often the only organized civilian forces that the despots could recruit to their cause. Consequently, the Communists were granted official sanction to infiltrate the labor unions, peasant organizations, and other politically significant groups. While the Democratic Left was being persecuted in those countries, the Communists were reaping the benefits of relatively unoppressed militancy. It is no wonder that they frequently emerged from the dictatorial regime better organized than their democratic foes.[34]

To add injury to insult, most contemporary dictatorships have even begun to forsake their traditional anti-communism on the international level. Though Batista, Pérez Jiménez, and Trujillo occasionally courted the local Communist

---

32. *Congresos Internacionales Demócrata-Cristianos*, p. 392.

33. Robert J. Alexander, *Communism in Latin America* (New Brunswick, N. J.: Rutgers University Press, 1957), p. 89; Romulo Betancourt, quoted in Luigi Einaudi, *Changing Contexts of Revolution in Latin America* (Santa Monica, Calif.: The Rand Corporation, 1966), p. 19.

34. Burr, *Our Troubled Hemisphere*, p. 63; Lieuwen, *Arms and Politics*, p. 228.

parties, they staunchly opposed the intrusion of Soviet power into the hemisphere. The newest dictatorships are intensely nationalistic and anxious to demonstrate their independence of the United States. The Peron dictatorship (1945 – 1955) was a harbinger of things to come. While advertising its anticommunism, the regime was also bent on manifesting its own personality by pursuing an independent foreign policy, no matter what the United States wanted.

The present dictatorships seem to be following Perón, thereby destroying another rationale for U.S. support. The Peruvian regime has clearly stated its intention to work with, trade with, and have diplomatic relations with Soviet bloc nations, despite the displeasure of the United States. It has established both diplomatic and trade relations with the Soviet Union and several satellites. In early 1970, the Peruvians began negotiations seeking Soviet technical and financial assistance for some internal development projects. The Bolivian dictatorship, established in late 1969, has advertised its affinity with the Peruvian military and seems ready to assume a similar international posture. Even the more conservative Brazilian authoritarian regime is now following a more independent foreign policy line. The interior minister announced that "we're not answerable to anybody outside our frontiers for what we do," and posited Peru and France as exemplars for its own policy.[35]

Furthermore, the new-style dictatorships in Latin America no longer support U.S. business and investments. Again, burgeoning nationalism has influenced the military tyrants just as much as it has infected their democratic opponents. If military dictatorship once meant anti-Russian, it also once meant that U.S. business was welcome and its investments safe. Many charged that aid to dictatorships was primarily based on that fact. If friendliness to U.S. capital were ever a cogent reason for U.S. support, it will probably be much less so in the future. The dictatorial regimes established in Peru and Bolivia in the late 1960's have nationalized American-owned oil industries, and the Brazilian despots have tightened their control over U.S. business in that nation.

The new-style dictatorships, in short, have destroyed many reasons for U.S. support and supplied the critics of aid to dictatorships with a devastating set of arguments against the continuation of U.S. assistance. Dictatorships that trade with the Soviet bloc nations, establish diplomatic relations with the Soviets, contract for Soviet technical assistance, and move against U.S. capital cannot be defended even on "realistic" grounds.

Finally, the critics reject the "dictator-as-modernizer" justification for aid to dictatorships. They deny that Latin American authoritarian governments can contribute to social, economic, and political development. Therefore, aid

---

35. See Virginia Prewett, "Brazilian Junta Challenges U.S.," *Washington Daily News*, January 8, 1969.

to despots based upon their supposed contribution to modernization is ill-conceived. A staff study of "The Political Aspects of the Alliance for Progress" undertaken for the Senate Latin American subcommittee states that "the trouble with *caudillos* is that they do not allow for political development because they see a threat to themselves in such development."[36]

Political development, say those who oppose aid to military dictatorships, demands the foundation and growth of political parties, labor unions, and interest groups of all kinds to recruit new participants into the political arena, to channel their political activity, and to cushion their impact on the political system. Progressive political growth also presupposes the evolution of well-trained, efficient bureaucracies free from the whimsical control of selfish and insecure despots. It means a division of labor among societal structures, which implies that parties, presidents, legislatures, and military men perform their own jobs. Both historical evidence and pragmatic logic prove that dictatorships have not, cannot, and will not contribute to the evolution of these elements of political growth.

A student of political modernization has set out the denial of the dictatorship as developer, alluding to the opinions in both Americas that look to "a Nasserite solution as the most promising path toward social, economic, and political development. These hopes," he continues, "have little chance of realization."

> Most Latin American societies are beyond the possibilities of Nasserism. They are too complex, too highly articulated, too far advanced economically to be susceptible to salvation by military men. As Latin America has modernized, the role of the military has become more conservative. . . . To say that the Brazil of the 1960's needed a Nasser was somewhat like saying that the Russia of the 1960's needed a Styolpin. The two types of leadership were simply irrelevant to the stage of development that these societies had reached.[37]

The Christian Democratic movement points to another dictatorial detriment to development. The movement proposes that international integration is necessary to the effective growth of Latin America. Despotic governments will not contribute to international integration; "The existence of dictatorships in Latin America is one of the worst obstacles in the task of achieving political and economic unity."[38] In sum, policy makers, Latin Americans, and scholars disagree that tyrannical governments can be effective agents of modernization.

---

36. Pat M. Holt, *Survey of the Alliance for Progress: The Political Aspects*, a study for a subcommittee of the Senate Committee on Foreign Relations (Washington, D.C.: U.S. Government Printing Office, 1967), p. 3.

37. Samuel P. Huntington, *Political Order in Changing Societies* (New Haven, Conn: Yale University Press, 1968), pp. 228–229. By way of scholarly objectivity, it should be noted that Huntington sees some possibility for dictatorial contributions in "Haiti, Paraguay, Nicaragua, or even the Dominican Republic. But the rest of the continent (is) simply too highly developed for such an attractively simple panacea."

38. Quoted in Edward J. Williams, *Latin American Christian Democratic Parties* (Knoxville: University of Tennessee Press, 1967), p. 144.

Because of the overlap of the aid to dictatorship and military assistance issues, most of the arguments proposed above are also broached by those who oppose U.S. support of the Latin military establishments. This section will also set out other criticisms more directly concerned with military functions, though not always necessarily a part of the aid-to-dictatorships theme.

The most frequently reiterated charge damns military aid as contributing to the rise and perpetuation of tyrants in Latin America and to the suppression of democratic groups dedicated to political and socio-economic modernization. An editorial in the *Denver Post* states the basic argument.

> Unfortunately, U.S. training and arms in Latin America have not always been used for the purposes for which they were envisioned. Instead, they have helped to make possible coups against legal Latin governments.
>
> Within the last three months, military groups — all beneficiaries of U.S. training and aid — have seized supreme power in three Latin nations, Peru, Panama, and Brazil.
>
> Of the 14 members of the military junta which overthrew the elected government of President Fernando Belaúnde Terry in Peru last October (1968), 11 had received military training in the United States.[39]

The suppression of the Latin American people is also a basic reason to discontinue military assistance. U.S. financed armies, says a Mexican intellectual, contribute to "continuous political stagnation" based on a "feudal structure (which) forbids the masses access to education and assures the concentration of political power in the hands of a fistful of landlords and city capitalists." Further on, he challenges the Yankee taxpayer:

> And do you think it just, as taxpayers, that your money should go to equip these caste armies? With your money, these armies prepare revolts, murder workers, torture students, and void elections.[40]

Beyond the evils emanating from U.S. support of Latin military establishments, the opposition charges that the investment has no tangible purpose and bears no political fruit. Military aid is simply unnecessary, because the premises on which it is granted are incorrect.[41] Military aid was at first justified as empowering the Latin defense establishments against an extra-hemispheric threat — an invasion of Latin America. That premise is clearly incorrect; it is ridiculous to posit that the Soviets or the Chinese have ever thought of invading Latin America. Even if they had, the Latin military would be unable to contribute much to the defense of the continent. North American forces would be necessary.

A more serious argument is made that U.S. aid has been important in developing the anti-subversive capabilities of the Latin American armed

---

39. Editorial, "Aid to Latin Military Men Misfires," *Denver Post*, December 29, 1968.

40. Fuentes, "The Argument of Latin America," pp. 491, 496.

41. For the general position, see Jeremiah O'Leary, "Latin Military Missions Hit as Costly U.S. 'Boondoggle'," Washington *Evening Star,* January 8, 1969.

forces. That is, U.S. military aid and training has made a significant contribution to the defeat of the New Left guerrillas. The objective observer might be more persuaded by that proposition, because American training may have been a factor in defeating the guerrillas, but other considerations seem equally important. A student has noted that guerrilla warfare "is not the facile, advantageous method that Castro has suggested it is." A commentator on the Guevara defeat in Bolivia points to "the profound weakness and incompetence of the current wave of 'Marxist' revolutionary struggles in Latin America." Further on, he chronicles "an almost incredible stupidity on the part of the guerrillas."[42] If these estimations of guerrilla capabilities are correct, U.S. aid was superfluous even in this situation. The Latin military forces were probably prepared to counter the threat without U.S. assistance.

Finally, the last premise of U.S. military assistance — to assure the friendship of the influential Latin military — no longer seems valid. Aid may once have assured the United States of sympathy among the Latin American military, but emerging trends indicate that it does no longer. The most recently established military dictatorships have been captured by anti-Yankee nationalism, as have all of the major political forces on the continent. No matter what aid the United States gives or withholds, the Latin military shows every sign of independence in both domestic and foreign affairs. If military aid were ever a tool of Yankee imperialism, it no longer is.

In sum, the critics of military assistance hold that it has been so much money wasted. The effects have been bad. The political goals have not been achieved. These large sums could have been employed more fruitfully in contributing to political and socio-economic modernization in Latin America.

Some Analysis

The aid-to-dictatorship controversy will probably continue to be a cogent theme of inter-American relations. It may never again achieve the importance that it had in the late 1950's, but trends in the 1960's and early 1970's point to its continued existence as a major controversy for the forseeable future.

The one major reservation to that point is that the military assistance aspect of the controversy will recede in the 70's, because the United States is making significant cuts in its military aid to Latin America. Before getting to that point, however, considerations contributing to a possible reduction in the aid-to-dictatorships theme will be discussed.

---

42. See David D. Burks, *Insurgency in Latin America,* a study prepared for a subcommittee of the Senate Committee on Foreign Relations (Washington, D.C.: U.S. Government Printing Office, 1968), p. 1; Norman Gall, "The Legacy of Che Guevara," *Commentary* Report with Study Guide, pp. 2, 4.

Some Considerations Leading to a Reduction of the Controversy

Though this analysis posits that the aid-to-dictatorships theme will continue to be a major issue, some facts and trends could reduce its cogency. U.S. hemispheric policy has been mightily influenced by its perception of extra-hemispheric intrusions as threatening U.S. interests and security.[43] When the traditional Great Powers or the Soviet Union challenged hemispheric hegemony, the United States reacted and the Latins caught hell. Imperialism, specific interventions, and aid to dictatorships were all triggered by challenges to the U.S. sphere of influence in the hemisphere. Conversely, when the threats receded, U.S. policy became more benign.

The 1970's should be characterized by little extra-hemispheric defiance of U.S. power in the Americas. The Yankee sphere of influence is again safe, and the United States may again have an opportunity to practice enlightened inter-American politics. The United States could launch an anti-dictatorial policy, in response to the opinion in both Americas that has always urged it to do so. In short, the time is ripe for the pursuance of democratic ideals.

The passing of Trujillo's tyranny may also lessen the impact of the aid-to-dictatorships theme. Trujillo was only one of many tyrants who have been praised and assisted by the United States, but he had become a symbol of the issue. His regime was particularly oppressive, his personality singularly obnoxious, and his international adventures peculiarly odious. No man was more despised by the Democratic Left of both Americas. No single example of U.S. affinity for dictatorships was more detested and more condemned than the long courting of the Dominican despot. With U.S. approval, if not assistance, he was finally assassinated in 1961, and an almost intolerable embarrassment to the United States disappeared.

The evolving trends among Latin American military dictatorships may also contribute to a lessening of readiness to assist them. The new breed of military dictators are intensely nationalistic; they demonstrate every evidence of repudiating Yankee leadership and striking a more independent posture. The Peron regime was the harbinger of this trend and the present Peruvian dictatorship is its contemporary archetype. The Peruvians, with the Bolivians and Brazilians not far behind, have announced that they intend to have political and economic dealings with whomever they please. Their domestic developmental policies will be framed and implemented with only the interests of Peru in mind. If Yankee interests stand in the way, then Yankee interests will be nationalized or sacrificed.

If these trends continue, Latin American authoritarian governments will cease to be the friends of old. Assuming that U.S. foreign policy is based on calculating self-interest, it may no longer be advantageous to support Latin

---

43. See particularly pp. 21–25.

tyrants. Hence, the objective conditions of Latin American politics may convince the policy makers that aid to dictatorships is no longer a prudent course of action.

Indeed, a strong domestic opposition to assisting dictatorships has always existed. The critics among the academic and political Left have constantly argued the hypocrisy and stupidity of aid to dictatorships. The critics have urged the policy makers to change the posture to one of official disapproval, if not out-right opposition shown by suspension of diplomatic relations and economic assistance. They have pressed Washington to exercise its influence in favor of democratic government. Hubert Humphrey advises that "in those instances when we must temporarily deal with non-constitutional governments, we should use all our levers of influence to restore constitutional government at the earliest possible time." In writing about the Castro regime, he has also cautioned that "it is important that throughout Cuba and all Latin America it be clearly understood that we want the Castro-Communist tyranny to be replaced with a progressive government, that we will not tolerate a right-wing dictatorship."[44] A student of Latin American politics wants a tougher policy vis-à-vis Latin American tyrants.

> Admittedly, nonrecognition has so far failed to prevent unrepresentative military regimes. But this is no reason to abandon all efforts to encourage democracy. The attempt to do so by eschewing all overt cooperation, including military and economic aid, with counter-revolutionary military regimes has not been given a full and fair trial as yet. Its trial in Peru, the Dominican Republic, and Honduras was abandoned too soon to have any effect.[45]

Another student of Latin politics posits that a tough policy toward military coups might be effective. In a study of the processes of Latin American military coups, he outlines the difficult task of establishing military support for government overthrows. The last, and frequently the most important, people to join the coup are the least committed to it. Therefore, they are liable to buckle if pressure is applied. The scholar concludes:

> In a coup situation, accordingly, even the mildest deterrent threat, such as a firmly stated non-recognition policy on the part of the United States, may still be effective, because of the structure of the pre-coup balance of forces.[46]

Finally, as the previous chapter on intervention attests,[47] the United States has opposed Latin American despots on numerous occasions. Some charge

---

44. Hubert H. Humphrey, "U.S. Policy in Latin America," *Foreign Affairs*, July 1964, 593; *A Report on the Alliance for Progress*, 1963, a report to the Senate Appropriations and Foreign Relations Committees (Washington: U.S. Government Printing Office, 1963), p. 37.

45. Lieuwen, *Generals vs. Presidents*, p. 145.

46. Needler, *Political Development*, p. 76. See pp. 66–76 for the argument.

47. See pp. 83–84.

that these attempts have been pursued with insufficient vigor. However, it is worth noting that U.S. recognition has been withheld and aid suspended in hopes of forcing dictatorships to modify their policies or of forcing their downfall. In the mid-1960's alone, Washington withheld diplomatic recognition or cut off aid against authoritarian regimes in Argentina, Bolivia, Brazil, the Dominican Republic, Honduras, Panama, Peru, and El Salvador. Even more dramatically, in 1963 the United States broke with long-honored hemispheric practices in extraditing Venezuela's Pérez Jiménez to stand trial before his democratic accusers.

The description of these anti-dictatorial moves is not intended to argue that the United States has not been guilty of assisting tyrants. It does indicate, however, that the opposition has sometimes been successful in influencing policy makers to move against despots. If some developments discussed in this section mature to create a more propitious domestic and international political climate, the opposition may be able to triumph and carry the day. The upshot of that unlikely turn of events would be to drastically reduce the aid-to-dictatorships theme as an element of inter-American politics.

Some Indications of Continued Aid to Dictatorships

As the previous discussion implies, the possibilities of continuing the aid-to-dictatorships theme seem significantly stronger than those of decreasing its cogency. Official policy continues to reject moves against tyrants, apologists increasingly paint a rosy picture of dictatorial developmental contributions, and the national political mood is not ripe for a dramatic revision of current practice. The policy makers in Washington have stated in unequivocal terms that the United States will continue to provide assistance to Latin American authoritarian governments. After a short-lived modification of the policy in the late 1950's and early 1960's, the pronouncements have again implied a readiness to deal with tyrants. Some contemporary apologists seem to have gone beyond mere acquiescence to dictatorships. The tone of positive approval is more effusive than at any time since the theme achieved fruition following World War II.

The present policy toward Latin American authoritarian regimes began under the Johnson administration. At that time, to quote a commentator, "the active promotion of democratic government in Latin America was . . . deemphasized as part of a general hardening of policy."[48] President Johnson's Latin American secretary, Thomas Mann, pursued a "realistic" policy and stated unequivocally that the United States would not take sanctions against many of the continent's dictators.[49]

48. Burr, *Our Troubled Hemisphere,* p. 31.
49. Thomas C. Mann, "The Democratic Ideal in Our Policy."

The position of the Nixon administration continued this realism. The Rockefeller Report noted that the United States "should recognize that diplomatic relations are practical conveniences and not measures of moral judgement." The Nixon pronouncement followed suit by positing that, "on the diplomatic level, we must deal realistically with governments in the inter-American system as they are."[50] It would be incorrect (as well as unkind) to posit that either the Johnson or the Nixon administrations were happy with Latin American dictatorships. Indeed, both administrations have pronounced to the contrary. Nonetheless, the present posture vis-à-vis Latin American despotic regimes seems as close to approval as it has been since World War II.

While some traditional reasons for approval of Latin dictatorships have eroded, other factors have arisen to take their place. These newer elements of the inter-American milieu explain Washington's increasing affinity for Latin American authoritarian regimes. The policy makers seem convinced that the new military dictatorships are authentically concerned with the redemption of the masses. Moreover, they seem equally convinced that the new military despots are capable of modernizing their countries.

The evolution of new military types in Latin America has, in a real sense, rescued Washington from a dilemma. Dictatorships were traditionally defended on the grounds that Cold War considerations necessitated that position. Even in the worst of times, however, the decision makers were uncomfortable with dictators because they oppressed the Latin American people. Hence, support of such regimes was frequently given reluctantly. At times, Washington's democratic sensitivities even overcame Cold War considerations and some attempts to discourage tyrannies were launched. Aid to dictatorships, in short, was seldom given with unflagging vigor, because Latin American authoritarian governments were never an unmixed blessing.

The emergence of the modernizing military has seemingly changed the situation, however, and the policy makers have embraced the regimes as the solution to their dilemma. Washington now thinks that it has the best of both worlds. Stability is maintained — thus serving the Cold War dictates of foreign policy. And, say the decision makers, military dictatorships are profoundly concerned with the Latin masses — thus responding to the residue of democratic sensitivity that has always impeded full-fledged support of such regimes. Hence a policy of aid to dictatorships emerges that may well be more enthusiastic than at any time in recent hemispheric history.

The U.S. sympathy with modernizing military dictatorships is well documented. Former inter-American Affairs Secretary Gordon has "effusively praised" the Brazilian military regime as an agent of modernizing change. A study of U.S. policy has characterized Gordon's position, "and others of a similar vein," as a "clear departure from traditional views of constitutional democracy and more akin to rationalizations for authoritarian govern-

---

50. "Rockefeller Report," p. 46; "Text of President Nixon's Address."

ment."[51] The position may be rationalization, but it is certainly not conscious excuse-making. On the contrary, a strong commitment to dictatorial government appears to be growing among influential U.S. decision makers. Representative Dante B. Fascell, Chairman of the House Inter-American subcommittee, has been described as "flexible" on the dictatorship issue; he seems to see merit in the Argentine and Brazilian dictatorial regimes because they are different from traditional despotic governments and because they have been "economically successful."[52] The Rockefeller Report, of course, was even more enthusiastic in its praise for the "new military leaders" in Latin America. They are described as "deeply motivated by the need for social and economic progress. They are searching for ways to bring education and better standards of living to their people while avoiding anarchy and violent revolution." The report advises that "in many cases it will be more useful for the United States to try to work with them in these efforts, rather than to abandon or insult them because we are conditioned by arbitrary ideological stereotypes."[53] Though not so strong as the Rockefeller Report, President Nixon's policy speech has also been interpreted as implying that the United States will look benignly upon these new-style authoritarian governments.

In addition to Washington's growing affinity for despotic governments, the current national mood will almost definitely decrease the possibilities of a vigorous anti-dictatorial policy. The nation has grown weary of foreign adventure; it is unsure of its ability to do good. Support of tyrants is less likely to get the United States involved in hemispheric controversy. The national will is simply not up to the task.

This same point was made concerning intervention in the analysis of the previous chapter. A dynamic policy in favor of democratic governments and against tyrants demands vigorous intervention. Public opinion in the United States will not tolerate any more interventionistic sallies. That fact is advantageous to the Latins because the Yankee will be much less obnoxious than in the past. Within the context of the aid-to-dictatorships theme, however, the contemporary isolationist mood destroys the hopes of those in both Americas who wish the United States to use its power and influence to topple tyrants and promote democrats.

The argument is already made — and will be made increasingly in the future — that the United States cannot influence the Latin American situation. The supposed failure of the anti-dictatorial policy of the late 1950's and early 1960's will be used to support the charge of political impotence. The position will be that the United States has tried and failed to bring down despots. It is useless to try again.

Emerging trends in Latin America, furthermore, will bolster the case of

---

51. Petras, "The United States and the New Equilibrium," pp. 113 – 114.

52. Jeremiah O'Leary, "Our Latin Policies Face a Shaking Up," *The* (Washington, D.C.) *Sunday Star,* March 16, 1969.

53. "Rockefeller Report," p. 51.

the supporters of continued aid to dictatorships. Sensitivities engendered by burgeoning nationalism will weaken the position of those who look to anti-dictatorial policies. Their opposition to interventionistic power, even against tyrants, is bound to overcome their hopes for a democratic continent.

Developments in the late sixties suggest the trend. The United States was reluctant to move against military dictatorships in both Brazil and Peru. When the Brazilian dictators saw the possibility of U.S. pressures to reform their regime, they responded belligerently. In the words of one commentator, "an open threat that the Brazilian generals would shift to anti-Americanism" was issued. The Peruvian dilemma was even more instructive. Pressure was not applied for fear of alienating the Latins.

> The Peruvian military have maneuvered the United States into a most disadvantageous position. If we allow them to grab United States investments without payment and keep on supplying Peru aid and guaranteeing their lucrative sugar quota, we strengthen the neo-Nazi tide.
>
> If we crack down, Peru will rally a damaging amount of nationalistic support, especially on the South American Pacific coast.[54]

The opposition to U.S. aid to dictatorships, in short, has fallen on bad times. The policy makers have accepted the new style military dictators in the name of long-range development. Contemporary pessimism has weakened the popular will to push for intervention against tyrants. Finally, burgeoning Latin American nationalism has raised the possible costs of U.S. interference and has added another reason to forsake an anti-dictatorial policy. The ambitions of democrats to use Yankee power for encouraging representative government have suffered a serious setback as the seventies begin.

Though it seems relatively clear that aid to dictatorships will continue in the future, military aid is just as clearly on the decline and may well end in the early 1970's. Military assistance to Latin America was reduced in the late 1960's, and despite the urging of the Rockefeller Report, the Nixon administration seemed prepared to continue the reductions in military aid to Latin America.

Before considering that trend, however, it is imperative to set straight the aid to dictatorships/military assistance relationship. It has been noted several times in this study that the two concepts, controversies, or themes are frequently equated. Critics of U.S. hemispheric policy seem to say that military aid *is* aid to dictatorships. The critics charge that military aid encourages the establishment of dictatorial government or at least contributes to the maintenance of Latin American despots. To erase these misunderstandings and to crystallize specific problems, it is useful to set them out for discussion.

First, military assistance cannot be equated with aid to dictatorships. Military subventions are also given to democratic regimes. The defenders of

---

54. Quotations from Virginia Prewett, "Brazilian Junta Challenges U. S." and "Dictatorship Problems Scar U.S.-Peru Row," *Washington Daily News,* January 8, 1969, and March 14, 1969.

military assistance have argued that U.S. training and assistance contributed mightily to the defeat of New Left guerrillas in several nations, thereby preserving democracy. Depending on the definition of Latin American democracy, about one half of U.S. support has gone to democracies since World War II. From 1950 to 1960, Chile and Uruguay received the largest amounts of United States aid on a per capita basis. During the same period those two nations, along with Costa Rica, were among the leading democracies in Latin America.[55]

Second, contemporary scholarship strongly suggests that U.S. military aid does not necessarily encourage military men to undertake coups and establish dictatorial regimes.

> No convincing evidence exists of a correlation between the American military aid and military involvement in politics. And, it must be pointed out, the opposite hypothesis also is not true: the hopes of many people that the propensity of foreign military to intervene would be reduced by courses at Leavenworth, indoctrination in Anglo-American doctrines of civilian supremacy, and association with professionalized American military officers have also turned to naught.

The author continues that some U.S.-aided armed forces have intervened, but others have not. In conclusion, he postulates that "military aid and military training are by themselves politically sterile: they neither encourage nor reduce the tendencies of military officers to play a political role."[56]

The third charge — that military aid contributes to the maintenance of tyrannical power by facilitating the oppression of political opponents — has been neither proved nor disproved. Informed intuition would seem to lend credence to the proposition. Dictators with modern weapons provided by the United States would logically enough seem better able to stave off challenge to their despotic rule. Though that charge may be correct, it is difficult to believe that it can be the only decisive factor. Castro's victory over the U.S.-supplied Cuban army is evidence enough to demonstrate that factors other than guns are involved in unseating a tyranny.

This explanation and crystallization of the aid to dictatorships/military assistance relationship is not offered in refutation of the critics of military aid. It is only posited as a way of contributing to a more concrete understanding of the elements involved. Opposition to military aid is well grounded. Many propose, understandably enough, that any aid is bad; one gun supplied is one gun too many; any peripheral chance that military assistance contributes to tyranny is sufficient evidence to stop all aid.

However surprising in view of the trends noted in this study, it seems that the critics of military aid are winning their battle. Military assistance has

---

55. See Charles Wolf, Jr., "The Political Effects of Military Programs: Some Indications from Latin America," *Orbis* 8 (Winter 1965), 880–881.

56. Huntington, *Political Order*, p. 193.

already been significantly cut back and will be decreased even further in the early 1970's. The 1969 proposed military program was the lowest since the early 1950's.The entire program is being reappraised. The emerging policy looks to phasing out military assistance as the Latin American nations achieve a basic level of internal security. Utilizing that criteria, grant aid to Argentina, Brazil, Chile, and Peru was terminated in fiscal year 1968.[57] Military missions in Latin America are also being reduced. By mid-1970, the number of United States advisors in Latin America is to be cut back to 505 from the mid-sixties level of over 800—a 35 percent reduction.

Three factors seem to explain the new reductions in military aid. First, the critics have been successful in dramatizing the supposed evils of military aid, even while failing to muster support for suspension of economic aid. Second, the success of the aid program in erasing the guerrilla threat has made its continuation unnecessary. Third, the Vietnam debacle has eroded the U.S. military's political punch with the decision makers. The military are very close to being in disrepute. They were an influential force in pushing military aid in Latin America, but no longer carry the weight of old, thereby relatively strengthening the hand of the opposition. Indeed, the ABM debates of mid-1969 may well have initiated a period in which the military's influence in all foreign policy decisions will decrease significantly.

---

57. *Foreign Assistance Act of 1969*, Part III, p. 656.

Five

The Rich Nations and the Poor Nations

Introduction

The political theme of the separation of the rich United States from poor Latin America is the most recent issue to complicate hemispheric affairs. This emerging theme may well have increased cogency in the 70's, but as yet is only barely sketched on the hemispheric canvas.

The rhetoric of Latin American politics and diplomacy increasingly identifies the poor Third World countries as ideological brethren and political allies. Some agreements and cooperative efforts have been wrought, but the ambitions of many for solidarity with the Third World are a long way from maturity. Though Latin America has backed away from the idea of a hemispheric community that includes the United States, it has not quite embraced the idea of a community that includes Africa and Asia. As the seventies begin, indeed, Latin America seems diplomatically, economically, and politically located somewhere between the rich, powerful nations to the north and the poor, weak nations of the southern half of the globe.

The rich nations and the poor nations theme began to intrude upon hemispheric relations at the beginning of the 1960's. Several factors explain the emergence of the theme at that time. First, it was not until then that all the nations of the Third World achieved independent existence. Many Asian and Near Eastern states attained independence in the late 1940's and early 1950's; other Asian countries and the North African nations joined them in the mid-fifties; but most of the Sub-Saharan African colonies became independent nations in the 1960's. The Cold War struggle also promoted the maturation of the rich versus the poor controversy. In the 1950's and early 1960's both the United States and the Soviet Union openly courted the underdeveloped

Southern Hemisphere. The importance imputed to the poor nations by Cold War propaganda increased their self-esteem and contributed to coordinated action. The Soviets particularly played on the anti-colonialistic passions of the Third World and aided in the emergence of an issue that elicited their political cooperation. Finally, the issue of economic development came to dominate North-South (rich-poor) world politics by the late 1950's and added still another catalyzing issue leading to increased cooperation among the nations of the Third World. Unlike colonialism, the problem of economic development is an issue that will contribute to long-range unity among the poor states of the Southern Hemisphere.

The Latin American move toward the Third World evolved in two identifiable stages. The first step essentially involved a more independent stance vis-à-vis U.S. Cold War policies. This step was most dramatically manifested by Juan Perón's "Third Position" in international politics, which repudiated both the East and the West along with their philosophic, ideologic, and programmatic baggage. Argentina had traditionally been the leading South American competitor of the United States for hemispheric leadership. The marked economic successes and revolutionary traditions of Mexico encouraged that country to a similar ambition after World War II. The independent policy of those two states had no immediate, specific meaning for Third World solidarity, but did imply a weakening of the Western Hemispheric idea that tied Latin America to the United States.

The transition from repudiation of the United States to increasing affinity with Afro-Asia is probably best exemplified by Brazil's Jânio Quadros. The mercurial president's short-lived reign in 1961 initiated a foreign policy combining Cold War neutralism with Third World unity. Quadros established relations with the Soviet Union and other Soviet bloc nations, and he designed a foreign policy that attempted to increase diplomatic intercourse and political friendship with Afro-Asia.[1] The second step of the rich nations and the poor nations theme, then, had emerged in fairly clear form by the beginning of the 1960's. Many Latin American states formulated a conscious policy to combine with the other poor nations in pursuit of specific political and economic goals. But the theme also encompassed an entirely new definition of Latin America, which shifted the emphasis from cultural, ideological, and philosophic association with the Western tradition to socio-economic identification with the poor states of Afro-Asia.[2]

---

1. See E. Bradford Burns, *Nationalism in Brazil* (New York: Frederick A. Praeger, 1968), pp. 95–97.

2. See Edward J. Williams, "Comparative Political Development: Latin America and Afro-Asia," *Comparative Studies in Society and History*, 11: 3 (June 1969), 342–354.

Latin America and the Poor Southern Nations

The Argument for Unity

In their evolving identification with the other parts of the poor Third World, the Latin Americans have pointed to a series of arguments that illustrate the common conditions, characteristics, and problems that tie them to Afro-Asia. As early as 1957, a pioneering work on the underdeveloped non-Western world had anticipated the emerging Latin American stance.

> The features that set Latin America apart from the mainstream of Western modernism are in many cases similar to features found in Asia and Africa. Latin America shares to a greater or lesser degree such elements as the yearnings and frustrations associated with poverty, past colonialism, weak and unstable national governments, severe economic instability, uncomfortably great dependence on major industrial nations, and a strong desire to abstain from excessive involvement in international rivalries and problems that seem far from home.[3]

The two most important foci of the Latin American argument are similarities in socio-economic underdevelopment and coincidental anti-colonialist international political policies. Racial similarities, a third common ground, have been noted from time to time, but have been less important than the other two elements.

Economic underdevelopment is the most important tie between the Latin Americans and other parts of the Third World. Both Latin America and Afro-Asia are poor. Common poverty breeds comparable social and political systems, making necessary similar domestic developmental programs. Common poverty also weakens both Latin America and Afro-Asia in their dealings with rich nations. Finally, it causes similar frustrations leading to a search for alliances and accords that will give power to the weak in their struggle with the strong.

A description of the Brazilian Catholic Left, for example, notes that the group has consciously nurtured an identification with Afro-Asia, "whose nations share the common characteristics of underdevelopment." These Catholic progressives, moreover, have repudiated the usual Catholic affinity for Portugal based on cultural grounds and replaced it with a tie to the poor nations based on economic similarity. "Cultural affinities," says the explanation, "cannot obscure a more fundamental worldwide division between prosperous and poor nations."

In a speech before Venezuelan professionals and *técnicos* in 1958, Rómulo Betancourt also pointed out the parallel problems facing under-

---

3. Vera Micheles Dean, *The Nature of the Non-Western World* (New York: Mentor Press, 1957), p. 173.

developed countries. He decried the lack of well-prepared technicians in his own country and continued that "this situation, in many aspects, is no different from that which confronts other underdeveloped areas . . . of the world. They are the same problems that are contemplated in India, in Pakistan, in Asia, and in Africa in general."

A leading Latin American trade unionist makes the same point in rejecting the East-West conflict as the dominant division in international politics.

> We Latin Americans, however, find the world divided along a different axis. There is a bloc of rich, economically developed countries and a bloc of poor, underdeveloped countries. In the rich bloc we see the United States, the Soviet Union and other wealthy nations, all located in the world's Northern Hemisphere. (We, alas, are in the Southern half).
>
> Thus, in our view the significant division is not between East and West, but between North and South. We feel more identified with the African nations than with the United States. For we and they have common needs and a common future to work out together. It is becoming clearer to us that we are a "third world."

Cuba also emphasizes a new identification. A Havana university student reports that the "critical words now are 'Third World' and 'underdevelopment,' with Cubans trying desperately to identify themselves with underdeveloped countries, to divorce themselves from the culture 90 miles away."[4]

The ambition of many Latin Americans is to develop increasing unity of action with their brethren in Africa and Asia. The poor nations, or poor continents, are too weak to resolve their problems in isolation. By working together, however, they may be able to overcome their weakness and poverty. In discussing the ideology of development, a Mexican sets out the argument.

> It implies the establishment of political and economic bonds between the weak, poor, and underindustrialized in order to strengthen their independence. From Caracas to Bandung and to the most recent congresses in Cairo the necessity of union, of cooperation, and alliance between former colonies with a common legacy or similar background — this has been the moving principle of independence for these countries. Isolation has been, and is, a symptom of weakness and colonialism. Union is symptomatic of, and a motivator of, independence.[5]

---

4. For the quotations and discussions cited above, see Thomas G. Sanders, "Catholicism and Development: The Catholic Left in Brazil," in Kalman H. Silvert, ed., *Churches and States: The Religious Institution and Modernization* (New York: American Universities Field Staff, 1967), p. 230; Rómulo Betancourt, *Posición y Doctrina* (Caracas: Editorial Cordillera, 1958), p. 146; José Goldsack, "Why a Christian Democratic Labor Organization?" *America*, 126 (January 28, 1967), 155; and Renata Adler, "Cultural Life in Cuba Thriving Despite Reign," *New York Times*, February 10, 1969.

5. Pablo Gonzáles Casanova, "Internal and External Politics of Underdeveloped Countries," in H. Barry Farrell, ed., *Approaches to Comparative and International Politics* (Evanston, Ill.: Northwestern University Press, 1966), p. 136.

Alberto Lleras Camargo, the Colombian statesman, carries the argument a step further in stating the division between the rich and the poor in Marxian terms. He forsees a "great crisis, apparently inevitable," resulting from "the somber panorama of our times, which seems to be translating itself in the international field into the class struggle predicated by Marx and Engels."[6]

The second major bond uniting Latin America with Afro-Asia is anti-colonialistic nationalism. Both areas are seeking a new national identity for themselves and the new personality is often heavily influenced by rejection of the former colonial master. Though the Latin Americans have been formally independent for almost 150 years, the United States has played the role of colonial mentor for most of that time. As the Africans and Asians reject the British, French, and other European imperialists, the Latins repudiate the United States. The nationalism of the entire Third World has similar roots in its rejection of Western European and Yankee hegemony.

During the 1950's and early 1960's, the Latin Americans began to actively back the Afro-Asians in their drive for independence. Most progressive political movements specifically supported the Afro-Asians and their rejection of Western Europe. For example, in 1958 one representative group of the Democratic Left declared its "frank solidarity with regions that are struggling to achieve their destinies as independent nations." At the same time another group sought "to promote increasing accord between the Latin American countries and the Afro-Asian bloc in matters concerning anti-colonialism.[7] During the mid-sixties the anti-colonial accord between Latin America and Afro-Asia achieved maturation and continues today to be one of the major areas of mutual inspiration and cooperation.

The third focus of Third World solidarity — race — is not so important as economic poverty and anti-colonialistic nationalism, but it has been used as a rally cry from time to time. The appeal to racial solidarity is based on the fact that Third World peoples are all non-white, besides being poor and politically subject to the white Northern Hemisphere. Many Latin Americans are as white as Yankees and Europeans, but about one half are non-white and the racial appeal has struck a responsive cord with that sector of the Latin American population. In discussing Quadros' courtship of Africa, for example, one student of Brazilian politics notes that "the Negro community in Brazil welcomed and approved the new attitude." Moreover, some hint of mestizo nationalism seemed to be influencing the policies of the military leaders who seized power in Peru in 1968.[8] In short, the racial issue is present in Latin

---

6. Alberto Lleras Camargo, "El Encuentro de Nueva Delhi," *Visión*, 24 de noviembre de 1967, 23.

7. John D. Martz, *Acción Democrática: Evolution of a Modern Political Party in Venezuela* (Princeton, N.J.: Princeton University Press, 1966), p. 229; *Congreso Internacional de la Democracia Cristiana: Anales del quinto . . .* (Lima: Editorial Universitaria, 1960), p. 219.

8. Burns, *Nationalism in Brazil*, p. 96; Thayer Waldo, "Nixon's New Latin Affairs Chief Must Face Soviet-Inspired Racism," *Denver Post,* March 28, 1969. For more discussion of racism, see p. 39 above.

America, and it sometimes influences the policies and programs of Latin governments. It is a much less important issue than economic underdevelopment or political nationalism, however, and its significance should not be exaggerated.

Cooperative Initiatives

Although Latin American-Afro-Asian solidarity is still a long way from maturity, the poor nations have launched cooperative initiatives in several areas to manifest their growing affinity. In the United Nations, Third World solidarity began to emerge as early as the mid-fifties. The trend has been strengthened yearly and has evolved into a rather formidable voting bloc. Formal liaison is maintained among the poor nations, and effective reciprocal support has developed. A study of voting patterns in the United Nations shows the solidarity characteristic of the Latin American and African positions.

> On an overall basis, the Latin American states voted with the African majority over 90 percent of the time on issues of specific concern to the Africans. The African states voted with the Latin American majority on matters of particular interest to them over 75 percent of the time. The two groups voted against each other on less than 8 percent of roll call votes on all categories of issues. The degree of cooperation and support that exists between these two groups is very great.[9]

Even greater cooperation among the poor nations has resulted from their activity in the United Nations Conference on Trade and Development (UNCTAD). The conference's business hits directly at the most cogent, cohesive issue of Third World politics, and the poor nations of Afro-Asia and Latin America have mustered a solid bloc against the rich nations of the Northern Hemisphere. Nowhere has Latin America's identification with the rest of the Third World been so dramatically and comprehensively evidenced. UNCTAD originally met in 1964 and again three years later in 1967. At both meetings the Latin Americans joined Afro-Asia in a united front against the northern countries. At the 1964 conclave Latin Americans voted down the line with their poor brethren. Because of the controversy of the first meeting, the 1967 conference passed only consensus agreements, but again the Latin Americans and the Afro-Asians joined to push for their interpretation of the consensus.

The specific economic demands of the poor nations have attained little success in UNCTAD, but the organization has crystallized and contributed to Third World solidarity. "From the Southern viewpoint," says a commentary, "the principal accomplishments of UNCTAD (1964) were the opportunities . . . to work together as a unified group to bring pressure on the North."[10]

---

9. Paul Saenz, "A Latin American-African Partnership," *Journal of Inter-American Studies,* 11: 2 (April 1969), 324.

10. John Pincus, *Trade, Aid, and Development: The Rich and Poor Nations* (New York:

In addition to their cooperation in the United Nations and UNCTAD, the poor nations have also collaborated in marketing their primary products. Agreements have been drawn, organizations founded, and cooperative efforts launched among Latin American and Afro-Asian producers and exporters of coffee, cocoa, tea, sugar, olive oil, wheat, oil, copper, and tin. UNCTAD constantly pushes a general, worldwide agreement on commodities.

All these efforts are basically an attempt to unify and empower the poor nations in their ongoing drive to modify trade relations with the rich. The arrangements seek to assure higher prices for the exports of the poor southern nations in compensation for the deterioration in the terms of trade that have resulted in lower export earnings. They also are directed to the establishment of more predictable yearly export earnings by the establishment of yearly quotas and fixed prices for commodity products. At present, argues the southern bloc, the free market frequently produces great fluctuations in prices, which strip those nations of their ability to plan long-range development. The commodity agreements sought by the southern bloc are similar to the domestic farm price-fixing programs in the United States and other northern nations.

The economic significance of these arrangements is less important for this study, however, than is the political implication of the poor nations identifying with one another and pursuing their mutual interests through organized groups including African, Asian, and Latin American countries. The economic arrangements add significantly to the emerging community of interests that has united the Third World in international affairs and points the direction that Latin America is taking in world politics. The composition of the several commodity groups exemplifies the nature of Third World cooperation. The Organization of Petroleum Exporting Countries (OPEC) includes Venezuela and the mid-Eastern nations. The iron ore group includes Africa's Gabon and Liberia, Asia's India, and Latin America's Chile, Peru, and Venezuela. The copper agreement includes Chile and Peru from Latin America and the Congo (Kinshasa) and Zambia from Africa.

The work of Fidel Castro's Cuba also points up the attempts of Latin America to work out a new identity. Castro's Cuba has joined the more radical elements of the Third World in fighting the "imperialism" of at least the western half of the Northern Hemisphere. Castro's collaboration with Afro-Asians has ranged from hosting conferences to providing Cuban soldiers for African revolutionary movements. In early 1966, for example, the Tri-Continental Conference met in Havana and founded the revolutionary Afro-Asian Latin American Peoples Solidarity Organization (AALAPSO). The group, according to a U.S. subcommittee staff report, "directs" and "coordinates" "subversive efforts . . . on all three continents." The Executive Secretariat of AALAPSO is composed of representatives from Africa, Asia, and Latin America.[11]

McGraw-Hill Book Co., 1967), p. 82.

11. *The First Conference of the Latin American Solidarity Organization*, a staff study for a

In addition to the Havana Conference and AALAPSO, Castro has undertaken other initiatives demonstrating the Cuban regime's collaboration with Third World revolutionary movements. A study of *Insurgency in Latin America* says

> Castro is ready to help fight "imperialism" in any hemisphere: his self-assigned mission is so broad it does not limit him geographically. He has pledged regular Cuban troops to North Vietnam if that country requests them. In Africa he has aided revolutionary movements against the Portuguese colonies. Dark-skinned Cuban soldiers have served in five African countries. Radio Havana has noticably stepped up its range of programs to Africa, some of them in indigenous languages.[12]

Other Arguments and Interpretations

Though the 1960's have witnessed a marked increase in the drive for Third World unity, the Latin Americans seeking ties with Afro-Asia have not yet carried the day. Some leading Latin American spokesmen accept the idea only with reservations. Others reject it altogether. Some argue for a united Third World under Latin American mentorship and leadership. Other Latin Americans propose the continent as the connecting link between the western and southern worlds. Some deny even the connecting link concept, and some see the continents of the southern bloc as locked in a competitive struggle for economic development.[13]

The idea of Latin American mentorship has been set out by the Uruguayan José Mora, former secretary-general of the Organization of American States. Writing in the early 1960's, Mora asked the question, "Will Latin America continue to adhere to the West?"[14] While responding affirmatively, the Uruguayan statesman mirrored the stance of many in proposing Latin America as mentor to the rest of the poor nations. "Latin America cannot help viewing sympathetically the newly independent nations of Africa and Asia as they take their place in world civilization," he allowed. Moreover, "the role of Latin America at the United Nations has been to favor and support the emancipation of all peoples." In projecting the future role of Latin America,

---

subcommittee of the Senate Committee on the Judiciary (Washington, D.C.: U.S. Government Printing Office, 1967), p. 5.

12. David D. Burks, *Insurgency in Latin America*, study for a subcommittee of the Senate Committee on Foreign Relations (Washington, D.C.: U.S. Government Printing Office, 1968), p. 6.

13. Though not specifically concerned with the subject of this discussion, John D. Martz has written a useful article covering some of the same general questions; see "The Place of Latin America in the Study of Comparative Politics," *Journal of Politics*, 28: 1 (February 1966), 57–80.

14. *The Annals*, 336 (July 1961), 98–105.

he promulgated what he believed to be the Latin American position as teacher to others.

> Latin America can, indeed, cooperate in the truest sense with the peoples of Asia and Africa who are now coming to enjoy their independence — an independence which the American peoples won many years ago at the cost of blood and sacrifice.
>
> Latin America cannot be disciple, but rather a teacher, in matters of revolution.[15]

Many would quarrel with the condescending tone of Mora's words, but his prognostication of Latin America as Third World leader has been fulfilled in some respects. Even though Latin America was late in aligning itself with the southern nations, it has taken a leading role. Modification of trade relations has become the principal controversy between the rich and the poor; the Latin Americans were the intellectual and propagandistic originators of the issue. Operating in the UN Economic Commission for Latin America under the leadership of Argentina's Raúl Prebisch, the Latins initiated the studies and conceived the arguments now propounded throughout the Third World. The debates in the first UNCTAD meeting in 1964 centered on "what was fundamentally the Latin American position on world trade."[16]

Indeed, Dr. Prebisch emerged as a leader of the poor nations in the mid-1960's. He chaired the first UNCTAD meeting and was appointed the first secretary-general of the organization when it achieved official status within the UN organizational structure. "More than any other single individual," says a commentator, "Dr. Prebisch . . . has succeeded in focusing attention over the years on the interrelationships between trade and development."[17] It is worth noting that in 1969 Prebisch was succeeded as UNCTAD secretary-general by another Latin American, Venezuela's Manuel Pérez Guerrero.

The Latin American nations have also influenced the formation of Third World commodity organizations. Venezuela took the lead in founding the Organization of Petroleum Exporting Countries (OPEC) in 1960. A year later, the Venezuelans again initiated negotiations toward an international agreement on iron ore. Brazil and Colombia have assumed a primary role in the coffee organization, and in the mid-1960's the Chilean government inaugurated cooperation among Latin American and African copper exporters.

Finally, Cuba has made a serious bid for leadership among the more radical nations of the Third World. Castro's defiance of the United States has given him a place of honor among the poor nations' leaders; he assiduously cultivates that position by periodic calls for the unity of the poor against the

---

15. *Ibid.*, p. 105.

16. Robert N. Burr, *Our Troubled Hemisphere: Perspectives on United States – Latin American Relations* (Washington, D.C.: The Brookings Institution, 1967), pp. 213 – 214.

17. Isaiah Frank, "Issues Before the U.N. Conference," *Foreign Affairs*, 42: 2 (January 1964), 214.

rich. The 1966 Tri-Continental Conference catapulted the Cubans into a position of eminence with the establishment of AALAPSO in Havana.[18]

Though many Latin Americans are ready to accept the mantle of Third World leadership, others repudiate the superior-inferior connotations and substitute a second interpretation of the poor nations' relationship — the concept of Latin America as connecting link between the rich West and the other parts of the poor South. The Quadros policy, for example, was consciously based on the belief "that his country could serve as a link between the newly independent African nations and the West." Gabriel Valdes, the Chilean foreign minister, set out the position before the United Nations. In discussing Latin America's role in the contemporary world, he stated:

> The transcendency of our participation can be decisive, since although belonging to the West by the common experience of fundamental values, we have with the East a concrete solidarity that is born from insufficiency of development.[19]

The role of connecting link or middleman is based on the proposition that Latin America understands both the poor nations of the South and the rich nations of Western Europe and the United States. Latin America shares economic underdevelopment, anti-colonialistic nationalism, and, to some degree, non-white racial characteristics with the Afro-Asian states. Latin Americans understand poverty, the problems of building an industrialized society, the frustrations of being dominated by a powerful country, and the indignity of racial discrimination. In short, Latin Americans understand the problems of the southern half of the world.

Unlike other elements of the Third World, however, Latin America has maintained a close relationship with the West. Latin American culture, economic relationships, languages, religion, and domestic politics have been molded by Western experience. Only in recent times have Latin Americans thought of themselves as being anything but a variation of Western civilization. In that sense, then, the Latins also understand the West.

The role of connecting link has several implications. On the highest level, Latin America is seen as transmitter of culture — as mentor to the rest of the poor nations. A more palatable connotation of the concept sees Latin America more as interpretor than mentor. Others see Latin America as having a

---

18. On a different plane, it is probably Afro-Asia and not Latin America which has been mentor. The militant nationalism found in the new Latin American unity with the Third World has been significantly influenced by Afro-Asian nationalism. One study notes that "as a result of the sweep of nationalism over Africa, the Middle East and Asia (and of the Communist-bloc policy of supporting it), Latin American nationalism has gained militant international interest and support." The author then specifically points to Nasser's seizure of the Suez Canal as having influenced Panamanian demands. See Daniel Goldrich, "Panama," in Martin C. Needler, ed., *Political Systems of Latin America* (New York: Van Nostrand – Reinhold, 1964), p. 136.

19. See Burns, *Nationalism in Brazil*, p. 96; and *News from Chile* (Washington, D.C.: Embassy of Chile), October 12, 1968.

special relationship with the United States — the richest and most powerful nation of the northern bloc. Whatever its interpretation, the connecting link concept is based on the proposition that Latin America is both western and southern. The two interpretations of Latin America's relationship with Afro-Asia (mentorship and connecting link) discussed thus far share the fundamental characteristic of affiliating Latin America with other poor nations. The implications of the two positions differ, but they both depict Latin America as an integral part of the emerging Third World bloc.

A third interpretation, however, rejects Latin American cooperation with Afro-Asia. The reasons for repudiation of Third World unity differ, but agreement on the incorrectness of Latin America's affiliation with the poor nations is shared. The traditional interpretations of Latin America put it in the western world. Many political thinkers posited variations of the essential Western character of Latin America, but the profound ties with Europe and the United States were seldom denied. Professor Herbert Eugene Bolton posited a fundamental interconnection between the histories, cultures, and political destinies of the United States and Latin America. The "Atlantic Trian- (Europe, North America, Latin America) concept of Arthur P. Whitaker makes a similar point. A leading Latin American statesman agrees with Whitaker in postulating that "both Americas are heirs of Western and Christian civilization. From that trunk was born two branches, so that they have the same profound origin and, in spite of many differences, a substantially common mind and a similar conception of man."[20]

This argument implicitly denies any substantial affiliation of Latin America with Afro-Asia. Latin America is basically Western oriented, says this position, and any cooperation with the other elements of the Third World is necessarily transient and tactical. Roberto de Oliveira Campos carries the argument further by proposing that identifying with other southern nations has diverted Latin America from realistically grappling with its own problems. In criticising the 1969 recommendations of the Comisión Económica de Coordinación Latino-Americano (CECLA), he scolds his fellow Latins:

> The formulation of a romantic "globalism," which has exaggerated the coincidence of our interests with those of the others of the Third World, erects obstacles to concrete solutions to our problems which we would be able to advance more easily within the Latin American region.[21]

Some in Latin America have pointed to the competitive economic systems of

---

20. On Bolton and Whitaker, see Lewis Hanke, ed., *Do the Americas Have a Common History?* (New York: Alfred A. Knopf, 1964). See Eduardo Frei Montalva, quoted in Edward J. Williams, *Latin American Christian Democratic Parties* (Knoxville: University of Tennessee Press, 1967), p. 152. See also much of the discussion of the "Shared Values" section of Chapter I of this work.

21. Roberto de Oliveira Campos, "El Continente Inmadura," *Visión*, 1 de agosto de 1969, 38.

Latin America and Afro-Asia as providing a source of friction between the two. Although in the contemporary period Latin America and Afro-Asia have attempted to cooperate in the production and marketing of their primary commodity products, the situation is fraught with difficulties. Brazilian coffee and cocoa competes with that of Ghana for a limited world market. Bolivian and Malaysian tin also compete, as does Near Eastern and Venezuelan oil and Zambian and Chilean copper. Moreover, the Afro-Asian nations have been getting a larger slice of the market,[22] and some Latin Americans are becoming disturbed about their role in the process. A writer sets out the problem.

> The first schemes to revitalize the economics of the so-called Black Continent were developed on the basis of introducing and intensifying the planting of the very tropical products that form the basis of Latin American exports. For the time being, the low cost of labor in Africa insured excellent return to whomever was connected with this operation, an operation that in the long run would shift an appreciable percentage of the cost of African emancipation to the shoulders of the Latin Americans. No thought was given to the possibility of future conflict between the economies of Africa and Latin America. Unwittingly, the United States contributed to this situation by favoring these schemes. The Latin Americans themselves showed a lack of foresight in approving with their votes the plans of technical assistance that FAO (the Food and Agriculture Organization of the UN) was preparing to promote coffee planting in Africa.[23]

The United States, Latin America, and the Poor Nations

The United States and the Poor Nations

U.S. relations with and conception of the poor nations have come close to going full circle since the close of World War II. There was little interest and minimal intercourse in the late 1940's and early 1950's. From the middle 50's to the middle 60's, the United States developed increasing concern with the poor nations. The poor nations receded in importance as the 60's progressed, and as the 70's begin, their relative position seems not too much different than it was immediately following the war. The poor nations have once again become a peripheral interest to American policy makers. The beginning of the Third World development policy was President Truman's

---

22. For the trends in commodity trade, see Pincus, *Trade, Aid and Development,* pp. 251–254.

23. Germán Arciniegas, "Latin America in a Developing World," in Mildred Adams, ed., *Latin America: Evolution or Explosion?* (New York: Dodd, Mead and Co., 1963), p. 206.

Point Four proposal, announced in 1949.[24] The program gave only technical assistance and involved relatively small sums of money. That modest program soon gave way to a more ambitious policy of U.S. assistance in the economic development of the poor nations. Particularly during the Kennedy and the first Johnson administrations, the policy aimed at building strong, stable economies throughout Africa, Asia, and Latin America. The goals of the U.S. aid program changed, and the number of recipient nations expanded dramatically. At its peak involvement, the United States was dispatching aid to practically every poor nation in the world. The American financial commitment to the Third World slipped in the late 60's and the policy for the 70's is a decrease in overall aid dispersed to fewer countries.

The conceptualization of the poor nations' relationship to American interests and security shows the same evolution. Immediately after the end of World War II, the United States reconstructed Europe to buttress its own security. Soviet bellicosity demanded a strong Europe lest the Russians overrun the entire continent. When that job was completed, American policy makers seemed to transfer the same principle to the Third World. The Cold War, went the argument, would ultimately be won by the power that rallied the poor nations to its side. India, for example, took on exaggerated symbolic importance in the East-West struggle, and this position came close to positing India (as representative of the Third World) as the key to American security. By a sort of domino-theory logic, the preservation of the United States became inextricably linked to the defeat of supposed Soviet ambitions within the southern bloc. The failure of the Soviets in the Third World, combined with increased sophistication in Washington, changed that conceptualization in the late 60's. By 1970 the Third World was passing to a relatively unimportant position in American security policy, despite the continuation of the tragic Vietnam adventure.

The U.S. response to the three major rallying cries of Third World unity also shows some ambiguity, although the evolution of policy has tended to favor the demands of the poor nations. The United States has grown increasingly willing to indulge the Third World in its drive for unencumbered independence. The United States has lessened pressures on the poor nations to assume an anti-Soviet stance in the Cold War struggle. As the policy was originally conceived by Secretary of State Dulles, there was little room for poor nations' independence. Dulles visualized the globe as being contested by the "Free" and "Communist" forces. No Third World nation could be independent in the sense that it was neutral in that struggle. To be neutral in a conflict between right and wrong, said Dulles, was to be immoral.

The Kennedy administration, however, contributed significantly to the independence of the poor nations in several ways. The president's general

24. The following discussion owes much to George W. Ball, *The Discipline of Power* (Boston: Little, Brown and Co., 1968), pp. 223 – 228.

conception of foreign policy was more "pluralistic" than his Republican predecessor's. The neutral nations were less condemned and their anti-Western propensities suffered more readily than they had during the 1950's. Neutralism among the poor nations became acceptable, but not ideal. Moreover, the United States became a much more vigorous proponent of the independence of the African nations. In the United Nations, for example, the United States pressured its Western allies to facilitate the independence of the impatient Africans. Furthermore, the emphasis on widespread economic aid reached its apogee in the early 1960's.[25]

This tone obtained during the remainder of the decade. Though the Nixon regime has spoken of applying more realistic criteria in its dealings with the Third World, the situation has not changed essentially. In sum, American policy toward Third World anti-colonialist nationalism and neutralism seems to have changed dramatically in favor of the position of the poor nations.

The U.S. response to the second major poor nations' issue — economic development — is not unlike the position concerning anti-colonialist nationalism and Cold War neutralism. Though American economic aid has decreased in recent years, direct aid is no longer the primary goal of the poor nations. Instead, they visualize a modification of rich-poor trade relations as the key economic issue. Developmental capital is not to be accumulated through aid, but rather through increased earnings for their primary exports. On that problem, the American position has evolved from opposition to increasing support.

At the outset the United States was against trade modifications and was wary even of discussing the issue in international conference. American opposition stemmed from its preference for free trade and from fear that the Soviet Union would use it in the Cold War. A scholar-diplomat explains the position.

> It is no secret that the United States was originally cool to the idea of a world trade conference under the aegis of the United Nations. For a number of years in the late fifties, the Soviet bloc had been pressing for such a conference primarily for the purpose of attacking Western, and particularly American, strategic trade controls as well as United States policy of denying most-favored nation treatment to the Soviet bloc . . . . Under the circumstances, a world trade conference such as that proposed by the Soviet bloc would merely provide a forum from which to attack Western "economic aggression" and appeal to the less developed countries for moral support for the "normalization" of East-West trade relations. In short, it would become an empty propaganda show.[26]

Opposition to Third World demands for trade revision was dramatically exemplified by the negative stance of the United States at the first UNCTAD conference in 1964. At that meeting, the United States frequently voted against

25. For a Latin American's interpretation of the evolution of United States policy, see Roberto de Oliveira Campos, "Relations between the United States and Latin America," in Adams, ed., *Latin America*, pp. 31 – 33.

26. Frank, "Issues Before the U. N. Conference," p. 210.

"unexceptionable statements" and "intentionally or unwittingly, put itself in the position of leading the opposition to virtually all of the Less Developed Country-sponsored resolutions, in some cases standing forth as the sole opponent."[27]

From that low point in 1964, the United States evolved an increasingly sympathetic position to the trade demands of the poor nations. At the 1967 UNCTAD conclave, the Americans inched toward acceptance of special trade arrangements. By 1970, the position had clearly changed and President Nixon, in his "State of the World" message, announced that "the United States will press for a liberal system of generalized tariff preferences for all developing countries."[28]

American response to the third rallying cry of the poor nations — racial solidarity — is more difficult to define than the stance on the first two issues. In the first place, the racial stance of the Third World is inextricably tied to the broader issue of anti-colonialist, anti-imperialist foreign policy. This means that Western colonialism and imperialism are often interpreted as being informed by racist considerations. In the second place, the issue is influenced by the U.S. domestic situation. The drive of the American black man for equality reverberates through the Third World. U.S. attitudes toward race are often extrapolated from the domestic to the international arena.

On the international level, U.S. involvement in Vietnam and its relations and attitudes vis-à-vis Rhodesia, South Africa, and Portugal have been the most important imperialistic-racial issues. Although American foreign policy interprets the Vietnam conflict as a Cold War confrontation, many in the poor nations see it as another attempt to subjugate the non-white peoples of the world. In this sense, the Vietnam conflict has been prejudicial to American efforts to counter the charge of racism.

Rhodesia has become an even more important racial issue in the mind of the Third World, and the United States has also suffered from its policies toward that nation. Many African nations have pressed for strong action against the white-supremacist government in Rhodesia. Though the United States has committed itself to black rule and has not supported the white Rhodesians, it has followed the middle road pursued by the United Kingdom, thereby eliciting criticism from black Africans and others in the Third World. This criticism reached a new high in early 1970 when the United States cast its first United Nations veto against a resolution that called upon the United Kingdom to employ armed force to suppress the white Rhodesians. Although the United States closed its consulate in Rhodesia that same day, the veto was interpreted throughout the Third World as a retreat from the U.S. position favoring black government in Africa.

The United States has been censored less for its relations with the Union

---

27. Pincus, *Trade, Aid and Development,* p. 78; see pp. 84 – 85 for an explanation of U.S. opposition to the poor nations' demands.

28. "Nixon's Report to the Congress on Foreign Policy," *New York Times*, February 19, 1970.

of South Africa, but some criticism has been expressed. American policy makers pleased the non-white Third World by imposing trade restrictions and arms embargos on South Africa. U.S. pronouncements in the United Nations have also been approved. Nonetheless, many in the poor nations feel that the United States has not acted so vigorously as it should.

The reaction to U.S. policies anent Portugal is similarly ambiguous. Though American policy makers long ago condemned Portuguese rule in Africa, many in the Third World accuse the United States of half-hearted support of its position. The United States has gone a long way in responding to the charge of racism, but that response has only partially satisfied the misgivings of the non-white peoples of the southern half of the globe.

The Rich United States and Poor Latin America

Only recently has Latin America begun to frame its inter-American policies and pronouncements in the rhetoric of the poor nations and the rich nations. Even now, much of the language of hemispheric politics retains the traditional framework of the Western Hemisphere idea or the Cold War. Also, the United States has only recently begun to envisage Latin America in terms of the poor nations syndrome. Some policies are framed in those terms, while others seem to be informed by the more traditional context of hemispheric intercourse.

As the 1970's begin, however, both Latin American charges and U.S. rejoinders are increasingly recognizing the theme of the rich and the poor nations. At the basic level of mutual understanding, for example, the Latin Americans often charge that the wealth and success of the United States has beclouded its ability to respond to the problems of the poor. A leading Latin statesman makes the argument.

> The United States is steadily moving further away from the underdeveloped world economically and, as a consequence of this, is moving further away psychologically. It is becoming more and more difficult for the United States as a nation to communicate with the rest of the world. When you have been rich for several generations, it is very difficult to gauge the emotions of people who have been poor. There is bound to be a great deal of misunderstanding. The misunderstanding exists and it is growing worse. It makes me anxious about the future of inter-American relations.[29]

The developmental experience of the United States, say some Latins, also befogs its perceptions of contemporary problems. The United States, goes the

---

29. José Figueres, quoted by José Rasco, "Inter-Americanism," in Samuel Shapiro, ed., *Integration of Man and Society in Latin America* (Notre Dame, Ind.: University of Notre Dame Press, 1967), p. 278.

charge, industrialized in a different epoch when different conditions obtained and different methods were applicable. Friendly Latin American critics depict the United States as being behind the times in its approach to the contemporary challenges faced by the poor nations.

> Many Latin American intellectuals, friends of the United States, argue that North American policy has not distinguished between the economics of the 19th century and what is appropriate to the revolutionary vigor of modern Latin America. New theories of growth are in vogue, with new perspectives on the law of comparative advantage, the marginal laws, inflation, and other economic matters.
>
> These groups recognize that the United States sincerely wants to help Latin America, but they believe it is like an 80 year old grandfather who does not understand the modern generation. To them, the International Monetary Fund is not a "lackey of the imperialists." Rather, it is a gentlemen's club, populated by well-intentioned, but old-fashioned conservatives.[30]

Although the United States has never been convinced about many specifics of the Latin American argument, its policies and policy pronouncements show readiness to grapple with Latin America as underdeveloped and poor. The United States is changing its conception of Latin America and responding with programs more attuned to the new definition of the continent.

Varying motives obviously inform the evolution of the new Yankee departure. The traditional special position of Latin America and Cold War strategy play roles. More important for this discussion, however, many in Washington seem to be accepting the Latin definition of the importance of rich-poor considerations in inter-American relations. The Rockefeller Report recognized the Latin American desire to coalesce with the poor nations of the world and warned policy makers against opposing that trend. "Each nation in the hemisphere has its own role and contacts throughout the world," the report said. "The quest for hemispheric unity and accelerated economic growth within the hemisphere should not be regarded as Western Hemispheric isolation." The "recommendation" for a "National Policy Objective" which followed proposed that "the United States should foster a worldwide outlook as complementary to rather than competitive with Western Hemisphere goals."[31]

More specific policy statements and analyses mirror the advice of the Rockefeller Report. When Peru's modernizing military nationalized Yankee business, established trade and diplomatic relations with Soviet bloc states, and began issuing anti-Yankee proclamations in 1969, Washington's retort was cast in the contemporary rich-poor context. The United States saw neither communism nor Latin passionate irrationality as the explanation. Rather,

---

30. John P. Powelson, *Latin America: Today's Economic and Social Revolution* (New York: McGraw-Hill Book Co., 1964), pp. 9–10.

31. "The Rockefeller Report," *Quality of Life in the Americas* (Washington, D.C.: Agency for International Development, 1969), p. 44.

differences were seen as coming from the disparity between developed and underdeveloped nations. Inter-American Affairs Secretary Charles A. Meyer explained the U.S. position.

> What we see in the Peruvian-United States relations at the present time in the broadest terms are differences between two long-time friends. It is partially a product of the changing aspirations of a developing country. It is by no means a unique phenomenon . . . . The difference of viewpoint is between large and small sovereign countries, between countries which export capital and those that receive capital.[32]

Furthermore, the United States also seems to accept the image of Latin America as connecting link between the rich West and the poor South. A U.S. scholar notes that "ideological, economic, and political artillery" are the weapons of the future in the battle for world supremacy and security. He then cites the connecting link argument in proposing that U.S. policy and practice in Latin America may well be a key element in its attempt to win the support of other poor nations.

> The United States, as it deploys these instruments in the Western Hemisphere, will show other underdeveloped lands what it really means by a "peaceful world community of free and independent states." If the United States, in relations with the Latin American nations, comprehends their interests as well as its own and consistently demonstrates a reasoning and conciliatory but firm attitude, rather than a blustering and intimidating one, it will indicate to the world its genuine support of a world order based upon a mutuality of interests rather than upon the purposes of the United States alone. Such comportment will appeal strongly to the numerous weaker nations of the world and encourage their cooperation with the United States.[33]

President Nixon's 1970 "State of the World" message mirrored the same cognizance of Latin America as a mediatory to other nations. The president posited that "our relationship with our sister republics has special relevance for this administration's general approach to foreign relations. We must be able to forge a constructive relationship with nations historically linked to us," he continued, "if we are to do so with nations more removed."[34]

Perhaps most important, official U.S. policy seems inclined to restructure trade relations with Latin America in line with the developmental demands of the Latins. The traditional American posture put heavy emphasis on private investment as the method of increasing capital in the Latin nations. The Alliance for Progress took a giant step in changing the emphasis to public

---

32. "Current U.S. – Peruvian Problems," *Department of State Bulletin*, 60: 1559 (May 12, 1969), 407 – 408.

33. Burr, *Our Troubled Hemisphere*, p. 40.

34. "Nixon's Report to the Congress on Foreign Policy."

assistance. Both private and public aid continue to be significant in U.S. developmental assistance, but Washington has looked sympathetically on the introduction of special tariff reductions and trade preferences for the Latin American nations. U.S. attitudes apparently began to change after the UNCTAD conference in 1964. In 1967, President Johnson broke with long-standing U.S. policy at a summit meeting of hemispheric presidents at Punta del Este, Uruguay. He endorsed in principle temporary tariff reductions for Latin American exports to the United States.

The Nixon administration inched even further in pursuit of the new policy. The Rockefeller Report recommended that the United States attempt to secure a worldwide agreement on the reduction of tariffs and the initiation of preferential treatment for all the nations of the Third World. Failing that, the report suggested, "Until such agreement is reached, the United States would extend preferences only to nations which are not receiving special treatment from other industrialized countries."[35] Because many African and Asian nations were receiving special consideration from the Common Market and the British Commonwealth, the United States would work out a special arrangement with the Latin American countries.

President Nixon's "State of the World" message, delivered in early 1970, announced immediate implementation of the first half of the Rockefeller Report's recommendation and suggested the approval of trade preferences in the near future. The president stated:

> The United States will press for a liberal system of generalized tariff preferences for all developing countries. We are working toward a system that would eliminate discriminations against South American exports that exist in other countries. Through the Organization for Economic Cooperation and Development and the UNCTAD, we are pressing other developed nations to recognize the need for a genuinely progressive tariff preference system.

Later in the speech the president came even closer to satisfying the demands of the Latin Americans. In discussing "increased pressures" in the 1970's, he recognized the Latin desire for entry into the U.S. market and proposed that "a liberal trade policy that can support development is necessary to sustain a harmonious hemispheric system."[36]

The Latin Americans would rather have seen the immediate implementation of trade preferences and tariff reductions, but U.S. policy is inching toward the satisfaction of their developmental demands. Assuming the probability that the United States will fail to effect a worldwide agreement, the next step, hopefully, will be the initiation of special treatment for Latin America.

---

35. *Quality of Life in the Americas*, p. 66.
36. "Nixon's Report to the Congress on Foreign Policy."

Some Analysis

Latin America and the Poor Nations

Latin America's identification and association with the other poor nations will continue in the 1970's. In some areas, cooperation may increase. In the United Nations, for example, the Latin American states will work even more closely with their poor brethren and will push even harder for developmental programs.

There are limits to poor nations' cooperation, however. Third World rivalries, the advantages of hemispheric cooperation, and the realities of world politics all impose limitations on the reorientation of Latin America's historic international posture. Before analyzing those factors, one advantage of Latin America's new identification demands postulation and discussion.

Latin America's new self-definition as a poor underdeveloped region may well imply a new realism among the Latins. Students of Latin America have long argued that the Latin Americans never quite knew who or what they were. Hence, for 150 years they searched about in bewilderment for self-definition.[37] The importation of foreign philosophic and ideological systems followed one another in chaos. The ideas of Jeremy Bentham, Thomas Jefferson, Auguste Comte and Karl Marx were unsuccessful; none was firmly rooted in the realities of the continent's psychological, sociological, or political substructure. None was able to define the Latin American reality.

With few exceptions, the Latin Americans have nurtured a proud tradition of Western civilization. Until recently they would have haughtily repudiated the proposition that they shared anything with the savages of Africa or the destitute masses of Asia. In their minds, they are only a slightly poorer version of Europe. That proposition, of course, is not entirely incorrect. What is crucially important, nonetheless, is that however "Western" Latin America may be, it is also economically and politically underdeveloped. Perhaps for the first time in Latin American history, the thinkers have begun to sort out that important element of the Latin American malady. In sum, the self-recognition and conscious self-definition of Latin America as a poor region may well be the first step in its redemption. Although the success of the poor nations' political bloc may be important for Latin America, its failure could not erase the new sense of realism that has become a part of the Latin American experience.

With that point aside it is important to take up the question of the

---

37. See W. Rex Crawford, *A Century of Latin American Thought*, rev. ed. (New York: Frederick A. Praeger, 1961), particularly the "Introduction," 3–11; and Edward J. Williams, "Christian Politics: The Significance for Latin America," *Duquesne Review*, 14: 1 (Spring 1969), 65–83.

continued viability of the poor nations' bloc and Latin America's position within it. The underdeveloped nations will certainly maintain a unified front in the coming years. The social and economic goals of Latin America and Afro-Asia are very similar,[38] and Latin America's political position is rapidly approaching the Cold War neutralism of the leading Afro-Asian states. All sectors of the poor world want more emphasis on developmental aid, the liquidation of the last remnants of the colonial system, and a free hand to repudiate or utilize the antagonisms of the Cold War as best suits their purposes. Latin Americans, Africans, and Asians share these goals and can be expected to pursue them vigorously in the future.

The most fruitful arenas for poor nation cooperation are the international organizations. Though the rich nations continue to hold sway in the United Nations, the poor states have made tremendous strides in the sixties and may be expected to gain more influence. The World Bank and the International Monetary Fund have also responded to the demands of the underdeveloped world. Their policies may be even more sympathetic in the future. In the most general sense, international organizations of every sort will be increasingly concerned with the problems of the poor nations.

Cooperation in the political arena implies more possibility for discord among the poor nations, but two general issues are conducive to continued unity of action. First, all agree that colonialism, neo-colonialism, imperialism, and Great Power intervention must go. Second, all have grown disenchanted with the Cold War — with the United States and the Soviet Union more specifically. The United States was distrusted from the outset, the Vietnam adventure has only solidified the original misgivings about the U.S. preoccupation with Cold War considerations. Though the Soviet Union made some headway in its attempt to exploit Third World anti-Westernism, the attraction soon dissipated. The Soviets lost the space race in the 1960's, lost face in the Cuban missile encounter, lost credibility when they failed to deliver much economic assistance, and lost trust when they invaded Czechoslovakia.

The level of Third World unity thus far achieved is solidly based on mutual self-interest. It will persevere and may well be enhanced through more cooperative action. On the other hand, there are very real limits to poor nations' unity. A cohesive, solidly unified policy encompassing all elements of the Third World is beyond the realm of possibility, at least for the foreseeable future. The optimistic hopes of many in Latin America and Afro-Asia are unrealistic.

Latin America is far more developed (or less underdeveloped) than Afro-Asia.[39] All indicators used by the developmentalists dramatize the differences. Latin America produces more electricity, its gross national product per capita

---

38. See Saenz, "A Latin American-African Partnership," p. 325.

39. For an expansion of the following discussion, see Williams, "Comparative Political Development."

is much greater, its literacy rates are higher, it is more urbanized, its interest groups are more clearly defined and better organized, and its political parties are more sophisticated. Furthermore, Latin America's international experience has been significantly different from Afro-Asia's. It has been independent for almost 150 years. It has experienced much intercourse with Europe and has had a special relationship with the United States. It has been a part of the Western World.[40]

In a recent book a student of the underdeveloped nations argues against the community of interests between Latin America and Afro-Asia. He suggests that Latin America is "something of a Fourth World, with characteristics of its own." He continues:

> Latin American independence preceded by more that a century the movement which has led to the vast post-war increase in independent states in Asia and Africa. The intervening period gave Latin America a form of experience which marked it off from other parts of the world. Its predominant culture was Latin, not indigenous; its dominant groups were European in origin; its relations with the United States, ever since the enunciation of the Monroe Doctrine, have been unique in world affairs, and remain unparalleled in the experience of Asia and Africa; its own interrelationships have been its main field of international concern, forming a distinct area of world politics, largely untouched by outside forces except that of the United States; and, even now, direct involvement of Latin America with the Afro-Asian countries is minimal, although it may be greater in the future.[41]

Third World unity, furthermore, is constantly threatened by the corrosive effects of nationalistic jealousies and economic self-interest. Nationalism is the ideology throughout the Third World. The curbing of nationalistic pride will not come easily for either Latin America or Afro-Asia. According to the Chilean foreign minister, a shadow of mistrust has always characterized the cooperative efforts of the poor nations. Speaking before the United Nations General Assembly in 1968, Gabriel Valdes noted:

> developing countries have been singularly incapable of exerting a constant, intelligent, and imaginative pressure on the developed countries. . . . The three continents (Asia, Africa, and Latin America), acted toward each other with misgiving and lack of confidence. The circumstantial unity attained on certain occasions has been demonstrated as always ephemeral, and consequently the vocal pressure exerted upon the developed countries has been without real conviction.[42]

---

40. On this point, see Theodore Geiger, *The Conflicted Relationship: The West and the Transformation of Asia, Africa, and Latin America* (New York: McGraw – Hill Book Co., 1967), pp. 264 – 271. He insists that Latin America must be conceived as part of the West, and that the correct policy will flow from that premise.

41. J. D. B. Miller, *The Politics of the Third World* (New York: Oxford University Press, 1967), pp. xi – xii. On the same point, see Campos, in Adams, ed., *Latin America*, pp. 37 – 38.

42. *News from Chile* (Washington, D.C.: Embassy of Chile), October 12, 1968.

Buttressing the divisive forces of nationalistic egocentrism, the problem of economic competition also endangers Third World unity. Some Latin Americans have already foreseen the essentially competitive nature of the Third World economies. They have implicitly predicted the possibilities of growing strain emanating from the battle for limited markets among the rich nations. The poor nations' unity will be severely tested when they are locked in a struggle to finance their own development. Political unity, in short, may well be sabotaged by economic competition.

Finally, Third World unity may suffer frustrations from its lack of success in achieving its pronounced goals. Though it is true that the rich nations have responded with some minimal sympathy to the demands of the poor, the underdeveloped world will be unable to wrest significant concessions from the rich. The selfish obstinance of the rich northern nations will weaken the unified resolve of the poor southern countries. The obstacles to unity among the underdeveloped seem to be more powerful than the factors contributing to it. Although some slight gains may be achieved in the 1970's, indications are that unity among the poor nations will not proceed much further than it has.

The Rich United States and Poor Latin America

Even though the poor nations' power bloc may not be the wave of the future, Latin America's new identification as a southern continent has some significance for inter-American relations. Combined with internal changes in Latin America and the United States and conditioned by the evolution of the east-west conflict, Latin America's underdeveloped, "poor" status has several implications.

First, it contributes to the general weakening of Yankee influence in Latin America. The Latin Americans vote solidly with the Afro-Asians, and frequently against the United States, on socio-economic and colonial issues in international forums. Those votes, of course, are informed by the theme of the north-south division of contemporary world politics. The United States is rich and northern; Latin America is poor and southern. Latin America has declared itself different from the United States and no longer blindly follows the lead of the powerful Yankee.

Moreover, the Organization of American States is increasingly concerned with issues and problems deriving from the rich-poor theme. The Latin Americans have essentially redefined the purposes of the organization. They refuse to accept the previous regional security emphasis and have compelled the United States to acquiesce to the new developmental focus. For example, the upgrading of the Economic and Social Council (ECOSOC) was probably the most important revision of the OAS structure dictated by the Protocol of Buenos Aires. The newly empowered ECOSOC is the OAS's developmental organ. Moreover, it is the structural proof of increased Latin American influence within the organization.

Perhaps even more significantly, the Latin Americans founded the Comisión Económica de Coordinación Latino-Americano (CECLA) in mid-1969. The organization is composed entirely of Latin American nations; the United States has no voice. The focus is developmental and nationalistic. The group first met in Chile, where it framed the Consensus of Viña del Mar. The consensus pointed up the independent tone struck by the Latin Americans. It was presented to President Nixon in June 1970. The first point of a summary of the consensus proposed:

> The emergence of a growing continental nationalism that seeks an affirmation of a Latin American personality, with concepts, values, and patterns of organization of its own must be accepted as legitimate and irreversible.[43]

Official U.S. policy recognizes the growing nationalistic sensitivities of the Latin Americans. President Nixon has launched a "low profile" posture in the southern half of the hemisphere. The policy is designed to acknowledge the independence of the Latin nations, to encourage their initiatives in inter-American forums, and to decrease the presence of the United States.

The second major policy implication flowing from Latin America's new identification concerns the U.S. commitment to assist its southern neighbors. An underdeveloped area demands a long-range commitment of developmental aid, not a ten-year crash program. Developmental aid includes building roads, constructing schools and hospitals, educating young people, and changing basic economic, political, and social attitudes and values. Unlike the Marshall Plan, which rebuilt the physical plant of Europe to assist an already sophisticated people, aid to Latin America must assist in the creation of a developed society. The task of creation is profoundly more difficult than rebuilding. It demands different skills, a much longer commitment, and infinite patience. The United States must develop an aid program stretching over the next generation or even the next 50 years. Latin America as underdeveloped implies a new departure in the conceptualization of U.S. assistance.

The third implication of Latin America as a poor continent connotes a developmental style different from that traditionally favored in the United States. The Latin Americans, like their brethren in other parts of the Southern Hemisphere, look to some variant of socialistic planning as their response to the problems of economic underdevelopment. A leading work on Latin American economics posits that "Latin Americans are more prone, *in general*, to seek collective solutions to economic problems (in which the government plays a significant role)." Two contemporary Latin American politicos emphasize the proposition. Rómulo Betancourt states unequivocally that "without planning, a coherent and progressive development of modern societies is impossible." Eduardo Frei Montalva agrees in proposing that "the planning of

---

43. *Documents of the First Part of the Meeting of the Special Committee of the IA–ECOSOC* (Washington: Pan American Union, 1969), p. 50. See Apendix II, pp. 51–65 for the consensus.

economic development and basic investments . . . are tasks that the state cannot renounce."[44]

In rough outline, the Latin Americans charge that the lack of time and money in the underdeveloped countries demands the establishment of priorities and careful planning. The happenstance and unfettered style of capitalistic development is too slow and too costly. Careful guidelines for the use of scarce resources are necessary. The agency that must plan is the government. Hence, the state assumes a major role in the developmental process. Thus, U.S. attempts to impose private initiative on the Latins have met with little success. As the developmental effort is pushed in Latin America in future, the socialistic styles characteristic of the underdeveloped world will continue to dominate the southern half of the hemisphere. The clash of differing philosophies will continue to be a strain on inter-American relations.

A Closed System

Finally, the theme of the rich nations and the poor nations portends some long-range possibility for an increase rather than a reduction of Yankee influence in Latin America. George Ball, a "realistic" diplomatic practitioner has analyzed competing conceptions of North-South relationships.

> At the moment there are two existing systems of North-South relations rarely acknowledged or differentiated. One is what we might call the Open System. The other consists of a series of Closed Systems. The basic assumption of the Open System is that all industrial countries of the free world will accept responsibility for the economic, commercial, and political well-being of all developing countries without discrimination. They will, through systematic consultation, concert their efforts to achieve that objective. The Closed System, on the other hand, assumes that specific industrial countries or groups of countries in the North will maintain special relationships with specific developing countries or groups of countries in the South, and will establish preferential and discriminatory arrangements to reinforce these relations. This is the situation, for example, that exists with regard to the African states of the French community and, to a lesser extent, within the British Commonwealth.[45]

Historically, the United States has been the champion of the Open System. Informed by a tradition that combines liberal free trade principles, messianic idealism, and hard-headed self-interest, the United States has opposed closed systems as being both unwise and unprofitable. In world forums it continues to press for that conception of political and economic relations. Solid indications, however, point to an erosion of the United States commitment to the Open System. The Vietnam fiasco has weakened the resolve of the policy

44. See Powelson, *Latin America*, p. 11; Betancourt, *Posición y Doctrina*, p. 148; and Williams, *Latin American Christian Democratic Parties*, p. 125.

45. Ball, *The Discipline of Power*, p. 237.

makers and led many to accept Senator J. William Fulbright's advice concerning the limits of power. Problems at home, combined with decreasing Soviet bellicosity, have encouraged the United States to lessen its commitments to Europe. General dissatisfaction with foreign aid has resulted in less presence in Africa. Finally, within the context of this book, the Latin Americans have insistently petitioned the United States to work out a special relationship involving the Western Hemisphere.

As noted earlier, recent policy analyses and pronouncements indicate increasing U.S. readiness to accede to the pleas of the Latins. The Johnson administration favored the principle, and President Nixon seems to be inching toward acceptance of the arrangement. A recent analysis, proposing possible acceptance of the program, hints at the significance for Yankee hegemony in Latin America.

> A United States – Latin American trade bloc, however, does contain the promise of both political and economic advantage. In many people's eyes, preferences for Latin America would cement Latin American political dependence on the United States with the bond of material interest. This is seen as a method of combating the growth of hostile political forces and as a way of preventing erosion of the United States' position as Latin America's principal supplier. It is probable that Congress would be willing to support one-way preference for Latin America, during a lengthy transition period, somewhat in the manner of EEC (European Community) relations with Greece, Turkey, and African associates.[46]

Whatever the dangerous consequences of preferred status, the Latin Americans may well be successful in convincing the United States to grant it. The purpose here is not to charge that U.S. policy makers are conniving to strengthen Yankee imperialism, but only to point out possible implications of the preference arrangements. They impose a closed system. They imply colonialism. They are the same arrangements that the United States granted to Cuba for some years. Fidel Castro and many others have accused the United States of imposing imperialistic control through the manipulation of preferences and special tariff arrangements. The same change may characterize inter-American relations in the future.

---

46. Pincus, *Trade, Aid, and Development*, p. 209.

Six

Conclusion

Some Prognostications

This book has defined and described the major political controversies of inter-American relations. It has discussed the points of contention between the two Americas and detailed how each side has framed its position. More ambitiously, the book has also analyzed and projected the evolution of the political themes of hemispheric intercourse.

The controversies herein discussed will remain key elements in inter-American affairs. The specific arguments and defenses will reappear in the future. Political relations among nations, like personal relations among men, are usually characterized by a dreary monotony in which the same issues and the same apologies appear and reappear decade after decade — indeed, century after century. Still, changes sometimes occur. For a short time in the present century, for example, intervention almost disappeared as a major controversy. U.S. aid to Latin American dictatorships, furthermore, evolved as a serious problem only after World War II. Latin American solidarity with the poor nations of Afro-Asia is an even more recent theme of inter-American relations. Changes evolve from varying sources and for varying reasons. The general trends of world politics affect how the United States interprets Latin America. Domestic changes in both halves of the hemisphere influence intercourse between the two. Equally important, men change their perception of the political universe and work for new relations to reflect the new image. All these factors play a role in hemispheric relations.

Three basic trends inform the emerging character of hemispheric politics: trends in the Cold War struggle between the United States and the Soviet Union; changes in American foreign policy emanating from the Vietnam War;

and changes in Latin American foreign policy deriving from the increasing intensity of Latin nationalism. As the seventies begin, the United States and the Soviet Union are creeping toward a rapprochement. The United States is no longer so concerned with Soviet encroachments in the Western Hemisphere. Castro and the New Left no longer pose the threat of old. Castro has increasingly addressed himself to the problems of his own country. The New Left guerrillas have suffered serious setbacks. In the United States, a general malaise has engulfed both people and government. The Vietnam debacle has raised questions of both national will and national purpose culminating in a searching appraisal of domestic and foreign policy. In Latin America, the forces of nationalism and the drive for internal development have produced new domestic and international equations. The environment of hemispheric politics has changed significantly.

The meaning of those environmental changes remains unclear, but the analysis of the several themes has attempted to outline some possibilities. Without again discussing all the possibilities, variations, and nuances of emerging hemispheric relations, informed speculation indicates the following picture in the 1970's.

1. U.S. imperialism will continue to be a major theme of inter-American relations. The discourse of that theme will continue to use the frames of reference contained in the "explanations of U.S. imperialism" set out in Chapter I. More specifically, the charge of economic imperialism will be featured in Latin American rhetoric, while the United States will have increasing recourse to a more sophisticated version of the White Man's Burden defense. North Americans and Latin Americans will be talking past one another, but they always have.

2. The Cold War and communism will continue to influence hemispheric intercourse, but its prominence may lessen. The objective realities of a passing Cold War and weakened Communist threat may well have some effect. Old habits maintained (and nurtured) over long periods die hard, however. The slightest hint of Soviet interest or Communist strength in the hemisphere will assuredly revive the Cold War paranoia.

3. Overt U.S. intervention will decline, but the theme will persevere. The lessening of outside threats to U.S. security and interests coupled with the growing material and political costs of intervention will dissuade the policy makers from interfering in Latin American affairs. Still, the increasing sensitivity of the Latins will produce constant cries of Yankee intervention. Furthermore, the United States will intervene if it believes it necessary. Some degree of intervention in Haiti is almost certain.

4. The United States will continue to aid dictatorships. Indeed, it will forsake almost all reticence to do so. Opposition to assisting despotisms will also continue, however, and the theme will persist as an important element of inter-American controversy. The only change in the theme may occur in the focus of the opposition. Latin American opposition will decrease for two reasons. First, Latin American nationalism will grow so intense that it will be

a shield for dictatorships. Those who propose bringing pressure against dictatorships will be shouted down in the name of non-intervention. Second, the traditional opposition to dictatorial regimes (the Betancourts, Hayas, Bosches, and others) are passing from influence. On the other hand, the U.S. New Left will keep the theme before the policy makers in Washington. Opposition to U.S. aid to dictatorships will play a key role in the New Left's struggle to cleanse U.S. foreign policy of imperialistic practices.

5. Latin American solidarity and cooperation with Afro-Asia will be maintained and will grow slightly, but the strides of the sixties will not be matched. Third World cooperation will not produce the achievements it needs for continued vitality. Moreover, the United States will wean Latin America from the southern bloc by offering special economic arrangements within the Western Hemisphere.

Some Prescriptions

In an age when both students and government leaders call for policy-relevant work from academia, a book of this sort would be remiss if it did not attempt to respond to those demands. If students and policy makers are confused and unsure of themselves, then it is the task of the scholar to help them by sorting out issues and offering possible courses of action. This book has sorted out the issues and implicitly suggested some ways to improve policy and better inter-American relations. It is now the time to set out some policy recommendations in more explicit form.

Imperialism

Although the discussion of imperialism in this book has been as much contextual as substantive, there are several lessons to be learned. First, inter-American political relations would be greatly improved if the issue of economic imperialism could be purged from hemispheric discourse. There is little chance of this happening, of course, but Washington might consider revising its emphasis on private investment as a contribution to Latin American development. A strong case could be made for the necessity of private capital in Latin America, if it did not imply the political problems that it so frequently does. But the point is that private investment (and the concomitant cry of economic imperialism) is simply counter-productive in its overall impact. It sets the stage for nationalistic opposition to the United States. It conjures up anti-Yankeeism. It invites nationalization, leading to reaction from the U.S. business community and the Congress. It leads to endless harangues and political imbroglios that poison hemispheric amity. Private capital's economic blessing is not worth the political grief that accompanies it.

Second, the United States ought to discipline its power, play down its influence, and lower its image in Latin America. As argued in the "strength vs. weakness" explanation of imperialism, U.S. wealth and power inevitably spill over. The very presence of the United States affects the Latins. Much of that presence is beyond the capacity of policy makers to change or revise, but much is susceptible to modification. The United States should talk less, listen more, posture not at all, and generally attempt to make itself less obnoxious. President Nixon's "low profile" policy is a solid step in the right direction. It should be pursued.

Last, the United States should strip the rhetoric from its pronouncements on hemispheric relations and attempt a straightforward approach. Manifest Destiny has happily been put to rest. The same should be done with the verbiage of shared values and the white man's burden. The straw man apologies are not worthy of a great power.

U.S. hemispheric policy should be based on two criteria — national security and national interest. National security considerations should be spelled out in specific terms. The subsequent discussion of intervention will suggest these terms. The national interest criterion should be modestly defined to avoid the claims of messianic idealism that have too frequently beclouded the real intentions (and possibilities) of foreign policy.

The Cold War and Communism

The United States must, once and for all, disavow its preoccupation with the Cold War and communism as a rationale for its hemispheric policies. The effects of policies resulting from that consideration have been little short of disastrous. Cold War paranoia has lead to a multitude of sins and stupidities. It has driven the United States to bless, bemedal, and buy dictatorships. It has forced the United States to undertake unnecessary armed interventions. It has led to undignified cajoling and pressuring of essentially friendly governments. It has distorted foreign aid programs. It has distorted academic research. Most seriously, it has kept the United States from the business of effectively responding to real and profoundly felt desires for economic, social, and political development.

The Cold War never had any real meaning for hemispheric politics except during a short time in the early sixties. It has no significance for inter-American relations in the seventies. Neither the Soviet Union nor Communist China entertains any ambition of intruding on the U.S. sphere of influence. Castro's zeal for continent-wide revolution has waned. The New Left guerrillas have failed. The United States ought to own up to these realities. It should purge Cold War rhetoric from its inter-American discourse and eliminate Cold War considerations from its hemispheric policies.

Intervention

With two specific exceptions, the United States ought not to intervene in the domestic affairs of the Latin American states. The prohibition of intervention should cover every kind from overt military intervention to diplomatic cajoling and pressuring and even to snotty remarks by government officials.

Intervention has always been a major complaint of the Latin Americans. For most of the history of hemispheric intercourse, it has been *the* most serious offense of Yankee imperialism. Given the increased sensitivity of Latin Americans resulting from contemporary nationalism, it is imperative that the United States be particularly careful not to intrude in the domestic affairs of its southern neighbors.

However good total nonintervention might be for inter-American friendship, there are two exceptions that must be posited. First, the United States may be compelled to intervene in pursuit of its national security. The conditions for such intervention must be defined very carefully, however. Moreover, they should be communicated so that the Latin Americans know exactly what condition will elicit intervention from the north. The condition should be a clear, immediate, and substantial (if not overwhelming) threat to U.S. territorial integrity or political independence. Intervention should not be employed to protect U.S. "interests," only its security. Governments should not be overturned because there is some anti-American influence within. Nor should nations be invaded because they might turn Communist. Indeed, nations should be permitted to function even if they are controlled by a Communist regime.

Only when such a regime imperils U.S. security is intervention merited. The only operational examples of security threats that should invite intervention are large-scale Soviet military presence in a Latin American country or large-scale import of offensive weapons by a hemispheric nation.

Aid to Dictatorships

The second justification for North American intervention concerns Latin American despotisms. The United States ought to stand unequivocally for democracy in Latin America. It should use its influence to discourage the implantation and perpetuation of dictatorial regimes. Physical intervention to impose democratic regimes is not advocated. The United States should not employ armed intervention against dictatorships of the left or the right, but it should use all measures up to armed intervention. It should break diplomatic relations, discontinue all but the most basic humanitarian aid, and actively encourage democrats in their fight against the tyranny. However idealistic this position may seem to the "realists," it is proposed on the realistic grounds that it will contribute to U.S. security and interests. If the United States wishes to maintain its leadership of the "free world," it must erase the stigmas of buying

Duvalier's vote, supporting Pérez Jiménez' tyranny, or buttressing Trujillo's dictatorship in the name of anti-Communist democracy.

The official line has long had it that the final battle in the Cold War will be a struggle for the allegiance of men's minds. That position has been exaggerated but is not totally without merit. If that struggle is to be won by the United States, then it must pursue a policy consonant with its claims to be on the side of democracy. Until now, U.S. practice in Latin America has made a lie of its official propaganda. Many in Latin America and elsewhere have become disillusioned with the United States and called its leadership into question. The United States needs the support of Latin America. An anti-dictatorial policy will contribute more to that support than a policy blessing dictatorships.

Furthermore, the supposed new-style dictatorships of the modernizing military should be repudiated along with their less sophisticated predecessors. No matter what their aims or their direction may be, their practices are as despicable and counter-productive as their less imaginative brethren. Torture by the contemporary Brazilian dictatorship is no different than Trujillo's practices. Transgressions of basic freedoms by the Peruvian military regime follow a time-worn pattern. Also, it is not obvious that dictatorship can be the midwife of democracy or development. Tyrannies introduce serious cleavages in the polity, nullifying the chance for national consensus. They refuse to permit participation by the masses in the governing process. They obviate the growth of responsible institutions and processes that are the stuff of a developed polity.

From the point of view of U.S. security, the time is ripe for a dynamic anti-dictatorial policy. Cold War necessities no longer demand the maintenance of the Latin American status quo. Threats to U.S. security no longer merit aid to dictatorships. The United States can pursue a morally and strategically sound policy with no danger to itself.

The Rich Nations and the Poor Nations

The policy implications of the rich nations and the poor nations theme have been strongly suggested in the analysis of the previous chapter. It will suffice here to affirm that those implications ought to become official U.S. policy. Latin America as a poor, underdeveloped continent means that the United States should be ready to give technical and financial assistance for as long as is necessary to make Latin America rich and self-sustaining. A convenient rule of thumb may be that the United States should pledge substantial assistance until a country achieves a gross national product per capita equal to the least prosperous state in the United States. Latin America as a developing area also means that the continent's nationalistic personality will frequently be manifested in demonstrations of anti-Yankeeism. However uncomfortable that may be, the United States should assume a posture of understanding forbearance. In the long run, a proud, independent Latin America is what the United States needs. Rich, strongly independent nations will be the best protection against foreign influence in the hemisphere and will contribute to U.S. security. Concomitantly, the United States should encourage Latin America's affiliation with the Afro-Asian nations, while at the same time offering special arrangements with the United States. Both avenues combined may lessen hemispheric tensions and contribute to Latin American development.

These suggestions have been posited by many over the last two decades. There is little that is new about them. Some of the ideas have been practiced by Washington from time to time, but the entire package has never been given a fair test. If amicable hemispheric relations within a secure international setting are the goal of the policy makers, these suggestions deserve a try. The policies followed for the last 25 years have not been successful. These may be better; they can hardly be worse.

Suggested Readings

Though hardly any of the literature on inter-American relations is written specifically within the context of this book, almost all of it deals, in one way or another, with the themes of inter-American controversy. Almost any book on inter-American relations describes and analyzes imperialism, the Cold War and communism, intervention, and aid to dictatorships. The rich nations and poor nations theme is the exception. Only the most recent works refer to that theme. Moreover, the best treatments are found in books on the Third World that refer to Latin America rather than in books on Latin America.

If a student is interested in learning more about these themes as they have been presented in this book, several tactics are appropriate. First, he may ferret out the few things that are specifically on the target of this book. Second, he may read chapters, sections, or pages in the general literature. Last, he may read the general literature, using the framework of this book as a guide to the political controversies of inter-American relations.

The readings listed below should help in any of these methods. A general list and a specific list for each major theme are recommended. Many of these books are paperbacks.

General

The diplomatic histories are the basis of the general literature on inter-American relations. The three basic texts are Samuel Flagg Bemis, *The Latin American Policy of the United States* (New York, 1943); Graham H. Stuart, *Latin America and the United States* (New York, 1955); and Dexter Perkins, *A History of the Monroe Doctrine* (Boston, 1963).

Books that combine diplomatic history with political analysis include J. Lloyd Mecham, *A Survey of United States-Latin American Relations* (Boston, 1965); Gordon Connell-Smith, *The Inter-American System* (London, 1966); Wilfred H. Callcott, *The Western Hemisphere* (Austin, Texas, 1968); and Norman A. Bailey, *Latin America in World Politics* (New York, 1967).

A good short survey of the political history of inter-American relations is Edwin Lieuwen, *U. S. Policy in Latin America* (New York, 1965).

Even more to the point of contemporary political and economic controversies are Robert N. Burr, *Our Troubled Hemisphere: Perspectives on United States-Latin American Relations* (Washington, D.C., 1967); William D. Rogers, *The Twilight Struggle: The Alliance for Progress and the Politics of Development in Latin America* (New York, 1967); Adolf A. Berle, *Latin America: Diplomacy and Reality* (New York, 1962); and Milton S. Eisenhower, *The Wine Is Bitter* (New York, 1963).

Finally, two first rate books on economic differences between the two Americas are John P. Powelson, *Latin America: Today's Economic and Social Revolution* (New York, 1964); and Albert O. Hirschman, *Latin American Issues: Essays and Comments* (New York, 1961).

Imperialism

Chapter I of this book attempted to posit "imperialism" as a neutral concept, implying that it could be either good or bad. The chapter then explained how the defenders and detractors of U. S. influence in Latin America framed their arguments. It seems appropriate to list the suggested readings in the same way.

Some authors listed previously defend U. S. policies in Latin America as being essentially good or absolutely necessary for U. S. security. See particularly the works of Bemis, Mecham, Perkins, and Stuart. Some have explained and defended specific aspects or epochs of United States influence. See Wilfred H. Callcott, *The Caribbean Policy of the United States, 1890–1920* (Baltimore, 1942); J. Lloyd Mecham, *The United States and Inter-American Security, 1889–1960* (Austin, Texas, 1961); and Dana G. Munro, *Intervention and Dollar Diplomacy in the Caribbean, 1900–1921* (Princeton, N.J., 1964).

Some other authors have been sympathetic to the United States, but critical of particular policies and practices. For that position, see Eisenhower and Powelson; Donald M. Dozer, *Are We Good Neighbors?* (Gainesville, Fla., 1959); and Bryce Wood, *The Making of the Good Neighbor Policy* (New York, 1961).

Much of the rhetorical framework for U. S. political and economic influence is contained in the official proclamations of policy made by governmental officials. President Kennedy's Alliance for Progress speech is packed with the images of hemispheric shared values and the role of the Americans in historical perspective. The same is true of President Nixon's speeches on Latin America, the Rockefeller Report (Chicago, 1969), and thousands of other speeches, proclamations, and policy statements made by Americans both North and South over 150 years of hemispheric intercourse. Scholars also have described and analyzed the philosophical and ideological context of U.S. influence in Latin America. Some recommended works include José Agustín Balseiro, *The Americas Look at Each Other* (Coral Gables, Fla., 1969); Donald M. Dozer, ed., *The Monroe Doctrine: Its Modern Significance* (New York, 1965); Lewis Hanke, ed., *Do the Americas Have a Common History?* (New York, 1964); Frederick Merk, *Manifest Destiny and Mission in American History* (New York, 1963); and Arthur P. Whitaker, *The Western Hemisphere Idea* (Ithaca, N.Y., 1954).

Negative interpretations of North American influence have always been around but may have become more numerous and more respectable in recent years. Two Latin Americans who have been critical of Yankee imperialism are Alonso Aguilar, *Pan Americanism from Monroe to the Present: A View from the Other Side* (New York, 1968); and Juan José Arévalo, *The Shark and the Sardines* (New York, 1961). For collections of critical articles written by both North and Latin Americans, see Carlos Fuentes et al., *Whither Latin America?* (New York, 1963); Irving Louis Horowitz, Josué de Castro, and John Gerassi, eds., *Latin American Radicalism: A Documentary Report on Left and Nationalist Movements* (New York, 1969); and James Petras and Maurice Zeitlin, *Latin America: Reform or Revolution?* (Greenwich, Conn., 1968). Finally, two North Americans have written very critically of U.S. imperialism in Latin America—Andre Gunder Frank, *Capitalism and Underdevelopment in Latin America* (New York, 1967); and John Gerassi, *The Great Fear in Latin America* (New York, 1965).

Communism and the Cold War

The activities in and ambitions for Latin America of the Soviet Union and communism have been repeatedly discussed in the literature. One can hardly pick up a book on Latin America without finding a chapter or so on the subject.

The two leading works on the domestic Communist movements are Robert J. Alexander, *Communism in Latin America* (New Brunswick, N. J., 1957); and Rollie E. Poppino *International Communism in Latin America* (New York, 1964). Luis Aguilar, ed., *Marxism in Latin America* (New York, 1968) is a book of readings that discuss both the traditional movement and the new variations. Two studies of a country are Karl M. Schmitt, *Communism in Mexico: A Study of Political Frustration* (Austin, Texas, 1965); and Ronald Schneider, *Communism in Guatemala, 1944–1954* (New York, 1958). On Soviet diplomatic, economic, and political penetration in Latin America, see Robert Loring Allen, *Soviet Influence in Latin America: The Role of Economic Relations* (Washington, 1959); Herbert S. Dinerstein, *Fifty Years of Soviet*

Policy (Baltimore, 1968), and "Soviet Policy in Latin America," *American Political Science Review* 61: 1 (March 1967) 80–90; D. Bruce Jackson, *Castro, the Kremlin, and Communism in Latin America* (Baltimore, 1969); and Salvador de Madariaga, *Latin America between the Eagle and the Bear* (New York, 1962).

Books on Castro's Cuba are almost as legion as those on communism more generally. Several of the better ones are Theodore Draper, *Castroism: Theory and Practice* (New York, 1965); Boris Goldenberg, *The Cuban Revolution and Latin America* (New York, 1965); Irving Louis Horowitz, ed., *Cuban Communism* (New York, 1970); and Andrés Suarez, *Cuba: Castroism and Communism, 1959–1966* (Cambridge, Mass., 1967).

The works on the New Left are mostly collections of speeches and books on strategy and tactics written by the activists themselves. Regis Debray's *Revolution in the Revolution?* (New York, 1967) and *The Diary of Che Guevara* (New York, 1968) are examples. Some analysis is found in Luigi Einaudi, *Changing Contexts of Revolution in Latin America* (Santa Monica, Calif., 1966); "Introduction" to John Gerassi, ed., *Venceremos! The Speeches and Writings of Che Guevara* (New York, 1968); Leo Huberman and Paul M. Sweezy, eds., *Regis Debray and the Latin American Revolution* (New York, 1968); and Luis Mercier Vega, *Guerrillas in Latin America: The Technique of the Counter State* (New York, 1969); and the Horowitz et al. and Petras and Zeitlin books noted in the imperialism section.

The U.S. response to the various faces of communism and Soviet penetration are included in the works cited in the general section above. Several other books dealing with more specific instances of the threat are Herbert S. Dinerstein, *Intervention against Communism* (Baltimore, 1967); David L. Larson, ed., *The Cuban Crisis of 1962: Selected Documents and Chronology* (Boston, 1963); Karl E. Meyer and Tad Szulc, *The Cuban Invasion: Chronicle of a Disaster* (New York, 1962); John Plank, ed., *Cuba and the United States: Long Range Perspectives* (Washington, D.C., 1967); Jerome Slater, *The OAS and United States Foreign Policy* (Columbus, Ohio, 1967); Tad Szulc, *Dominican Diary* (New York, 1965); and Center for Strategic Studies, *Dominican Action — 1965: Intervention or Cooperation?* (Washington, D.C., 1966).

Intervention

Two books on intervention are C. Neale Ronning, ed., *Intervention in Latin America* (New York, 1970); and A.V.W. Thomas and A. J. Thomas, *Nonintervention: The Law and Its Import in the Americas* (Dallas, 1956).

The descriptions and analyses of the intervention theme in inter-American relations are frequently paralleled to that of imperialism. Hence, almost all citations listed in the imperialism section provide extensive treatment of intervention.

For explanations, criticisms, and defenses of U.S. interventions in the early part of the century, see especially the works of Bemis, Callcott, Connell-Smith, Dozer, Mecham, Munro, Stuart, and Wood.

Since World War II, real or imagined Communist threats have been the major catalysts for U.S. intervention. Hence, the works listed in the Communist and Cold War section are rich sources of material for intervention during that period. The authors listed there who are particularly pertinent include Dinerstein, Meyer and Szulc, Plank, the Center for Strategic Studies, and Szulc. Other works that reach the issue include those by Horowitz et al. and Petras and Zeitlin. Two other selections that analyze contemporary interventions are Richard J. Barnet, *Intervention and Revolution* (New York, 1968); and Philip B. Taylor, Jr., "The Guatemalan Affair: A Critique of United States Foreign Policy," *American Political Science Review* 50:3 (September 1956), 787 - 806.

Collective intervention is most thoroughly discussed in the literature on the Organization of American States. Some of the leading works are M. Margaret Ball, *The OAS in Transition* (Durham, N.C., 1969); John C. Dreir, *The Organization of American States and the Hemispheric Crisis* (New York, 1962); O. C. Stoetzer, *The Organization of American States* (New York, 1965); A. V. W. Thomas and A. J. Thomas, *The Organization of American States* (Dallas, 1963) and Slater's book cited in the intervention section.

Aid to Dictatorships

Aid to dictatorships emerged as a cogent inter-American controversy only after World War II. Moreover, it was usually contained within the context of communism and the Cold War. Therefore, systematic descriptions and analyses of the issue are much rarer than for other themes in this book. Even more than usual, the student is compelled to read bits and pieces of general works to interpret the issue within the context of this study.

Furthermore, the controversy is difficult to join because few are ready to offer a strong defense of aid to dictatorships. With that reservation made, the best justifications of aid to dictatorships are to be found in the speeches and congressional testimony of the policy makers. President Nixon's speech of October 31, 1969, defends the practice, as does the Rockefeller Report. A defense is also offered by Mecham.

Though they seldom advocate the same complete break with dictators that this book does, academic critics are much more numerous than defenders. Robert Alexander and Edwin Lieuwen criticize U.S. policy toward dictators in almost all their works; see, for example, Robert Alexander and Charles O. Porter, *The Struggle for Democracy in Latin America* (New York, 1961); and Edwin Lieuwen, *Generals vs. Presidents* (New York, 1965). Other critics include Gordon Connell-Smith; George I. Blanksten, *Perón's Argentina* (New York, 1953, 1967); Renato Poblete, "The Phenomenon of Dictatorship," in

John J. Considine, ed., *Social Revolution in the New Latin America* (Notre Dame, Ind., 1965); and J. Fred Rippy, *Globe and Hemisphere* (Chicago, 1958). Martin Needler's analysis of the coup process has real implications for U.S. recognition of dictators; see *Political Development in Latin America* (New York, 1968).

The contemporary literature from the Left is even more critical of aid to dictatorships. A number of these were listed in the imperialism section of this bibliography. See Aguilar, Arévalo, Gerassi, Fuentes, Horowitz, and Petras and Zeitlin.

The literature on the Latin American military is fairly limited, though growing of late. Sympathetic analyses are found in John J. Johnson, ed., *The Role of the Military in Underdeveloped Countries* (Princeton, N.J., 1962); and John J. Johnson, *The Military and Society in Latin America* (Stanford, Calif., 1964). Edwin Lieuwen is the leading critic; see *Arms and Politics in Latin America* (New York, 1961). A useful comparison of the two positions, along with a good bibliography, is found in Martin Needler, "The Latin American Military: Predatory Reactionaries or Modernizing Patriots?" *Journal of Inter-American Studies* 11:1 (April 1969), 237 – 244. A special element of the military is described and analyzed in Willard F. Barber and C. Neale Ronning, *Internal Security and Military Power: Counterinsurgency and Civic Action in Latin America* (Columbus, Ohio, 1966).

The particular problems of inter-American relations posed by the emergence of the new, modernizing military are noted in most of the above works, but it receives more comprehensive treatment in the Rockefeller Report; James Petras, "The United States and the New Equilibrium in Latin America," *Public Policy* 18:1 (Fall 1969), 95 – 132; and Luigi Einaudi, *Peruvian Military Relations with the United States* (Santa Monica, Calif., 1970).

The Rich Nations and the Poor Nations

The attempt to understand Latin America's connection with Afro-Asia is very new to the literature. Even newer, of course, is the meaning for inter-American relations. Most references to Latin America's place in the Third World are found in the more general literature on underdeveloped areas. Some books and articles that deal explicitly or implicitly with the theme are Charles W. Anderson, Fred R. von der Mehden, and Crawford Young, *Issues of Political Development* (Englewood Cliffs, N. J., 1967); Barnet; Vera Micheles Dean, *The Nature of the Non-Western World* (New York, 1957); Theodore Geiger, *The Conflicted Relationship: The West and the Transformation of Asia, Africa, and Latin America* (New York, 1967); J. Ronald Pennock, ed., *Self-Government in Modernizing Nations* (Englewood Cliffs, N. J., 1964); John Pincus, *Trade, Aid, and Development: The Rich and Poor Nations* (New York, 1967); Paul E. Sigmund, ed., *The Ideologies of the Developing Nations* (New York, 1963); and Edward J. Williams "Comparative Political Development: Latin America and Afro-Asia," *Comparative Studies in Society and History* 11:3 (June 1969), 342 – 354. Other works that sometimes hit the theme more directly are Mildred Adams, ed., *Latin America: Evolution or Explosion?* (New York, 1963); E. Bradford Burns, *Nationalism in Brazil* (New York, 1968); José A. Mora, "Will Latin America Continue to Adhere to the West?" *The Annals of the American Academy of Political and Social Science* July 1961, 98 – 105; José Honório Rodrigues, *Brazil and Africa* (Berkeley and Los Angeles, 1965); the Rockefeller Report; Paul Saenz, "A Latin American-African Partnership," *Journal of Inter-American Studies* 11:2 (April 1969), 317 – 327: and Leopold Zea, *Latin America and the World* (Norman, Okla., 1969).

Finally, the writings of the Latin American New Left refer to the unity of Third World revolutionaries. See the works of the New Left noted in the communism and Cold War section above. See also *The First Conference of the Latin American Solidarity Organization* (Washington, D.C., 1967).

Index